Oregon and Washington National Forest

Campground Directory and Recreation Guide

This directory is dedicated to the memory of one of its creators, Dick Dodge, who served the Forest Service and its visitors well.

USDA Forest Service
Pacific Northwest Region

Published by
Pacific Northwest National
Parks and Forests Association

Printed in the United States of America

Compiled by Dale Farley and Edited by Shirley Moore

Design by Diane Lynn Converse

Cover Photos *Pack Trip, Hells Canyon National Recreation Area,*
Wallowa-Whitman National Forest by Jim Hughes
Running the Illinois Wild and Scenic River,
Siskiyou National Forest by Jim Hughes
Sunset, Hood Canal, Olympic National Forest by Jim Hughes

CONTENTS

The Pacific Northwest Region of the U.S. Department of Agriculture Forest Service includes the 19 National Forests in Oregon and Washington. A National Grassland is included on the Ochoco National Forest. Also, small portions of California and Idaho are administered by the Region.

Each National Forest is under the direction of a Forest Supervisor and three to seven District Forest Rangers. Each ranger is responsible for the on-the-ground multiple use management of a district of from 100,000 to 700,000 acres.

Over 24.5 million acres in these states include the most beautiful mountainous and forested lands. Camping, picnicking, hunting, fishing, hiking, horseback riding, mountain climbing, sports, and scenic drives through the National Forests of our nation are enjoyed by millions of Americans. Because of increasing use, Forest Service recreation management is becoming more dependent upon visitor self-service and volunteer assistance to meet the mushrooming demand.

Pacific Northwest National Forests are lands of great contrast, beauty, and productivity. Within their boundaries are surf-splashed coastline and beaches, vast coastal and interior forests, deep blue lakes carved from the mountains, glaciers, white-water rivers, a live volcano, and high desert dotted with sage and juniper.

The Forests produce about half the timber sold annually from the entire National Forest System. The favorable climate and soils of the Pacific Northwest provide some of the world's most productive coniferous forests.They are treasures that can provide continuous supplies of timber forever. Also, one-sixth of the total recreation use on all the country's National Forests occurs here. Important as timber and recreation use are, the wildlife habitat, the forage produced for big game, cattle, and sheep, and the watersheds providing pure water for fish, cities, agriculture, and power are essential to life in the Northwest.

New Campground Reservation System

Advance reservations are now available for a few popular campsites. Both family and group campgrounds are included in the system. Reservations will be available year-round by toll free telephone request. This system is operated by Mistix, Inc., a reservation company in San Diego, California. Fees are charged in advance by credit card, money order, or personal check. The system is a trial and will be adjusted to meet public needs. Please check with the Forest Service or with Mistix, Inc. for current information.

All other campsites will still be available on a first-come, first-served basis.

Reservations can be made and you can obtain information by calling: 1-800-283-CAMP (2267) or, from Canada, 1-619-452-1950. Call 9 a.m. to 6 p.m. Monday through Friday, or 9 a.m. to 2 p.m. Saturday and Sunday, Pacific time. A reservation fee of $6 for family units and $10 for group units will be charged in addition to the normal user fee for each reservation made. At least ten days advance notice is needed to reserve family units, and at least three days advance notice for group sites. On a three-day holiday weekend, you must reserve a minimum of two consecutive nights at family units.

User Fees

Recreation use fees are charged for many of the recreation sites listed on the following pages. Fees and also reservations are required for group sites. Information about fees is available at Ranger Stations and is posted at recreation sites.

Concession Campgrounds

Some fee sites are operated by private parties, under special-use authorizations. This authorization to operate and maintain the government-owned facilities and provide public services is awarded on a competitive basis through a prospectus and bid process.

Permit holders are required to operate, maintain, and provide the services as specified in the prospectus, special-use permit, and site operating and maintenance plan. The Forest Service monitors and regulates the operation to ensure compliance with policy and standards. This in review and approval of fees and services. The Golden Age/Gol Access passports are honored at all concessionaire-operated ca grounds.

Volunteers

The "Volunteers in the National Forest" program provides a means for interested persons to become involved and assist in the conservation work of the Forest. Campground Host and Wilderness Information Specialist are just two of the job titles for volunteers who provide a long list of services in the program. The varied tasks are listed under major headings which include public contact and assistance, operation and maintenance, administration, and information and education. Anyone interested in becoming involved in the program should contact one of the Ranger Stations, the Forest Supervisor's Office or the Regional Office.

Wilderness

The Pacific Northwest National Forests include 59 wildernesses totaling nearly 4.6 million acres. These areas are dedicated to preserving a part of our national heritage in its natural state. Roads, motorized travel, logging, resorts, or other commercial developments are not allowed in wilderness. However, prior established grazing use is permitted. Anyone able and willing to ride a horse, pack a burro, ski, or just plain hike may travel over the many trails available. Here one may enjoy the challenge of wilderness hunting, fishing, climbing, camping or relaxing surrounded by undisturbed beauty. Wilderness permits are not required except in the Enchantment Lakes area of the Alpine Lakes Wilderness.

Special Areas

Through the years the importance of certain lands has been recognized by Congress and by the Forest Service. Some areas are so special that politically it became important to safeguard them with Congressional Designations which directed particular management of those lands within the National Forest System.

First, in 1964, was the Wilderness Act. Additions through the years have spread from the National Forests to National Parks and to National Wildlife Refuges.

The Oregon Dunes National Recreation Area (within the Siuslaw National Forest) came next in this Region.

More recently, Hells Canyon National Recreation Area, Mount St. Helens National Volcanic Monument, and Columbia River Gorge National Scenic Area have been established within the Wallowa-Whitman, Gifford Pinchot, and Mt. Hood National Forests respectively.

Winter Sports

All 25 ski areas in Oregon and Washington are in whole or in part on National Forest administered lands. Also, hundreds of miles of marked cross-country ski trails and snowmobile routes attract ever-increasing numbers of people seeking the rejuvenation of the outdoors. Ski lift facilities are privately owned and operated under permits issued by the Forest Service. For your safety, ski patrols are on duty during operating hours.

Historical and Archaeological Sites

National Forest visitors may encounter historical and archaeological sites. These sites are protected by the Antiquities Act of 1906 and the Archaeological Resources Protection Act of 1979. Visitors CANNOT dig in or remove any object from these sites. If you encounter someone digging in or vandalizing a site, please report it to the nearest Forest Service office. Help to preserve our cultural heritage for all to enjoy. Other important historic sites like Timberline Lodge invite visitors and are interpreted to enhance enjoyment.

Know and Obey Rules

A new understanding and appreciation of National Forest System lands is urgently needed. Many visitors unknowingly "love the land to death" and while enjoying the freedoms afforded by our recreation resources may cause serious scars of overuse upon the land. We each must develop an ecological conscience or low-impact ethic. It has been said that we should "walk softly upon the land, taking only pictures and leaving only footprints." This is a challenge, to leave each place, insofar as is humanly possible, without a trace of your presence, or your passing. We must recognize that a complex ecological interrelationship exists in the forest which can easily be upset, damaged, or even destroyed. Once damaged, some plants and soil may not recover in one or several lifetimes.

Rules and regulations governing the use of developed National Forest recreation sites, as well as dispersed areas, are posted at developed sites and available in pamphlet form at Forest Service offices. These are common sense rules to help increase the enjoyment of all visitors to the National Forests and to protect the natural resources. The rules are enforced and violators may expect penalties.

Also available are pamphlets and interpretive programs to help visitors enjoy their National Forests through better understanding and appreciation. Such programs are available at visitor centers as well as numerous other developed sites.

Golden Access/Golden Age Passports

Persons older than 62 and those who are handicapped may receive free lifetime Golden Access/Golden Age Passports which provide a 50% discount on campground use fees. Passports are available at Forest Service offices, National Parks and Monuments, and Federal Information Centers. Applicants must apply in person and provide proof of handicap or age by federal certificate, driver's license, or birth certificate as appropriate.

Dispersed Recreation

This directory gives information about developed recreation sites. These sites are often heavily used, and the pressure mounts each year. Why not use some of the thousands of acres of National Forest land with little or no development? "Dispersed recreation" pays dividends in restful solitude, freedom from noise, natural scenery, and uncrowded picnicking, camping, fishing, or hunting.

Wherever you go, keep all recreation lands clean and attractive for future visitors. Pack out what you pack in. Leave no sign of your visit. Trash left behind not only spoils the environment but can be hazardous to the health of people and wildlife. Be especially alert to possible campfire restrictions and always be careful with fire.

Maps

Detailed 1/2" per mile maps of National Forests and 1" per mile maps of most wildernesses are available for $2 per copy from Forest Service offices on that particular Forest. Also, maps of all National Forests are available by mail or in person for $2 per copy from the Forest Service Regional Office, Office of Information, 319 SW Pine Street, P.O. Box 3623, Portland, Oregon 97208 (telephone (503) 326-2877). An order sheet is enclosed.

Getting Around on National Forest Roads

Getting around on National Forest roads is different from driving on a city street or state highway. This section tells how to determine road conditions from signs, maps, and road entrance conditions. This will help you choose which National Forest roads will best fit your vehicle capabilities and the driving experiences you desire. It also provides safe driving information.

You will find out...

how route markers help describe conditions;
which roads are not suitable for automobile use.

Please remember...

Most National Forest roads in Oregon and Washington are low-standard, one-lane roads with turnouts for meeting oncoming traffic. Many roads on the east side of the Cascade Mountains are not graveled. Most roads are not maintained or snowplowed in winter weather.

Food, gas, and lodging are seldom available along National Forest roads.

Encounters with logging trucks are possible even on weekends.

Driving rules used on state highways apply to National Forest roads.

The first step for enjoyable travel is to obtain a map of the National Forest you plan to visit. Maps are sold both at Forest Service offices and through the mail. For a minimal fee (presently $2) information on roads, trails, campgrounds, and more is at your fingertips.

The route markers shown are posted on National Forest roads maintained for automobile travel. These markers are posted at the entrance of primary and secondary routes. Primary routes usually offer the better choice for the traveler; secondary routes may not be as smooth or as well maintained.

National Forest primary route marker.

2490 National Forest secondary route marker.

These signs use white numbers on a brown background and are found at road entrances and intersections.

Roads not suitable for automobile travel can be identified by one or more of the following:

> route markers numbered vertically or placed away from road entrance;
>
> obvious obstructions in the roadway such as crossditches, scattered rocks, limbs, or ruts;
>
> drainage ditch across the road entrance;
>
> painted road-edge line across the road entrance.

These low-standard roads are not always shown on National Forest maps.

If you choose to drive these roads, plan to encounter rocks and boulders, road washouts, downed trees and brush encroaching on the roadway.

For safety, use a vehicle suitable for rough travel and carry extra equipment such as ax, shovel, gloves, and extra fuel.

Notes About the Directories

A "family camp unit" usually includes parking space for a vehicle, a table, and a fire pit or fireplace.

"Season of use" is generally from before Memorial Day to just after Labor Day. Weather, road or site repair, agency finances, or numerous other factors can alter these dates and cause closures. If you need definite dates, check with nearby National Forest offices.

Drivers of large motor homes, trailers, and campers should note and benefit from road condition warnings and maximum length recommendations for camp trailers. Forest Service campgrounds are not normally equipped with utility hookups. Sanitary disposal stations and centralized water hydrants are provided to serve some campgrounds as indicated. Direct connections are permitted at only a few individual family units equipped for hookups. Units designated as Tent/Trailer Sites will usually accommodate a 22-foot trailer. Smaller limits are noted in the text.

Abbreviations used: I= Interstate, St. Hwy.= State Highway, Cty. Rd.= County Road, FR or FRs= Forest Road(s)

If this guide does not supply all the information you need, please call or visit the Forest Service offices nearest the area in question.

Barrier-Free Access ♿

Campgrounds in the listing that will accommodate wheelchairs to some or all of their facilities are designated by the symbol shown above. The level of accessibility is described below. If barrier-free facilities do not include camping or picnic units, only the symbol is shown and the type of facility is described. Please consult with the local Ranger District, Supervisor's office or Visitors Center for detailed access information.

❶* Fully Accessible

Sites include a full range of interconnected accessible facilities. Parking for both cars and vans is available. Pathways between the parking and recreation facilities are wide enough for a wheelchair and pedestrian to pass and are paved with a hard, smooth surface. Toilets are fully accessible and conveniently located.

❷ Usable

Sites are more challenging than Level 1 sites. Parking is available with appropriate access aisles, but slopes and ramps may have slopes steeper than the ANSI Standard, and surface materials, although firm, may be more difficult to traverse. Accessible toilets are provided.

❸ Difficult

Sites provide more challenging experience that Levels 1 and 2. An accessible parking, loading zone is provided. Pathways are wide enough for a wheelchair, but may be unpaved and rough. At least one accessible toilet is available.

* These number codes appear throughout the directory below the campground units to which they apply.

Colville National Forest

Peewee Falls, Colville National Forest

A sense of peace and solitude is felt when traveling through the forest's scenic 7,000-foot mountains and beautiful valleys, hiking the trails, or camping by picturesque lakes. Here one has a sense of being away from it all. The 1.1-million-acre forest, located in the northeast corner of Washington and bordering Canada, is known for its rolling wooded slopes, ranging from large lodgepole pine stands in the west to extensive cedar groves on the eastern slopes. The forest's great salmon runs first attracted Native Americans to the area and miners, fur trappers, and homesteaders made their way here later to tap the area's abundant resources. Hudson's Bay Company established a fur-trading post at Fort Colville in 1825. Gold was discovered in 1855, leading the way for mineral exploration; and today, old cabins, mining shafts, and trails are reminders of days gone by.

Special places of interest to the visitor include a major recreation area with wildlife viewing opportunities, nestled in the mountains at Sullivan Lake; Chewelah Mountain for winter sports; Little Pend Oreille Lakes chain; Bangs Mountain auto tour for geology; Sherman Pass, the highest pass in Washington; the Salmo-Priest Wilderness; Thirteen-mile National Trail; and the Log Flume interpretive trail.

Further information about recreation opportunities, campground locations and facilities, as well as current maps of the area, are available at the following offices:

Colville National Forest
Supervisor's Office
695 S. Main
Colville, WA 99114
(509) 684-3711

Colville Ranger District
755 South Main St.
Colville, WA 99114
(509) 684-4557

Kettle Falls Ranger District
255 West 11th
Kettle Falls, WA 99141
(509) 738-6111

Republic Ranger District
180 N. Jefferson St.
Republic, WA 99166
(509) 775-3305

Sullivan Lake Ranger District
Metaline, WA 99153
(509) 446-2681

Spokane Information Office
West 920 Riverside, Room 112
Spokane, WA 99201
(509) 353-2574

Newport Ranger District
P.O. Box 770
Newport, WA 99156
(509) 447-3129

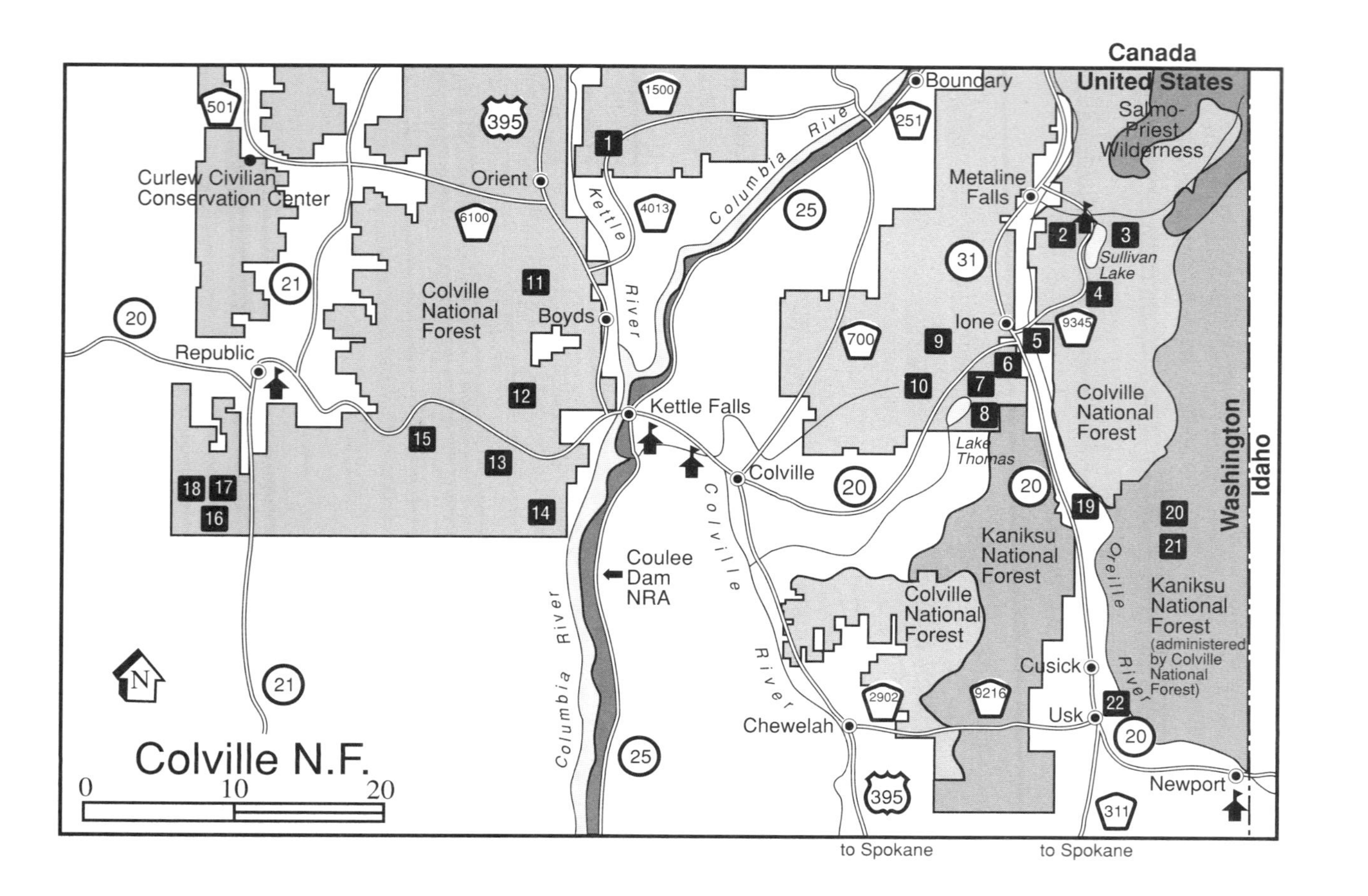
Canada
United States
Salmo-Priest Wilderness
Boundary
Metaline Falls
Sullivan Lake
Ione
Curlew Civilian Conservation Center
Orient
Colville National Forest
Boyds
Republic
Kettle River
Columbia River
Kettle Falls
Colville
Lake Thomas
Colville National Forest
Washington
Idaho
Kaniksu National Forest
Colville National Forest
Coulee Dam NRA
Colville River
Oreille River
Kaniksu National Forest (administered by Colville National Forest)
Cusick
Usk
Chewelah
Newport
to Spokane
to Spokane
Colville N.F.
0
10
20

COLVILLE NATIONAL FOREST

	Map Location	Elevation	Picnic Units	Tent Units	Tent-Trailer Units	Fee	Drinking Water

Colville Ranger District

Developed Sites

Big Meadow Lake

Access: 20 miles NE of Colville on the Aladdin Hwy., then right for 5 miles on the Meadow Creek Rd. Or, 8 miles W of Ione on the Meadow Cr. Rd.

Special Activities & Facilities: Interpretive trail with barrier -free loop, wildlife viewing platform, picnicking, boating, fishing.

	Map Location	Elevation	Picnic Units	Tent Units	Tent-Trailer Units	Fee	Drinking Water
♿	9	3430			16❶		

Gillette

Access: 20 miles E of Colville via St. Hwy. 20.

Special Activities & Facilities: Interpretive trail, picnicking, boating, fishing, off-road motorcycle trail system.

	Map Location	Elevation	Picnic Units	Tent Units	Tent-Trailer Units	Fee	Drinking Water
♿	8*	3200			30❷	x	x

Lake Leo

Access: 23 miles E of Colville via St. Hwy. 20.

Special Activities & Facilities: cross-country skiing, swimming, boating, and fishing, ORV trails.

	Map Location	Elevation	Picnic Units	Tent Units	Tent-Trailer Units	Fee	Drinking Water
	6	3200			8	x	x

Lake Thomas

Access: 20 miles E of Colville via St. Hwy. 20, FR 4987.

Special Activities & Facilities: Fishing.

	Map Location	Elevation	Picnic Units	Tent Units	Tent-Trailer Units	Fee	Drinking Water
♿	7	3200		15❸		x	x

Lake Gillette

Access: 20 miles E of Colville via St. Hwy. 20.

Special Activities & Facilities: Six multiple family sites available, picnicking, boating, and fishing.

	Map Location	Elevation	Picnic Units	Tent Units	Tent-Trailer Units	Fee	Drinking Water
	8*	3200	6		14	x	x

Little Twin Lakes

Access: 18 miles NE of Colville via Cty. Rd 4939, FR 94B.

Special Activities & Facilities: Fishing, picnicking, RV's to 16', high clearance vehicles only.

	Map Location	Elevation	Picnic Units	Tent Units	Tent-Trailer Units	Fee	Drinking Water
	10	3900			20		x

Lake Leo, Colville National Forest

Map Location	*Elevation*	*Picnic Units*	*Tent Units*	*Tent-Trailer Units*	*Fee*	*Drinking Water*

Kettle Falls Ranger District

Pierre Lake

Access: 20 miles N of Kettle Falls via St. Hwy. 395, Cty. Rd. 4013.
Special Activities & Facilities: Fishing, boating, hiking, swimming.

Map Location	*Elevation*	*Picnic Units*	*Tent Units*	*Tent-Trailer Units*	*Fee*	*Drinking Water*
1	*2100*	*9*		*15*		*x*

Davis Lake

Access: 16 miles NW of Kettle Falls via St. Hwy. 395, FR 480.
Special Activities & Facilities: Boat launch, fishing, RVs to 16'.

Map Location	*Elevation*	*Picnic Units*	*Tent Units*	*Tent-Trailer Units*	*Fee*	*Drinking Water*
11	*3900*			*4*		

Trout Lake

Access: 14 miles W of Kettle Falls via St. Hwy. 20, FR 020.
Special Activities & Facilities: Fishing, boating, swimming.

Map Location	*Elevation*	*Picnic Units*	*Tent Units*	*Tent-Trailer Units*	*Fee*	*Drinking Water*
12	*3000*		*4*			*x*

Kettle Range

Access: 18 miles E of Republic via St. Hwy. 20.
Special Activities & Facilities: Hiking, viewing area, picnicking.

Map Location	*Elevation*	*Picnic Units*	*Tent Units*	*Tent-Trailer Units*	*Fee*	*Drinking Water*
15	*5300*	*7*		*9*		*x*

Canyon Creek

Access: 8 miles W of Kettle Falls via US 395, St. Hwy. 20.
Special Activities & Facilities: Hiking.

Map Location	*Elevation*	*Picnic Units*	*Tent Units*	*Tent-Trailer Units*	*Fee*	*Drinking Water*
13	*2200*			*12*		*x*

Lake Ellen

Access: 15 miles SW of Kettle Falls via US 395, St. Hwy. 20, Cty. Rd. 412.
Special Activities & Facilities: Fishing, boating.

Map Location	*Elevation*	*Picnic Units*	*Tent Units*	*Tent-Trailer Units*	*Fee*	*Drinking Water*
14	*2300*			*11*		*x*

Map Location	Elevation	Picnic Units	Tent Units	Tent-Trailer Units	Fee	Drinking Water

Newport Ranger District

Panhandle

Access: 15 miles N of Usk via Cty. Rd. 9325.
Special Activities & Facilities: Fishing, boating, interpretive site.

Map Location	Elevation	Picnic Units	Tent Units	Tent-Trailer Units	Fee	Drinking Water
19	2000			11	x	x

Brown's Lake

Access: 25 miles N of Newport via Cty. Rds. 9325, 3389, FR 5030.
Special Activities & Facilities: Fishing (fly fishing only), non-motorized boating, trails.

Map Location	Elevation	Picnic Units	Tent Units	Tent-Trailer Units	Fee	Drinking Water
20	3400			18	x	x

South Skookum Lake

Access: 20 miles N of Newport via Cty. Rds. 9325, 3389, FR 5032.
Special Activities & Facilities: Boating, barrier-free, fishing, trails.

♿

Map Location	Elevation	Picnic Units	Tent Units	Tent-Trailer Units	Fee	Drinking Water
21	3500	10	10	15	x	x

Pioneer Park

Access: 2.5 miles N of Newport via Cty. Rd. 9305.
Special Activities & Facilities: Fishing, boating on Box Canyon Reservoir, interpretive site.

♿

Map Location	Elevation	Picnic Units	Tent Units	Tent-Trailer Units	Fee	Drinking Water
22	2000	9		14 ❶	x	x

Republic Ranger District

Ferry Lake

Access 14 miles SW of Republic via St. Hwy. 21, FRs 53, 800.
Special Activities & Facilities: Fishing, boating.

Map Location	Elevation	Picnic Units	Tent Units	Tent-Trailer Units	Fee	Drinking Water
17	3300		9	9	x	x

Swan Lake

Access: 15 miles SW of Republic via St. Hwy. 21 FR 353.
Special Activities & Facilities: Swimming, fishing.

Map Location	Elevation	Picnic Units	Tent Units	Tent-Trailer Units	Fee	Drinking Water
18	3700	17	4	25	x	x

Long Lake

Access: 16 miles S of Republic via St. Hwy. 21, FRs 53, 400.
Special Activities & Facilities: Swimming, fly fishing only.

Map Location	Elevation	Picnic Units	Tent Units	Tent-Trailer Units	Fee	Drinking Water
16	3300			12	x	x

Sullivan Lake Ranger District

Millpond

Access: 5 miles E of Metaline Falls via Cty. Rd. 9345.
Special Activities & Facilities: Fishing.

Map Location	*Elevation*	*Picnic Units*	*Tent Units*	*Tent-Trailer Units*	*Fee*	*Drinking Water*
2	2400			10	x	x

Sullivan Lake

Access: (East & West) 6.5 miles E of Metaline Falls via St. Hwy. 31, Cty. Rd. 9345.
Special Activities & Facilities: Boating, fishing, waterskiing, swimming.

Map Location	*Elevation*	*Picnic Units*	*Tent Units*	*Tent-Trailer Units*	*Fee*	*Drinking Water*
3	2600	15		35	x	x

Noisy Creek

Access: 10 miles S of Metaline Falls on Cty. Rd. 9345.
Special Activities & Facilities: Fishing, boating, swimming.

Map Location	*Elevation*	*Picnic Units*	*Tent Units*	*Tent-Trailer Units*	*Fee*	*Drinking Water*
4	2600			19	x	x

Edgewater

Access: 2 miles NE of Ione via Cty. Rds. 9345, 3669.
Special Activities & Facilities: Picnicking.

Map Location	*Elevation*	*Picnic Units*	*Tent Units*	*Tent-Trailer Units*	*Fee*	*Drinking Water*
5	2200	6		23		x

*Indicates more than one site in an area.

Handicapped Accessibility Codes
❶ Fully Accessible
❷ Usable
❸ Difficult
See page 7 for full description.

Deschutes National Forest

Mt. Bachelor and Elk Lake, Deschutes National Forest

Diversity is the word best used to describe Central Oregon's Deschutes National Forest. Start with a scenic backdrop of volcanic mountains that form the crest of the Cascade Divide, then add alpine forests, volcanic attractions, dense evergreen forests, mountain lakes, caves, desert areas, and alpine meadows. Elevations range from 2,000 feet at Lake Billy Chinook to 10,497 feet on Mt. Jefferson, the second highest peak in Oregon. Year-round recreation opportunities abound.

Special places of interest to the visitor include Lava Lands Visitor Center, Lava Butte where you can view lava fields and a fire lookout, Lava River Cave where you can rent a lantern and explore a lava tube, roaring Benham Falls, Lava Cast Forest Geologic Site, scenic Odell and Crescent lakes which straddle the Oregon Cascades, and the Upper Deschutes Recreation and Scenic River. In addition, there is the head of the Metolius where a river emerges from the ground, Camp Sherman fish-viewing bridge, tranquil head of Jack Creek,Wizard Falls fish hatchery, scenic Suttle Lake, Newberry Crater containing two lakes and an obsidian flow, spectacular Paulina Peak Overlook, Paulina Creek Falls, Mt. Bachelor for winter sports or summer viewing, Tumalo Falls, the Lava Island Indian rockshelter, and the Cascades Lakes Scenic Byway that skirts three major volcanoes and passes numerous lakes. The forest is also home to the Bend Pine Nursery, the Fire-Silviculture Research Laboratory, and the Redmond Fire and Aviation Center.

Further information about recreation opportunities, campground locations and facilities, as well as current maps of the area, are available at the following offices:

Deschutes National Forest
Supervisor's Office
1645 Highway 20 East
Bend, OR 97701
(503) 388-2715

Bend Ranger District
1230 NE 3rd, Suite A-262
Bend, OR 97701
(503) 388-5664

Crescent Ranger District
P.O. Box 208
Crescent, OR 97733
(503) 433-2234

Fort Rock Ranger District
1230 NE 3rd, Suite A262
Bend, OR 97701
(503) 388-5664

Sisters Ranger District
P.O. Box 249
Sisters, OR 97759
(503) 549-2111

Lava Lands Visitor Center
58201 South Highway 97
Bend, OR 97707
(503) 593-2421

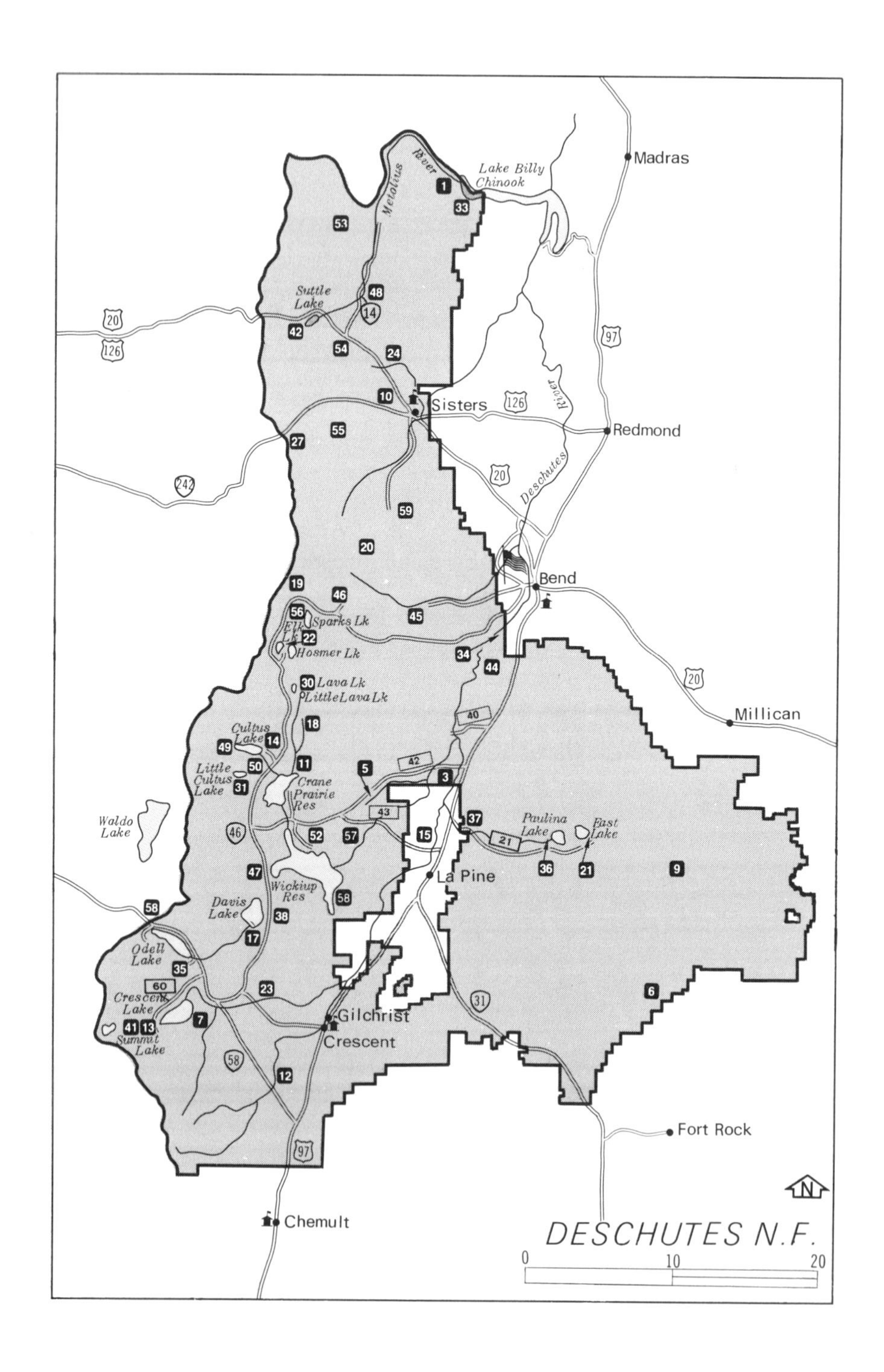

Madras
Lake Billy Chinook
Metolius River
Suttle Lake
Sisters
Redmond
Deschutes River
Bend
Sparks Lk
Elk Lk
Hosmer Lk
Lava Lk
Little Lava Lk
Cultus Lake
Little Cultus Lake
Crane Prairie Res
Waldo Lake
Paulina Lake
East Lake
La Pine
Wickiup Res
Davis Lake
Odell Lake
Crescent Lake
Summit Lake
Gilchrist
Crescent
Millican
Fort Rock
Chemult
DESCHUTES N.F.
0
10
20

DESCHUTES NATIONAL FOREST

Bend Ranger District

Big River

Access: 22 miles S of Bend on Cty. Rd. 42.
Special Activities & Facilities: Boating, fishing.

Map Location	Elevation	Picnic Units	Tent Units	Tent-Trailer Units	Fee	Drinking Water
3	4200		4	9		

Cow Meadow

Access: 46 miles SW of Bend via Hwy. 46, FR 620.
Special Activities & Facilities: N end of Crane Prairie Res., boating, fishing on Crane Prairie Res.

Map Location	Elevation	Picnic Units	Tent Units	Tent-Trailer Units	Fee	Drinking Water
11*	4400		4	16		

Crane Prairie

Access: 55 miles SW of Bend via Hwy. 46, FR 4270.
Special Activities & Facilities: Boating, fishing.

Map Location	Elevation	Picnic Units	Tent Units	Tent-Trailer Units	Fee	Drinking Water
♿ 11 *	4400	6	6❷	141❷	x	x

Cultus Lake

Access: 55 miles SW of Bend via Hwy. 46, FR 4635.
Special Activities & Facilities: Boating, fishing, swimming, waterskiing, trails.

Map Location	Elevation	Picnic Units	Tent Units	Tent-Trailer Units	Fee	Drinking Water
14*	4700	10		54	x	x

Deschutes Bridge

Access: 41 miles SW of Bend via Hwy. 46.
Special Activities & Facilities: Fishing.

Map Location	Elevation	Picnic Units	Tent Units	Tent-Trailer Units	Fee	Drinking Water
18*	4600	4		15	x	x

Devils Lake

Access: 28 miles SW of Bend via Hwy. 46.
Special Activities & Facilities: Fishing, trails.

Map Location	Elevation	Picnic Units	Tent Units	Tent-Trailer Units	Fee	Drinking Water
19	5500		6			

Elk Lake

Access: 33 miles SW of Bend via Hwy. 46.
Special Activities & Facilities: On SW side of lake, boating, sailing, fishing, swimming, trails.

Map Location	Elevation	Picnic Units	Tent Units	Tent-Trailer Units	Fee	Drinking Water
22*	4900			22	x	x

Fall River

Access: 30 miles S of Bend via US 97, Cty. Rd. 42.
Special Activities & Facilities: Fly fishing, barrier-free trails and toilets.

	Map Location	Elevation	Picnic Units	Tent Units	Tent-Trailer Units	Fee	Drinking Water
♿	5	4300	5❸		12		

Gull Point

Access: 39.5 miles SW of Bend via US 97, Cty. Rd. 42, FRs 42, 4260.
Special Activities & Facilities: Boating, fishing, swimming, waterskiing, concessionaire operated.

Map Location	Elevation	Picnic Units	Tent Units	Tent-Trailer Units	Fee	Drinking Water
52*	4300	10		80	x	x

Lava Lake

Access: 38 miles SW of Bend via Hwy. 46, FR 4600-500.
Special Activities & Facilities: Boating, fishing.

Map Location	Elevation	Picnic Units	Tent Units	Tent-Trailer Units	Fee	Drinking Water
30	4800	8		45	x	x

Little Cultus

Access: 50 miles SW of Bend via Hwy. 46, FR 4630.
Special Activities & Facilities: Boating, fishing, swimming, trails.

Map Location	Elevation	Picnic Units	Tent Units	Tent-Trailer Units	Fee	Drinking Water
31	4800			12		x

Little Fawn

Access: 38 miles SW of Bend via Hwy. 46, FR 4625.
Special Activities & Facilities: E side of Elk Lake, fishing, boating, swimming, group area reservations.

Map Location	Elevation	Picnic Units	Tent Units	Tent-Trailer Units	Fee	Drinking Water
22*	4900	4	4	29	x	x

Little Lava Lake

Access: 38 miles SW of Bend via Hwy. 46, FR 4600500.
Special Activities & Facilities: Boating, fishing, swimming.

Map Location	Elevation	Picnic Units	Tent Units	Tent-Trailer Units	Fee	Drinking Water
30*	4800			14		x

Mallard Marsh

Access: 34 miles SW of Bend via Hwy. 46, FR 4625.
Special Activities & Facilities: On Hosmer Lake, boating, fishing, good canoe lake.

Map Location	Elevation	Picnic Units	Tent Units	Tent-Trailer Units	Fee	Drinking Water
22*	4900			15		

Map Location	Elevation	Picnic Units	Tent Units	Tent-Trailer Units	Fee	Drinking Water

Mile Camp

Access: 40 miles SW of Bend via Hwy. 46, 1 mile before Deschutes Bridge.
Special Activities & Facilities: Fishing on Deschutes River.

Map Location	Elevation	Picnic Units	Tent Units	Tent-Trailer Units	Fee	Drinking Water
18*	4600			8		

North Davis Creek

Access: 26 miles W of La Pine, follow Hwy. 46 from Bend.
Special Activities & Facilities: W end of Wickiup Res., boating and fishing.

Map Location	Elevation	Picnic Units	Tent Units	Tent-Trailer Units	Fee	Drinking Water
47	4400	3		17	x	x

North Twin

Access: 38 miles SW of Bend via US 97, Cty. Rd. 42, FR 42.
Special Activities & Facilities: Boating, fishing, swimming.

Map Location	Elevation	Picnic Units	Tent Units	Tent-Trailer Units	Fee	Drinking Water
52*	4300			10		

Point

Access; 34 miles SW of Bend via Hwy. 46.
Special Activities & Facilities: On Elk Lake, boating, sailing, fishing, swimming, trails.

Map Location	Elevation	Picnic Units	Tent Units	Tent-Trailer Units	Fee	Drinking Water
22*	4900			9	x	x

Pringle Falls

Access: 9 miles NW of La Pine via US97, FR 43 just off FR 43.
Special Activities & Facilities: Lightly improved, fishing, canoe launching point.

Map Location	Elevation	Picnic Units	Tent Units	Tent-Trailer Units	Fee	Drinking Water
57	4300			7		

Quinn River

Access: 50 miles SW of Bend on Hwy. 46.
Special Activities & Facilities: On W side Crane Prairie Res., boating, fishing.

Map Location	Elevation	Picnic Units	Tent Units	Tent-Trailer Units	Fee	Drinking Water
50*	4400	2		41	x	x

Rock Creek

Access: 51 miles SW of Bend on Hwy. 46.
Special Activities & Facilities: On W side Crane Prairie Res., boating, fishing.

Map Location	Elevation	Picnic Units	Tent Units	Tent-Trailer Units	Fee	Drinking Water
50*	4400	3		32	x	x

Map Location	Elevation	Picnic Units	Tent Units	Tent-Trailer Units	Fee	Drinking Water

Sheep Bridge

Access: 19 miles W of La Pine via US 97N, Cty. Rd. 43, FR 42.
Special Activities & Facilities: On Wickiup Res., fishing.

*52**	*4400*			*17*		*x*

Soda Creek

Access: 26 miles W of Bend on Hwy. 46.
Special Activities & Facilities: On Sparks Lake, boating, fishing, trails, good canoe lake.

*56**	*5400*		*4*	*8*		

South

Access: 34 miles SW of Bend via Hwy. 46, FR 4625.
Special Activities & Facilities: On Hosmer Lake, boating, fishing, good canoeing.

*22**	*4900*			*23*		

South Twin Lake

Access: 19 miles SW of La Pine via US 97N, Cty. Rd. 43, FRs 42, 4260.
Special Activities & Facilities: Boating, fishing, swimming, concessionaire operated.

*52**	*4800*	*12*		*21*	*x*	*x*

Todd Lake

Access: 25 miles W of Bend 1 mile N of Hwy. 46.
Special Activities & Facilities: Site is lightly improved. Hike in campground.

46	*6200*	*4*	*4*			

Tumalo Falls

Access: 16 miles W of Bend via Hwy. 46, FR 4601 and 4603.
Special Activities & Facilities: Fishing.

45	*5000*	*4*	*4*			

West Cultus

Access: 48.6 miles SW of Bend via Hwy. 46, FR 4635, boat or hike in.
Special Activities & Facilities: No road access, boating, fishing, swimming, waterskiing.

49	*4700*		*15*			

Map Location	Elevation	Picnic Units	Tent Units	Tent-Trailer Units	Fee	Drinking Water

West South Twin

Access: 20 miles W of La Pine via US 97N, FRs 43, 42, 4260.
Special Activities & Facilities: Boating, swimming, fishing, concessionaire operated.

*52**	*4300*			*24*	*x*	*x*

Reservoir

Access: 27 miles W of La Pine on Wickiup Res. Follow Hwy. 46, FR 44 from Bend.
Special Activities & Facilities: Boating, fishing.

47	*4400*	*4*		*28*		

Dillon Falls

Access: 11 miles SW of Bend via Hwy. 46, FR 41.
Special Activities & Facilities: Boating, fishing.

*34**	*4000*			*7*		

Wickiup Butte

Access: 18.3 miles W of La Pine via Cty. Rd. 43, FRs 44, 4260.
Special Activities & Facilities: Boating, fishing, E shore Wickiup Reservoir.

58	*4400*			*5*		

Bend Ranger District

Day Use Areas

Meadow Camp

Access: 7 miles W of Bend off Hwy. 46.
Special Activities & Facilities: On Deschutes River, fishing.

*34 **	*3800*	*10*				

Beach

Access: 33 miles SW of Bend on Hwy. 46.
Special Activities & Facilities: On Elk Lake, boating, sailing, fishing, swimming, trails.

*22**	*4900*	*6*				*x*

Map Location	Elevation	Picnic Units	Tent Units	Tent-Trailer Units	Fee	Drinking Water

Sunset View

Access: 36 miles SW of Bend via Hwy. 46, FR 4625.
Special Activities & Facilities: E side of Elk Lake, fishing, swimming.

Map Location	Elevation	Picnic Units	Tent Units	Tent-Trailer Units	Fee	Drinking Water
*22**	*4900*	*5*				

Lava Lake

Access: 38 miles SW of Bend via Hwy. 46, FR 4625.
Special Activities & Facilities: Boating, fishing.

Map Location	Elevation	Picnic Units	Tent Units	Tent-Trailer Units	Fee	Drinking Water
30	*4800*	*8*				

Horse Camp

Quinn Meadow

Access: 34 miles W of Bend via Hwy. 46, FR 450.
Special Activities & Facilities: Reservation, fishing, trails.

Map Location	Elevation	Picnic Units	Tent Units	Tent-Trailer Units	Fee	Drinking Water
*22**	*5200*			*27*	*x*	*x*

Crescent Ranger District

Contorta Point

Access: 8 miles SW of Hwy. 58 & FR 60 Jct. via FR 60.
Special Activities & Facilities: Boating, fishing, swimming, and waterskiing at S end Crescent Lake.

Map Location	Elevation	Picnic Units	Tent Units	Tent-Trailer Units	Fee	Drinking Water
*13**	*4800*			*12*		

Crescent Creek

Access: 9 miles NW of Crescent on Cty. Rd. 61.
Special Activities & Facilities: Fishing.

Map Location	Elevation	Picnic Units	Tent Units	Tent-Trailer Units	Fee	Drinking Water
23	*4500*			*10*	*x*	*x*

Crescent Lake

Access: 3 miles SW of Crescent Lake Junction with Hwy. 58 on FR 60.
Special Activities & Facilities: Boating, fishing, swimming, windsurfing, waterskiing, trails.

Map Location	Elevation	Picnic Units	Tent Units	Tent-Trailer Units	Fee	Drinking Water
♿ *7**	*4800*	*5❸*		*46❸*	*x*	*x*

<table>
<tr><th>Map Location</th><th>Elevation</th><th>Picnic Units</th><th>Tent Units</th><th>Tent-Trailer Units</th><th>Fee</th><th>Drinking Water</th></tr>
<tr><td colspan="7">East Davis Lake
Access: 11 miles NW of Hwy 58/61 Jct. via Hwy. 46 on Davis Lake.
Special Activities & Facilities: Boating and fishing (very shallow lake). Fly fishing only.</td></tr>
<tr><td>17*</td><td>4400</td><td></td><td></td><td>33</td><td>x</td><td>x</td></tr>
<tr><td colspan="7">Lava Flow
Access: 14 miles NW of Hwy. 58/61 Jct. via Hwy. 46.
Special Activities & Facilities: Boating, fishing, and duck hunting (very shallow lake), fly fishing only.</td></tr>
<tr><td>38</td><td>4400</td><td></td><td></td><td>12</td><td></td><td></td></tr>
<tr><td colspan="7">Odell Creek
Access: Just off Hwy. 58 at SE end of Odell Lake.
Special Activities & Facilities: Boating, fishing, and trails.</td></tr>
<tr><td>35*</td><td>4800</td><td></td><td></td><td>22</td><td>x</td><td>x</td></tr>
<tr><td colspan="7">Princess Creek
Access: 2 miles E of Willamette Pass on Hwy. 58 on N side of Odell Lake.
Special Activities & Facilities: Boating, fishing, waterskiing.</td></tr>
<tr><td>58*</td><td>4800</td><td>5</td><td></td><td>46</td><td>x</td><td>x</td></tr>
<tr><td colspan="7">Spring
Access: 6.5 miles SW of Crescent Lake Jct with Hwy. 58 on FR 60.
Special Activities & Facilities: Boating, fishing, swimming, windsurfing, waterskiing, trails, on Crescent Lake.</td></tr>
<tr><td>13*</td><td>4800</td><td>8</td><td></td><td>68</td><td>x</td><td>x</td></tr>
<tr><td colspan="7">Summit Lake
Access: 12 miles SW of Crescent Lake Jct with Hwy. 58 via FRs 60, 6010. Narrow, primitive road.
Special Activities & Facilities: Canoeing, fishing, and trails.</td></tr>
<tr><td>41</td><td>5600</td><td></td><td></td><td>3</td><td></td><td></td></tr>
<tr><td colspan="7">Sunset Cove
Access: Hwy. 58, 5 miles E of Willamette Pass on N side of Odell Lake.
Special Activities & Facilities: Boating, fishing, windsurfing.</td></tr>
<tr><td>35*</td><td>4800</td><td>4❸</td><td></td><td>26</td><td>x</td><td>x</td></tr>
</table>

Map Location	Elevation	Picnic Units	Tent Units	Tent-Trailer Units	Fee	Drinking Water

Trapper Creek

Access: Via Hwy. 58, Fr 5810, near Willamette Pass.
Special Activities & Facilities: Boating, fishing, and trails.

58*	4800			32	x	x

West Davis Lake

Access: 13 miles NW of Hwys. 58/61 Jct. via Hwy. 46. On S end of Davis Lake.
Special Activities & Facilities: Boating and fishing (very shallow lake). Fly fishing only.

17*	4400			25	x	x

Day Use Areas

Tandy Bay

Access: 6 miles SW of Hwy. 58 and FR 60 Jct., on FR 60.
Special Activities & Facilities: Boating, fishing, swimming, and waterskiing.

13*	4800	2				

Tranquil Cove

Access: 5 miles SW Hwy. 58 and FR 60 Jct., on FR 60.
Special Activities & Facilities: Boating, fishing, and swimming, waterskiing.

13*	4800	5				

Simax Beach

Access: 4 miles SW of Hwy. 58 and FR 60 Jct. via FRs 60, 110. At NE end of Crescent Lake.
Special Activities & Facilities: Waterskiing, swimming, windsurfing.

7	4800	16				

Horse Camps

Whitefish Camp

Access: 7 miles SW of Hwy. 58 and FR 60 Jct., on FR 60.
Special Activities & Facilities: Horse use and trails, fishing, hiking, boating nearby; reservation advised.

13*	4800			19	x	

Map Location	Elevation	Picnic Units	Tent Units	Tent-Trailer Units	Fee	Drinking Water

Fort Rock Ranger District

Cabin Lake

Access: 10 miles N of Ft. Rock via Cty. Rd. 18.
Special Activities & Facilities: Hunting and bird watching, lightly improved.

Map Location	Elevation	Picnic Units	Tent Units	Tent-Trailer Units	Fee	Drinking Water
6	*4500*			*14*		*x*

China Hat

Access: 32 miles SE of Bend via US 97, FR 18.
Special Activities & Facilities: Hunting, lightly improved.

Map Location	Elevation	Picnic Units	Tent Units	Tent-Trailer Units	Fee	Drinking Water
9	*5100*			*14*		*x*

Cinder Hill

Access: 18 miles E of US 97 via Cty. Rd. 21.
Special Activities & Facilities: Boating, fishing, viewpoint and trails, on East Lake.

Map Location	Elevation	Picnic Units	Tent Units	Tent-Trailer Units	Fee	Drinking Water
*21**	*6370*			*110*	*x*	*x*

East Lake

Access: 17 mile SE of US 97 via Cty. Rd. 21.
Special Activities & Facilities: Boating, fishing, viewpoint, barrier-tree trails and toilets.

Map Location	Elevation	Picnic Units	Tent Units	Tent-Trailer Units	Fee	Drinking Water
♿ *21**	*6370*			*29*	*x*	*x*

Hot Springs

Access: 17 mile SE of US 97 via Cty. Rd. 21.
Special Activities & Facilities: Boating, fishing, trails, viewpoint and picnicking.

Map Location	Elevation	Picnic Units	Tent Units	Tent-Trailer Units	Fee	Drinking Water
*21**	*6370*	*5*		*42*	*x*	*x*

Little Crater

Access: 15 miles E of US 97 via Cty. Rd. 21.
Special Activities & Facilities: Boating, fishing, trails, sailing, picnicking and viewpoint, Newberry Crater.

Map Location	Elevation	Picnic Units	Tent Units	Tent-Trailer Units	Fee	Drinking Water
*36**	*6330*	*5*		*50*	*x*	*x*

Map Location	Elevation	Picnic Units	Tent Units	Tent-Trailer Units	Fee	Drinking Water

Paulina Lake

Access: 13 miles E of US 97 via Cty. Rd. 21.
Special Activities & Facilities: Boating, sailing, fishing, playground, picnicking, viewpoint and trails, Newberry Crater.

Map Location	Elevation	Picnic Units	Tent Units	Tent-Trailer Units	Fee	Drinking Water
36*	6330	7		69	x	x

Prairie

Access: Just off Cty. Rd. 21, 3 miles SE of US 97.
Special Activities & Facilities: Trails.

Map Location	Elevation	Picnic Units	Tent Units	Tent-Trailer Units	Fee	Drinking Water
37*	4300			16	x	x

Rosland

Access: 2 miles W of Wickiup Jct. on Cty. Rd. 43.
Special Activities & Facilities: Fishing.

Map Location	Elevation	Picnic Units	Tent Units	Tent-Trailer Units	Fee	Drinking Water
15	4200	1		10		

McKay Crossing

Access: 5 miles E of US 97 via Cty. Rd. 21, FR 2120.
Special Activities & Facilities: Fishing, lightly improved.

Map Location	Elevation	Picnic Units	Tent Units	Tent-Trailer Units	Fee	Drinking Water
37*	4400		10			

Day Use Areas

Benham Falls

Access: 4 miles W of Lava Butte on FR 9702.
Special Activities & Facilities: Boating, fishing, and trails.

Map Location	Elevation	Picnic Units	Tent Units	Tent-Trailer Units	Fee	Drinking Water
44	4100	6				

Paulina Creek Falls

Access: 13 miles E US 97 on Cty. Rd. 21.
Special Activities & Facilities: Trails.

Map Location	Elevation	Picnic Units	Tent Units	Tent-Trailer Units	Fee	Drinking Water
36*	6240	5				

Horse Camps

Chief Paulina

Access: 14 miles E of US 97 on FR 21.
Special Activities & Facilities: Horse trails and viewpoint, Paulina Lake, (reservations available).

Map Location	Elevation	Picnic Units	Tent Units	Tent-Trailer Units	Fee	Drinking Water
36*	6330			13	x	

Map Location	Elevation	Picnic Units	Tent Units	Tent-Trailer Units	Fee	Drinking Water

Group Camps

Ogden Group

Access: 4 miles E of US 97 on Cty. Rd. 21.
Special Activities & Facilities: Large flat area near stream suitable for family reunions, company campouts, etc., trails, reservations.

Map Location	Elevation	Picnic Units	Tent Units	Tent-Trailer Units	Fee	Drinking Water
37*	4300			64	x	x

Newberry Group

Access: 14 miles E of US 97 on Cty. Rd. 21 at Paulina Lake.
Special Activities & Facilities: Located on shore of Paulina Lake, suitable for family reunions, company campouts, etc., barrier-free trails and toilets, reservations.

Map Location	Elevation	Picnic Units	Tent Units	Tent-Trailer Units	Fee	Drinking Water
36*	6330			32	x	x

Sisters Ranger District

Allen Springs

Access: N of Sisters via US 20, Cty. Rd. 14, then 5 miles N of Camp Sherman Store on the Metolius River.
Special Activities & Facilities: Fishing and trails.

Map Location	Elevation	Picnic Units	Tent Units	Tent-Trailer Units	Fee	Drinking Water
48*	2800		4	13	x	x

Allingham

Access: N of Sisters via Us 20, Cty. Rd. 14, then 1 mile N of Camp Sherman Store on the Metolius River.
Special Activities & Facilities: Fishing and trails.

Map Location	Elevation	Picnic Units	Tent Units	Tent-Trailer Units	Fee	Drinking Water
48*	2900			10	x	x

Blue Bay

Access: 14 miles NW of Sisters on Suttle Lake via US 20, FR 2070.
Special Activities & Facilities: Fishing, boating, waterskiing, and trails.

Map Location	Elevation	Picnic Units	Tent Units	Tent-Trailer Units	Fee	Drinking Water
42*	3400			25	x	x

<table>
<tr><th>Map Location</th><th>Elevation</th><th>Picnic Units</th><th>Tent Units</th><th>Tent-Trailer Units</th><th>Fee</th><th>Drinking Water</th></tr>
<tr><td colspan="7">Camp Sherman
Access: N of Sisters via US 20, Cty. Rd. 14, then 1/2 mile N of Camp Sherman Store on the Metolius River.
Special Activities & Facilities: Fishing and trails.</td></tr>
<tr><td>48*</td><td>3000</td><td>1</td><td></td><td>15</td><td>x</td><td>x</td></tr>
<tr><td colspan="7">Cold Springs
Access: 5 miles W of Sisters on Hwy. 242.
Special Activities & Facilities:</td></tr>
<tr><td>10</td><td>3400</td><td>5</td><td></td><td>23</td><td>x</td><td>x</td></tr>
<tr><td colspan="7">Driftwood
Access: 18 miles S of Sisters on FR 16.
Special Activities & Facilities: Fishing and trails, RVs under 16' on Three Creek Lake.</td></tr>
<tr><td>20 *</td><td>6400</td><td></td><td></td><td>14</td><td></td><td></td></tr>
<tr><td colspan="7">Gorge
Access: N of Sisters via US 20, Cty. Rd. 14, then 2 miles N of Camp Sherman Store on the Metolius River.
Special Activities & Facilities: Fishing and trails.</td></tr>
<tr><td>48*</td><td>2900</td><td></td><td></td><td>18</td><td>x</td><td>x</td></tr>
<tr><td colspan="7">Indian Ford
Access: 5 miles NW of Sisters on US 20.
Special Activities & Facilities: Fishing.</td></tr>
<tr><td>24</td><td>3200</td><td>3</td><td></td><td>25</td><td>x</td><td>x</td></tr>
<tr><td colspan="7">Lava Camp Lake
Access: 12 miles West of Sisters at McKenzie Pass via Hwy. 242.
Special Activities & Facilities: Fishing and trails.</td></tr>
<tr><td>27</td><td>5200</td><td></td><td>2</td><td>10</td><td></td><td></td></tr>
<tr><td colspan="7">Black Pine
Access: 8 miles S of Sisters on FR 16.
Special Activities & Facilities: Lightly improved.</td></tr>
<tr><td>59</td><td>4400</td><td></td><td></td><td>7</td><td></td><td></td></tr>
</table>

Map Location	Elevation	Picnic Units	Tent Units	Tent-Trailer Units	Fee	Drinking Water

Link Creek

Access: 15 miles NW of Sisters via US 20 at W end of Suttle Lake.
Special Activities & Facilities: Boating, fishing, swimming, waterskiing, and trails.

Map Location	Elevation	Picnic Units	Tent Units	Tent-Trailer Units	Fee	Drinking Water
42*	3400			33	x	x

Lower Bridge

Access: N of Sisters via US 20, Cty. Rd. 14, then 9 miles N of Camp Sherman Store on the Metolius River.
Special Activities & Facilities: Fishing and trails.

Map Location	Elevation	Picnic Units	Tent Units	Tent-Trailer Units	Fee	Drinking Water
48*	2800	3		12	x	x

Monty

Access: 30 miles NW of Culver via Cove State Park on Lower Metolius River.
Special Activities & Facilities: Fishing.

Map Location	Elevation	Picnic Units	Tent Units	Tent-Trailer Units	Fee	Drinking Water
1	2100			45		

Perry South

Access: 25 miles NW of Culver via Cove State Park near Lake Billy Chinook.
Special Activities & Facilities: Fishing, boating and swimming.

Map Location	Elevation	Picnic Units	Tent Units	Tent-Trailer Units	Fee	Drinking Water
33	2000	6	4	62	x	x

Pine Rest

Access: N of Sisters via US 20, Cty. Rd. 14, then 1-1/2 miles N of Camp Sherman Store on the Metolius River.
Special Activities & Facilities: Fishing and trails.

Map Location	Elevation	Picnic Units	Tent Units	Tent-Trailer Units	Fee	Drinking Water
48*	2900		8		x	x

Pioneer Ford

Access: N of Sisters via US 20, Cty. Rd. 14, then 6-1/2 miles N of Camp Sherman Store on the Metolius River.
Special Activities & Facilities: Fishing and trails.

Map Location	Elevation	Picnic Units	Tent Units	Tent-Trailer Units	Fee	Drinking Water
♿ 48*	2800	1	2	18❸	x	x

Riverside

Access: N of Sisters via US 20, Cty. Rd. 14, then 2 miles S of Camp Sherman Store on the Metolius River.
Special Activities & Facilities: Fishing, lightly improved.

Map Location	Elevation	Picnic Units	Tent Units	Tent-Trailer Units	Fee	Drinking Water
48*	3000			22	x	x

<table>
<tr><th>Map Location</th><th>Elevation</th><th>Picnic Units</th><th>Tent Units</th><th>Tent-Trailer Units</th><th>Fee</th><th>Drinking Water</th></tr>
<tr><td colspan="7">Scout Lake</td></tr>
<tr><td colspan="7">Access: 14 miles NW of Sisters via US 20, FRs 2070, 2066 just S of Suttle Lake.
Special Activities & Facilities: Swimming and trails (group area reservations).</td></tr>
<tr><td>42*</td><td>3700</td><td>14</td><td>3</td><td>19</td><td>x</td><td>x</td></tr>
<tr><td colspan="7">Smiling River</td></tr>
<tr><td colspan="7">Access: N of Sisters via US 20, Cty. Rd. 14, then 1 mile N of Camp Sherman Store on the Metolius River.
Special Activities & Facilities: Fishing and trails.</td></tr>
<tr><td>48*</td><td>2900</td><td></td><td></td><td>37</td><td>x</td><td>x</td></tr>
<tr><td colspan="7">South Shore</td></tr>
<tr><td colspan="7">Access: 14 miles NW of Sisters via US 20, FR 2070 on Suttle Lake.
Special Activities & Facilities: Fishing, boating, swimming, and trails.</td></tr>
<tr><td>42*</td><td>3400</td><td>4</td><td></td><td>38</td><td>x</td><td>x</td></tr>
<tr><td colspan="7">Three Creeks Lake</td></tr>
<tr><td colspan="7">Access: 18 miles S of Sisters on FR 16.
Special Activities & Facilities: Fishing and trails, RVs under 16'.</td></tr>
<tr><td>20*</td><td>6400</td><td></td><td></td><td>10</td><td></td><td></td></tr>
<tr><td colspan="7">Jack Creek</td></tr>
<tr><td colspan="7">Access: N of Sisters via US 20, FRs 12, 1230.
Special Activities & Facilities: Fishing, hiking trails.</td></tr>
<tr><td>48*</td><td>3100</td><td></td><td></td><td>9</td><td></td><td></td></tr>
</table>

Handicapped Accessibility Codes

- ❶ Fully Accessible
- ❷ Usable
- ❸ Difficult

See page 7 for full description.

*Indicates more than one site in area.

Map Location	Elevation	Picnic Units	Tent Units	Tent-Trailer Units	Fee	Drinking Water

Day Use Areas

Suttle Lake Picnic

Access: 14 miles NW of Sisters via US 20 at the E end of lake (on Suttle Lake Resort Road).
Special Activities & Facilities: Fishing and trails (barrier-free toilet facilities).

Map Location	Elevation	Picnic Units	Tent Units	Tent-Trailer Units	Fee	Drinking Water
42*	3400	7				x

Suttle Lake Water Ski

Access: 14 miles NW of Sisters via US 20 at W end of lake.
Special Activities & Facilities: Waterskiing.

Map Location	Elevation	Picnic Units	Tent Units	Tent-Trailer Units	Fee	Drinking Water
42*	3400	3				

Horse Camps

Sheep Springs

Access: (Reservation) 22 miles NW of Sisters via US 20, FRs 12, 1230 just off FR 1230.
Special Activities & Facilities: Horse use and trails (40 box stalls, Metolius-Windigo Horse Trail).

Map Location	Elevation	Picnic Units	Tent Units	Tent-Trailer Units	Fee	Drinking Water
53	3200			10	x	x

Graham Corral

Access: 9 miles NW of Sisters via US 20, FRs 1012, 1012300, 342.
Special Activities & Facilities: Horse use and trails (corral, Metolius-Windogo Horse Trail).

Map Location	Elevation	Picnic Units	Tent Units	Tent-Trailer Units	Fee	Drinking Water
54	3400			10		x

Three Creek Meadow

Access: 16 miles S of Sisters on FR 16.
Special Activities & Facilities: Horse use and trails (32 box stalls, Meolius-Windigo Horse Trail).

Map Location	Elevation	Picnic Units	Tent Units	Tent-Trailer Units	Fee	Drinking Water
20	6300			19		

Whispering Pine

Access: 11 miles SW Sisters via Hwy. 242 W, FR 1018.
Special Activities & Facilities: Fishing, horse use, 28 box stalls.

Map Location	Elevation	Picnic Units	Tent Units	Tent-Trailer Units	Fee	Drinking Water
55	4400			7		

Fremont National Forest

Warner Mountains, Fremont National Forest

Encompassing some 1.2 million acres in south-central Oregon, the Fremont National Forest is characterized by expansive views, dramatic cliffs, and distinctive rock outcroppings. A beautiful contrast of colors throughout the year is created by open meadows and mixed stands of aspen and pine. You will find forest vistas from many of the prominent peaks. The Gearhart Mountain Wilderness, one of the most scenic areas in the forest, provides outstanding opportunities for solitude. Several indigenous Indian tribes inhabit the area and ancient tribal sites are protected.

Special places of interest to the visitor include the rugged and remote Gearhart Mountain; Abert Rim viewpoint, over 2,500 feet above the valley floor; Big Hole, which is a huge explosion crater; a giant prehistoric landslide at Slide Mountain Geologic Area; a dramatic overlook of Crooked Creek Canyon from North Warner viewpoint; Mitchell Monument; Drake Peak lookout; and a panoramic vista of Summer Lake from Winter Ridge viewpoint.

Further information about recreation opportunities, campground locations and facilities, as well as current maps of the area, are available at the following offices:

Fremont National Forest
Supervisor's Office
524 North G Street
Lakeview, OR 97630
(503) 947-2151

Bly Ranger District
Bly, OR 97622
(503) 353-2427

Lakeview Ranger District
HC-64 Box 60
Lakeview, OR 97630
(503) 947-3334

Paisley Ranger District
Paisley, OR 97636
(503) 943-3114

Silver Lake Ranger District
Silver Lake, OR 97638
(503) 576-2107

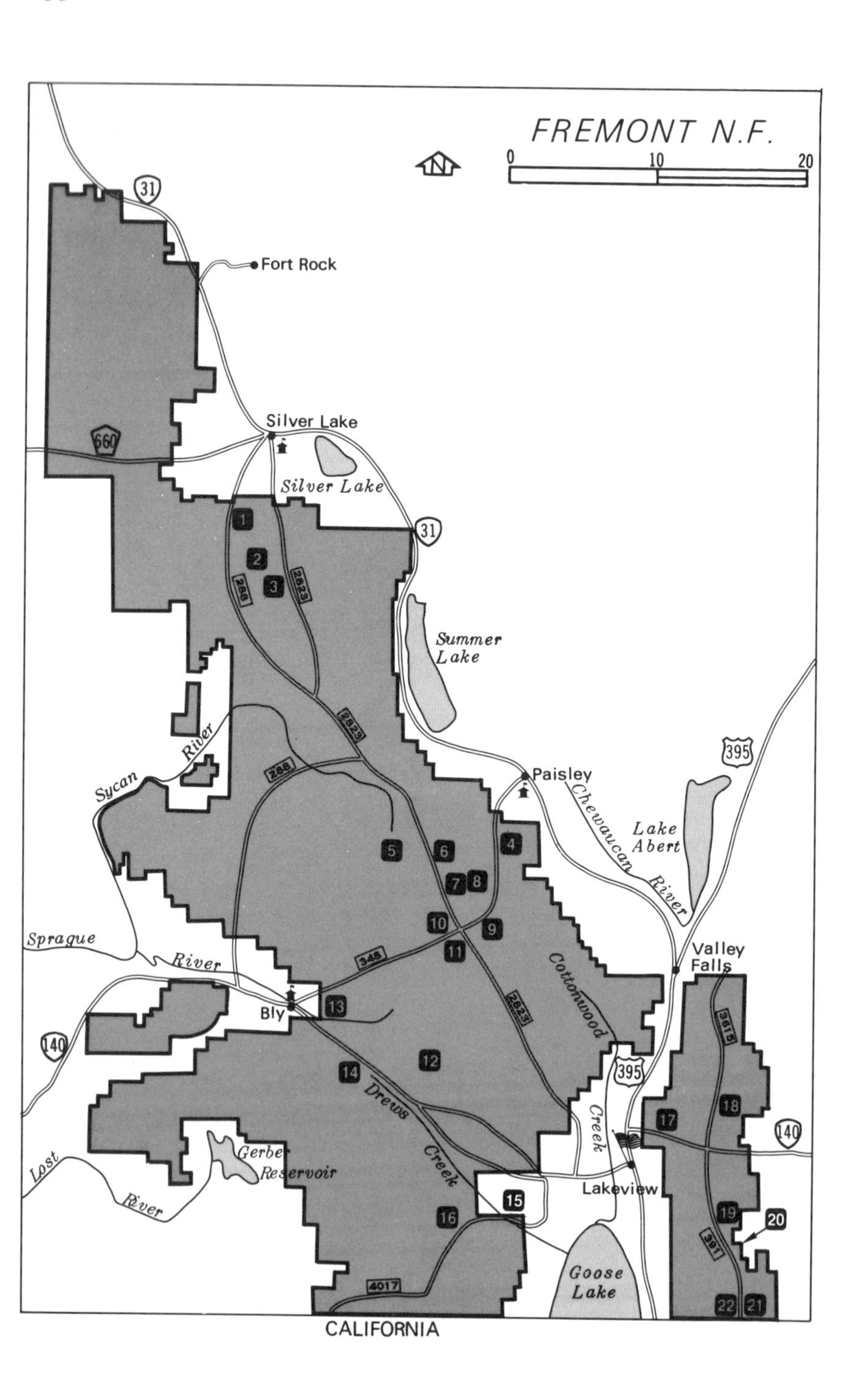
FREMONT N.F.
0
10
20
N
31
Fort Rock
660
Silver Lake
Silver Lake
31
Summer Lake
Sycan River
Paisley
Chewaucan River
Lake Abert
395
Sprague River
Valley Falls
Cottonwood
Bly
140
395
Drews Creek
Creek
Gerber Reservoir
Lost River
Lakeview
140
Goose Lake
CALIFORNIA
1
2
3
4
5
6
7
8
9
10
11
12
13
14
15
16
17
18
19
20
21
22
266
2823
348
4017
3615
391

FREMONT NATIONAL FOREST

Map Location	*Elevation*	*Picnic Units*	*Tent Units*	*Tent-Trailer Units*	*Fee*	*Drinking Water*

Developed Sites

Silver Creek Marsh

Access: 10 miles SW of Silver Lake via Cty. Rd. 4-11, on FR 27.
Special Activities & Facilities: Fishing, hunting.

Map Location	Elevation	Picnic Units	Tent Units	Tent-Trailer Units	Fee	Drinking Water
1	*5000*	*1*	*7*			*x*

Thompson Reservoir

Access: 14.2 miles S of Silver Lake via Cty. Rd. 4-11 off FR 27.
Special Activities & Facilities: Boat launch, fishing, hunting.

Map Location	Elevation	Picnic Units	Tent Units	Tent-Trailer Units	Fee	Drinking Water
2	*5000*	*3*		*19*		*x*

East Bay

Access: 14 miles S of Silver Lake via Cty. Rd. 4-12 off FR 28.
Special Activities & Facilities: Boat launch, fishing, hunting.

Map Location	Elevation	Picnic Units	Tent Units	Tent-Trailer Units	Fee	Drinking Water
3	*5000*			*10*		*x*

Marsters Spring

Access: 8.1 miles S of Paisley via Cty. Rd. 2-8, on FR 33.
Special Activities & Facilities: Fishing, hunting.

Map Location	Elevation	Picnic Units	Tent Units	Tent-Trailer Units	Fee	Drinking Water
4	*5400*			*10*		*x*

Sandhill Crossing

Access: 30.2 miles SW of Paisley via Cty. Rd. 2-8, FRs 3315, S on 28, 3411.
Special Activities & Facilities: Fishing, hunting.

Map Location	Elevation	Picnic Units	Tent Units	Tent-Trailer Units	Fee	Drinking Water
5	*5900*			*5*		*x*

Lee Thomas

Access: 27.9 miles SW of Paisley via Cty. Rd. 2-8, FRs 3315, S on 28, 3411.
Special Activities & Facilities: Fishing, hunting.

Map Location	Elevation	Picnic Units	Tent Units	Tent-Trailer Units	Fee	Drinking Water
6	*6200*			*7*		*x*

Deadhorse Lake

Access: 27 miles SW of Paisley via Cty. Rd. 2-8, FRs 3315, S on 28, 033.
Special Activities & Facilities: Fishing, hiking.

Map Location	Elevation	Picnic Units	Tent Units	Tent-Trailer Units	Fee	Drinking Water
7	*7400*	*6*	*6*	*9*		*x*

Campbell Lake

Access: 26 miles SW of Paisley via Cty. Rd. 2-8, FRs 3315, S on 28, 033.
Special Activities & Facilities: Boat launch, fishing, hiking.

Map Location	Elevation	Picnic Units	Tent Units	Tent-Trailer Units	Fee	Drinking Water
8	*7200*	*2*		*15*		*x*

Map Location	Elevation	Picnic Units	Tent Units	Tent-Trailer Units	Fee	Drinking Water

Happy Camp

Access: 24.7 miles SW of Paisley via Cty. Rd. 2-8, FRs 33, 28, 2800-047.
Special Activities & Facilities: Fishing, hunting.

Map Location	Elevation	Picnic Units	Tent Units	Tent-Trailer Units	Fee	Drinking Water
9	5200			9		x

Corral Creek

Access: 19 miles E of Bly via St. Hwy. 140, FRs 34, 012.
Special Activities & Facilities: Lightly improved, wilderness access, hunting, fishing, wildlife viewing.

Map Location	Elevation	Picnic Units	Tent Units	Tent-Trailer Units	Fee	Drinking Water
NA	6000		5			

Dairy Point

Access: 21.2 miles SW of Paisley via Cty. Rd. 2-8, FRs 33, 28, Jct. with 3428.
Special Activities & Facilities: Fishing, hunting.

Map Location	Elevation	Picnic Units	Tent Units	Tent-Trailer Units	Fee	Drinking Water
11	5200			4		x

Cottonwood Meadows

Access: 25 miles NW of Lakeview via St. Hwy. 140, FR 3870.
Special Activities & Facilities: Fishing, hunting, boat launch, RVs under 16', trails.

Map Location	Elevation	Picnic Units	Tent Units	Tent-Trailer Units	Fee	Drinking Water
12	6100	10	7	9		x

Sprague River

Access: 4.2 miles SE of Bly via St. Hwy. 140.
Special Activities & Facilities: Fishing.

Map Location	Elevation	Picnic Units	Tent Units	Tent-Trailer Units	Fee	Drinking Water
13	4400	11				x

Lofton Reservoir

Access: 21.0 miles SE of Bly via St. Hwy. 140, FRs 3715, 013.
Special Activities & Facilities: Fishing, boat launching.

Map Location	Elevation	Picnic Units	Tent Units	Tent-Trailer Units	Fee	Drinking Water
14	6200			14		x

Drews Creek

Access: 13.7 miles SW of Lakeview via St. Hwy. 140, Cty. Rds. 1-13, 1-11-0, FR 4017.
Special Activities & Facilities: Fishing, hunting, group picnicking, RVs under 16'.

Map Location	Elevation	Picnic Units	Tent Units	Tent-Trailer Units	Fee	Drinking Water
15	4900	10	1	4		x

Map Location	*Elevation*	*Picnic Units*	*Tent Units*	*Tent-Trailer Units*	*Fee*	*Drinking Water*

Dog Lake

Access: 25 miles SW of Lakeview via St. Hwy. 140, Cty. Rds 1-13, 1-11-0, FR 4017.
Special Activities & Facilities: Boat launch, fishing, hunting, RVs under 16'.

16	*5100*	*1*	*3*	*6*		

Warner Canyon Ski Area

Access: 11 miles NE of Lakeview on St. Hwy. 140.
Special Activities & Facilities: Downhill and cross-country skiing. Food service.

17	*5700*				*x*	*x*

Mud Creek

Access: 18 miles NE of Lakeview via St. Hwy. 140, on FR 3615.
Special Activities & Facilities: Fishing, hunting, RVs under 16'.

18	*6600*			*7*		*x*

Willow Creek

Access: 22 miles SE of Lakeview via St. Hwy. 140, FRs 3915, 4011.
Special Activities & Facilities: Fishing, hunting.

19	*5800*			*8*		*x*

Deep Creek

Access: 28 miles SE of Lakeview via St. Hwy. 140, FRs 3915, 4015.
Special Activities & Facilities: Fishing, hunting.

20	*5600*		*1*	*4*		

Cave Lake (California)

Access: 10 miles E of New Pine Creek on FR 2.
Special Activities & Facilities: Fishing, boating.

21	*5800*			*6*		*x*

Lily Lake (California)

Access: 10 miles E of New Pine Creek on FR 2.
Special Activities & Facilities: Fishing, boating

22	*5800*		*6*			*x*

...rd Pinchot National Forest

Mt. Adams and Takhlakh Lake, Gifford Pinchot National Forest

On the densely forested slopes of the Cascade Mountains in s
Washington, you will find the Gifford Pinchot National Forest between the Columbia River Gorge on the south and Mt. Rainier National Park to the north. Mount St. Helens, the volcanic dynamo that announced itself in May 1980, and Mt. Adams, a dormant volcano, are within the forest boundary. These mountains exist in old Indian folklore and are significant in the lives and religious customs of local Native American tribes. Heavily forested with Douglas-fir, hemlock, western redcedar, and true firs, the forest offers scenic drives and year-round recreation activities. For backcountry hikers, there are seven wilderness areas, dotted with many lakes and streams and home to an abundant range of wildlife.

Special places of interest to the visitor include Mount St. Helens National Volcanic Monument; Mt. Adams, a glorious white peak over 12,000 feet; an area of alpine meadows and mountain peaks, called the Goat Rocks Wilderness; the secluded Indian Heaven Wilderness; extensive Big Lava Bed; Packwood Lake near Mt. Rainier; Wind River Nursery with thousands of young tree seedlings; a spectacular wildflower display at Silver Star Mountain; Bear Meadow, on the edge of the Mount St. Helens blast zone; the Sawtooth huckleberry fields; Lewis River country; secluded Walupt Lake; scenic Takhlakh Lake; and Quartz Creek Big Trees.

Further information about recreation opportunities, campground locations and facilities, as well as current maps of the area, are available at the following offices:

Gifford Pinchot National Forest
Supervisor's Office
6926 E. 4th Plain Blvd.
Vancouver, WA 98668-8944
(206) 696-7500

Mt. Adams Ranger District
2455 Hwy. 141
Trout Lake, WA 98650-9724
(509) 395-2501

Packwood Ranger District
P.O. Box 539
Packwood, WA 98361-0559
(206) 494-5515

Randle Ranger District
Randle, WA 98377-9105
(206) 497-7565

Wind River Ranger District
Carson, WA 98610-9725
(509) 427-5645

Mount St. Helens National Volcanic
Monument Headquarters
Rt. 1, Box 369
Amboy, WA 98601-9715
(206) 247-5473

Mount St. Helens National Volcanic
Monument Visitor Center
3029 Spirit Lake Highway
Castle Rock, WA 98611
(206) 274-4038 (24-hr. recording)
(206) 274-6644 (office)

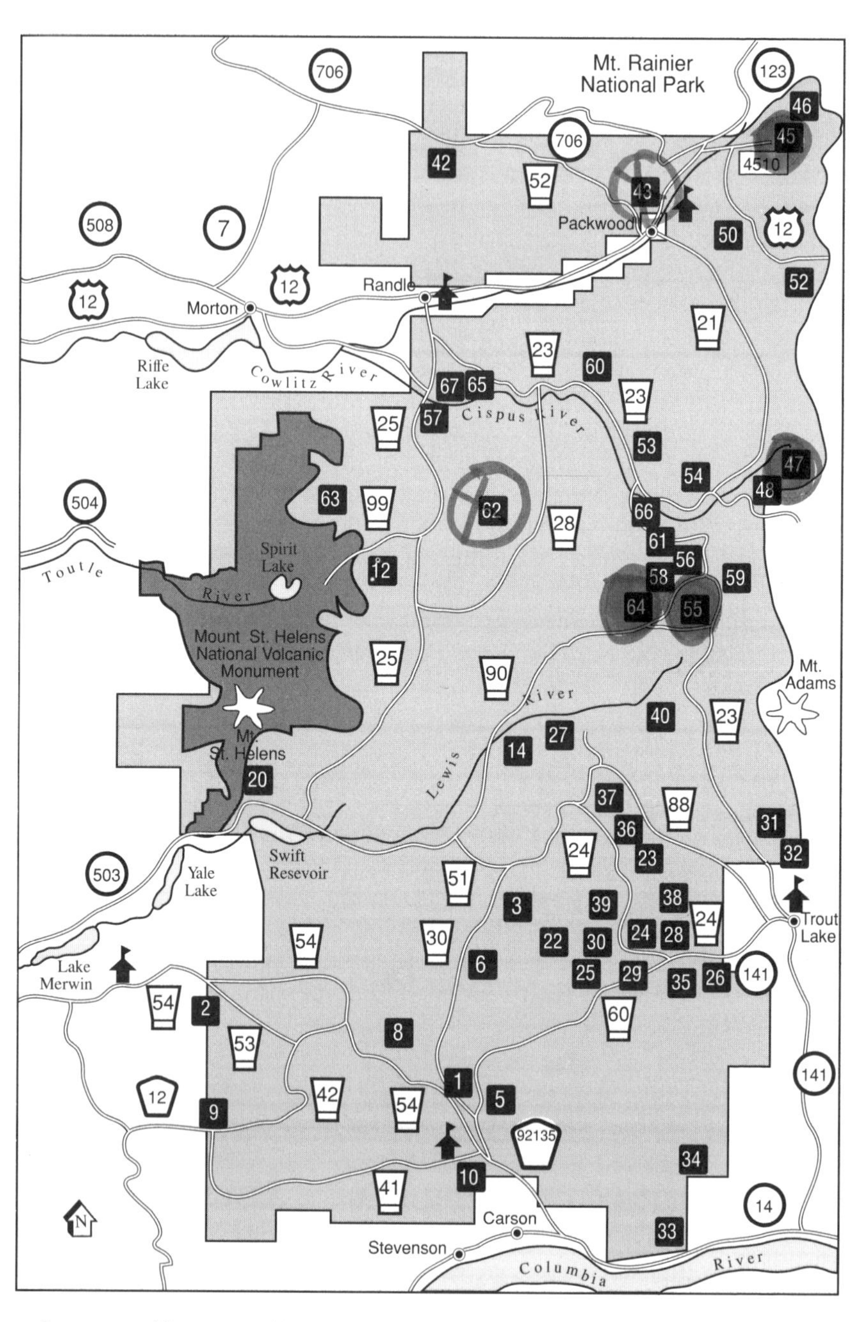

0 10 20

Gifford Pinchot National Forest

Map Location	Elevation	Picnic Units	Tent Units	Tent-Trailer Units	Fee	Drinking Water

Wind River Ranger District

Developed Sites–Campgrounds

Beaver

Access: 12 miles NW of Carson via Cty. Rd. 92135 on Wind River.
Special Activities & Facilities: Fishing, mushrooming.

1*	1100		1	23	x	x

Falls Creek Horse Camp

Access: 23 miles NW of Carson via Cty. Rd. 92135, FR 65.
Special Activities & Facilities: Riding, hiking, berry picking, RVs under 20'.

3	3600		3	8		

Panther Creek

Access: 11 miles N of Carson via Cty. Rd. 92135, FR 65.
Special Activities & Facilities: Fishing, trailhead to PCNST.

5	900		2	31	x	x

Paradise Creek

Access: 20 miles N of Carson via Cty. Rd. 92135, FR 30.
Special Activities & Facilities: Fishing, hiking, berry picking.

6	1500			42	x	x

Sunset

Access: 11 miles E of Yacolt on Cty. Rd. 12.
Special Activities & Facilities: Hiking, waterfall, near Silver Star Mountain.

9	1000	20		10	x	x

Group Camps

Beaver

Access: 12 miles NW of Carson on Cty. Rd. 92135.
Special Activities & Facilities: Reservations, fishing, hiking, mushrooming.

1*	1100			14	x	x

Map Location	Elevation	Picnic Units	Tent Units	Tent-Trailer Units	Fee	Drinking Water

Day Use Sites

Government Mineral Springs

Access: 15 miles N of Carson via Cty. Rd. 92135, FR 3065.
Special Activities & Facilities: Mineral water, big trees, hiking.

8	1200	10				x

Trout Creek (Hemlock Lake)

Access: 9 miles N of Carson off Cty. Rd. 92135, near Wind River Ranger Station.
Special Activities & Facilities: Fishing, swimming, boating (non-motorized).

10	1100	15				x

Mt. Adams Ranger District

Campgrounds

Note: Certain campgrounds designated "Indian Camp" are lightly developed sites used by Native Americans for huckleberry picking.

Cold Springs Indian Camp

Access: 22 miles NW of Trout Lake via St. Hwy. 141, FR 24.
Special Activities & Facilities: Berry picking.

23	4200			9		

Cultus Creek

Access: 18 miles NW of Trout Lake via St. Hwy. 141, FR 24.
Special Activities & Facilities: Hiking, berry picking, barrier-free toilet.

♿ 24	4000			51	x	x

Forlorn Lakes

Access: 14 miles W of Trout Lake via St. Hwy. 141, FRs 24, 60, 6035.
Special Activities & Facilities: Fishing, RVs under 16'.

22	3600		8			

Goose Lake

Access: 13 miles SW of Trout Lake via St. Hwy. 141, FRs 24, 60.
Special Activities & Facilities: Fishing, boating, RVs under 16'.

25	3200		24			

Ice Cave

Access: 7 miles SW of Trout Lake via St. Hwy. 141, FR 24.
Special Activities & Facilities: Spelunking.

Map Location	*Elevation*	*Picnic Units*	*Tent Units*	*Tent-Trailer Units*	*Fee*	*Drinking Water*
*26**	*2800*	*3*		*12*		

Lewis River

Access: 26 miles NW of Trout Lake via St. Hwy. 141, FRs 88, 8851, 3241.
Special Activities & Facilities: Fishing, hiking.

Map Location	*Elevation*	*Picnic Units*	*Tent Units*	*Tent-Trailer Units*	*Fee*	*Drinking Water*
27	*1500*					

Little Goose

Access: 16 miles NW of Trout Lake via St. Hwy. 141, FR 24.
Special Activities & Facilities: Hiking, berry picking, RVs to 16', 3-unit horse camp.

Map Location	*Elevation*	*Picnic Units*	*Tent Units*	*Tent-Trailer Units*	*Fee*	*Drinking Water*
*28**	*4000*		*18*	*10*		*x*

Meadow Creek Indian Camp

Access: 20 miles NW of Trout Lake via St. Hwy. 141, FR 24.
Special Activities & Facilities: Berry picking.

Map Location	*Elevation*	*Picnic Units*	*Tent Units*	*Tent-Trailer Units*	*Fee*	*Drinking Water*
30	*4100*		*8*			

Morrison Creek

Access: 12 miles N of Trout Lake via FRs 80, 8040.
Special Activities & Facilities: Hiking, scenic, horse camp nearby.

Map Location	*Elevation*	*Picnic Units*	*Tent Units*	*Tent-Trailer Units*	*Fee*	*Drinking Water*
*31**	*4600*		*14*			

Moss Creek

Access: 8 miles N of Cook via St. Hwy 14, Cty. Rd. 86.
Special Activities & Facilities: Fishing.

Map Location	*Elevation*	*Picnic Units*	*Tent Units*	*Tent-Trailer Units*	*Fee*	*Drinking Water*
33	*1400*			*18*	*x*	*x*

Oklahoma

Access: 14 miles N of Cook via St. Hwy. 14, Cty. Rd. 86, FR 18.
Special Activities & Facilities: Fishing.

Map Location	*Elevation*	*Picnic Units*	*Tent Units*	*Tent-Trailer Units*	*Fee*	*Drinking Water*
34	*1700*			*23*	*x*	*x*

Peterson Prairie

Access: Via St. Hwy. 141, FR 24, 8 miles SW of Trout Lake.
Special Activities & Facilities: Hiking, berry picking, barrier-free toilet.

Map Location	*Elevation*	*Picnic Units*	*Tent Units*	*Tent-Trailer Units*	*Fee*	*Drinking Water*
*35**	*2800*			*30*	*x*	*x*

Map Location	Elevation	Picnic Units	Tent Units	Tent-Trailer Units	Fee	Drinking Water

Saddle

Access: Via St. Hwy. 141, FRs 24 and 2480, 24 miles NW of Trout Lake.

Special Activities & Facilities: Berry picking.

Map Location	Elevation	Picnic Units	Tent Units	Tent-Trailer Units	Fee	Drinking Water
36	*4200*			*12*		

South

Access: Via St. Hwy. 141, FRs 24 and 2480, 25 miles NW of Trout Lake.

Special Activities & Facilities: Berry picking, RVs to 16'.

Map Location	Elevation	Picnic Units	Tent Units	Tent-Trailer Units	Fee	Drinking Water
37	*4000*			*9*		*x*

Surprise Lakes Indian Camp

Access: Via St. Hwy. 141, FR 24, 22 miles NW of Trout Lake.

Special Activities & Facilities: Fishing, berry picking.

Map Location	Elevation	Picnic Units	Tent Units	Tent-Trailer Units	Fee	Drinking Water
38	*4100*			*9*		

Tillicum

Access: Via St. Hwy. 141, FR 24, 25 miles NW of Trout Lake.

Special Activities & Facilities: Berry picking, RVs to 16'.

Map Location	Elevation	Picnic Units	Tent Units	Tent-Trailer Units	Fee	Drinking Water
39	*4300*			*49*		*x*

Smokey Creek

Access: 12.3 miles W of Trout Lake via St. Hwy. 141, FR 24.

Special Activities & Facilities: Berry picking.

Map Location	Elevation	Picnic Units	Tent Units	Tent-Trailer Units	Fee	Drinking Water
28	*3700*			*5*		

Group Camps

Peterson Prairie

Access: 8 miles SW of Trout Lake via St. Hwy. 141, FR 24.

Special Activities & Facilities: Special charge, reservations, call Mt. Adams RD (509)395-2501, hiking, mushrooming, berry picking.

Map Location	Elevation	Picnic Units	Tent Units	Tent-Trailer Units	Fee	Drinking Water
*35**	*2800*			*10*	*x*	*x*

Atkisson

Access: 5 miles SW of Trout Lake via St. Hwy. 141.

Special Activities & Facilities: Reservations: call Mt. Adams R.D. (509) 395-393-2501, hiking, mushrooming, berry picking, shelter.

Map Location	Elevation	Picnic Units	Tent Units	Tent-Trailer Units	Fee	Drinking Water
*26**	*2700*			*8*		

	Map Location	Elevation	Picnic Units	Tent Units	Tent-Trailer Units	Fee	Drinking Water

Packwood Ranger District

Big Creek

Access: 4 miles SE of Ashford via St. Hwy. 706, FR 52.
Special Activities & Facilities: Fishing, hiking, visit Mt. Rainier NP.

	Map Location	Elevation	Picnic Units	Tent Units	Tent-Trailer Units	Fee	Drinking Water
♿	42	1800			30❸	x	x

La Wis Wis

Access: 7 miles NE of Packwood via US 12, FR 1272.
Special Activities & Facilities: Fishing, hiking, waterfall.

	Map Location	Elevation	Picnic Units	Tent Units	Tent-Trailer Units	Fee	Drinking Water
♿	43*	1400	12	78	40❷	x	x

Soda Springs

Access: 15 miles NE of Packwood via US 12, FRs 45, 4510.
Special Activities & Facilities: Trailhead to William O. Douglas Wilderness.

	Map Location	Elevation	Picnic Units	Tent Units	Tent-Trailer Units	Fee	Drinking Water
	45	3200		8			

Summit Creek

Access: 12 miles NE of Packwood via US 12, FRs 45, 4510.
Special Activities & Facilities: Fishing, hiking.

	Map Location	Elevation	Picnic Units	Tent Units	Tent-Trailer Units	Fee	Drinking Water
	46	2400		5			

Walupt Lake

Access: 24 miles SE of Packwood via US 12, FRs 21, 2160.
Special Activities & Facilities: Fishing, hiking, boating, limited number of sites for RVs over 16'.

	Map Location	Elevation	Picnic Units	Tent Units	Tent-Trailer Units	Fee	Drinking Water
	47*	3900		9	35	x	x

Walupt Lake Horse Camp

Access: 23 miles SE of Packwood via US 12, FRs 21, 2160.
Special Activities & Facilities: Trail access, limited facilities.

	Map Location	Elevation	Picnic Units	Tent Units	Tent-Trailer Units	Fee	Drinking Water
	48*	3900		6			

Map Location	Elevation	Picnic Units	Tent Units	Tent-Trailer Units	Fee	Drinking Water

Day-Use Sites

Knuppenburg

Access: 18 miles E of Packwood on US 12.
Special Activities & Facilities: Fishing.

Map Location	Elevation	Picnic Units	Tent Units	Tent-Trailer Units	Fee	Drinking Water
52	4100	7				

Palisades

Access: 12 miles NE of Packwood via US 12.
Special Activities & Facilities: Geologic, scenic viewpoint.

Map Location	Elevation	Picnic Units	Tent Units	Tent-Trailer Units	Fee	Drinking Water
50	2500					

Randle Ranger District

Campgrounds

Adams Fork

Access: 24 miles SE of Randle via FRs 23 & 21.
Special Activities & Facilities: Fishing, hiking on Cispus River.

Map Location	Elevation	Picnic Units	Tent Units	Tent-Trailer Units	Fee	Drinking Water
66	2600			24	x	x

Blue Lake Creek

Access: 16 miles SE of Randle via FR 23.
Special Activities & Facilities: Fishing, hiking on Cispus River.

Map Location	Elevation	Picnic Units	Tent Units	Tent-Trailer Units	Fee	Drinking Water
53	1900			11	x	x

Cat Creek

Access: 25 miles SE of Randle via FRs 23, 21.
Special Activities & Facilities: Fishing on Cispus River, RVs under 16', lightly developed.

Map Location	Elevation	Picnic Units	Tent Units	Tent-Trailer Units	Fee	Drinking Water
54	3000		6			

Council Lake

Access: 35 miles SE of Randle via FRs 23, 2334.
Special Activities & Facilities: Fishing, hiking, boating, carry-in boat launch.

Map Location	Elevation	Picnic Units	Tent Units	Tent-Trailer Units	Fee	Drinking Water
55	4300		6	5		

Horseshoe Lake

Access: 40 miles SE of Randle via FRs 23, 2329.

Special Activities & Facilities: Fishing, hiking, boating, primitive boat launch, RVs under 16'.

Map Location	Elevation	Picnic Units	Tent Units	Tent-Trailer Units	Fee	Drinking Water
56	4200			10		

Iron Creek

Access: 10 miles S of Randle via FR 25.

Special Activities & Facilities: Fishing, hiking, near Mount St. Helens National Volcanic Monument.

Map Location	Elevation	Picnic Units	Tent Units	Tent-Trailer Units	Fee	Drinking Water
57	1200			98 ➊	x	x

Keenes Horse Camp

Access: 39 miles SE of Randle via FRs 23, 2329.

Special Activities & Facilities: Riding, scenic, hiking, corral, views of Mt. Adams.

Map Location	Elevation	Picnic Units	Tent Units	Tent-Trailer Units	Fee	Drinking Water
58	4300			15		

Killen Creek

Access: 38 miles SE of Randle via FRs 23, 2329.

Special Activities & Facilities: Hiking, scenic, berry picking.

Map Location	Elevation	Picnic Units	Tent Units	Tent-Trailer Units	Fee	Drinking Water
59	4400			8		

North Fork

Access: 12 miles SE of Randle on FR 23.

Special Activities & Facilities: Fishing, hiking.

Map Location	Elevation	Picnic Units	Tent Units	Tent-Trailer Units	Fee	Drinking Water
60*	1500			33	x	x

Olallie Lake

Access: 33 miles SE of Randle via FRs 23, 2329, 5601.

Special Activities & Facilities: Views of Mt. Adams, fishing, boating.

Map Location	Elevation	Picnic Units	Tent Units	Tent-Trailer Units	Fee	Drinking Water
61	4200			6		

Pole Patch

Access: 31 miles S of Randle via FRs 23, 28, 76, 77.
Special Activities & Facilities: Berry picking, scenic, primitive access road.

Map Location	Elevation	Picnic Units	Tent Units	Tent-Trailer Units	Fee	Drinking Water
62	4400		8	4		

Takhlakh

Access: 34 mile SE Randle via FRs 23, 2329.
Special Activities & Facilities: Views of Mt. Adams, fishing, hiking, boating.

Map Location	Elevation	Picnic Units	Tent Units	Tent-Trailer Units	Fee	Drinking Water
♿ 64	4500			54 ❷	x	x

Tower Rock

Access: 12 miles SE of Randle via FRs 23, 28, 76.
Special Activities & Facilities: Fishing, near Cispus Learning Center.

Map Location	Elevation	Picnic Units	Tent Units	Tent-Trailer Units	Fee	Drinking Water
67	1100			22	x	x

Group Camps

North Fork

Access: 12 miles SE of Randle on FR 23.
Special Activities & Facilities: Fishing, hiking, reservation, each site's capacity is 30 people.

Map Location	Elevation	Picnic Units	Tent Units	Tent-Trailer Units	Fee	Drinking Water
60*	1500			3	x	x

Day-Use Sites

Yellow Jacket

Access: 10 miles SE of Randle via FRs 23, 28.
Special Activities & Facilities: Stocked fishing ponds.

Map Location	Elevation	Picnic Units	Tent Units	Tent-Trailer Units	Fee	Drinking Water
65	1100	6				

Ryan Lake

Access: 10 miles S of Randle via FRs 25, 26.
Special Activities & Facilities: Interpretive site related to Mount St. Helens eruption, barrier-free toilet.

Map Location	Elevation	Picnic Units	Tent Units	Tent-Trailer Units	Fee	Drinking Water
♿ 63	3300					

* Indicates more than one site in an area

Windy Point, Mount St. Helens National Volcanic Monument, Gifford Pinchot National Forest

Handicapped Accessibility Codes
- ❶ Fully Accessible
- ❷ Usable
- ❸ Difficult

See page 7 for full description.

MOUNT ST. HELENS NATIONAL VOLCANIC MONUMENT
Gifford Pinchot National Forest

After 123 quiet years, Mount St. Helens reawakened in a massive eruption on May 18, 1980. Triggered by an earthquake, the north flank of the mountain slid into the Spirit Lake basin and down the North Fork Toutle River valley, forming the largest landslide in recorded history. A lateral blast of ash and hot gas, traveling at speeds up to 330 miles per hour, toppled 150 square miles of forest north of Mount St. Helens, and volcanic mudflows, known as lahars, flowed down all slopes of the volcano. A vertical column of ash billowed from the newly formed crater to a height of 12 miles and, spread eastward by prevailing winds, circled the earth in just two weeks. When the ash cleared, Mount St. Helens was 1,300 feet shorter, Spirit Lake was much larger, and the lush green forest around it had been transformed into a blown-down grey landscape.

The 110,000-acre Mount St. Helens National Volcanic Monument, created through Congressional legislation in 1982, provides a rare opportunity to view an active volcano and observe the astonishing resurgence of life in the area surrounding it. Visitors may drive and hike into the fascinating landscape, so dramatically altered by the 1980 eruption, and look right into the crater with its steaming lava dome.

Special places of interest include the exhibits and audio-visual programs at the visitor center; the drive into the heart of the blowdown area at Windy Ridge; Meta Lake, where patches of life survived the blast; crater and lava dome views from Norway Pass; the remains of the Miners' car; views of Spirit Lake from Independence Pass and Cedar Creek vista; Lava Cast Trail; Muddy River viewpoint; Ape Cave, which was formed by an ancient lava flow; and the Lahar viewpoint where mud flows occurred in the 1980 eruption.

Further information about recreation opportunities, campground locations and facilities, as well as current maps of the area, are available at the following offices:

Mount St. Helens National Volcanic
Monument Visitor Center
3029 Spirit Lake Highway
(exit 49 on Interstate 5)
Castle Rock, WA 98611
(206) 274-4038 (24-hr. recording)
(206) 274-6644 (office)

Mount St. Helens National
Volcanic Monument Headquarters
Rt. 1, Box 369
Amboy, WA 98601-9715
(206) 247-5473

Gifford Pinchot National Forest
Supervisor's Office
6926 E. 4th Plain Blvd.
Vancouver, WA 98668-8944
(206) 696-7500

	Map Location	*Elevation*	*Picnic Units*	*Tent Units*	*Tent-Trailer Units*	*Fee*	*Drinking Water*

Mount St. Helens National Volcanic Monument
Campgrounds

Lower Falls

Access: 30 miles NE of Cougar via St. Hwy. 503, FR 90.
Special Activities & Facilities: Hiking, fishing on North Fork Lewis River.

	14	*1610*			*20*		

Day-Use Sites

Mount St Helens Visitor Center

Access: 5 miles E of I-5 on State Hwy. 504.
Special Activities & Facilities: Interpretive programs, information, mountain viewing, exhibits, barrier-free. Seaquest State Park across highway.

♿		*450*					*x*

Ape Cave

Access: 9 miles NE of Cougar via St. Hwy. 503, FRs 90, 83, 8303.
Special Activities & Facilities: Hiking, spelunking, volcano viewing, barrier-free toilet and trail.

♿	*20**	*2100*					

Lava Cast

Access: 9 miles NE of Cougar via St. Hwy. 503, FRs 90, 83, 8303.
Special Activities & Facilities: Hiking, spelunking, interpretive trail.

	*20**	*1800*	*5*				

Bear Meadow

Access: 44 miles NE of Cougar via St. Hwy. 503, FRs 90, 25, 99.
Special Activities & Facilities: Volcano viewing and information, hiking.

♿	*12*		*5*❸				

Other sites of particular interest near Bear Meadow are: Meta Lake/ Miners' car; Windy Ridge; Norway Pass; Pine Creek Information Station (at the junction of FRs 90 and 25). Obtain detailed information at the Visitor Center, Ranger Stations or Inf. Stations.

Malheur National Forest

Strawberry Lake, Strawberry Mountain Wilderness, Malheur National Forest

In the Blue Mountains of eastern Oregon lies the 1.46-million-acre Malheur National Forest, a place of dramatic landscape and scenery. Solitude, tranquility, and beauty abound in this forest where there is no fast lane. On over 200 miles of trails, one can walk through forests of pine and fir, climb timbered slopes to scenic alpine lakes and meadows, or enjoy the grasslands, sage, and juniper. The Strawberry Mountain Wilderness, with its 9,038-foot peak, extends east to west through the heart of the forest, and the Monument Rock Wilderness overlooks the eastern boundary.

Special places of interest to the visitor include the wild and rugged Strawberry Mountain; the Cedar Grove Botanical Area where Alaska-cedar can be found; the Vinegar Hill-Indian Rock Scenic Area which is mostly above timberline and is road accessible; Lake Magone formed by a great landslide; a 15-foot-high opening called Arch Rock; the Malheur River National Recreation Trail through an interesting geologic canyon; and scenic driving on Highway 26.

Further information about recreation opportunities, campground locations and facilities, as well as current maps of the area, are available at the following offices:

Malheur National Forest
Supervisor's Office
139 N.E. Dayton St.
John Day, OR 97845
(503) 575-1731

Bear Valley Ranger District
528 E. Main St.
John Day, OR 97845
(503) 575-2110

Burns Ranger District
Star Rt. 4-12870 Hwy 20
Hines, OR 97738
(503) 573-7292

Long Creek Ranger District
528 E. Main St.
John Day, OR 97845
(503) 575-2110

Prairie City Ranger District
327 S.W. Front
Prairie City, OR 97869
(503) 820-3311

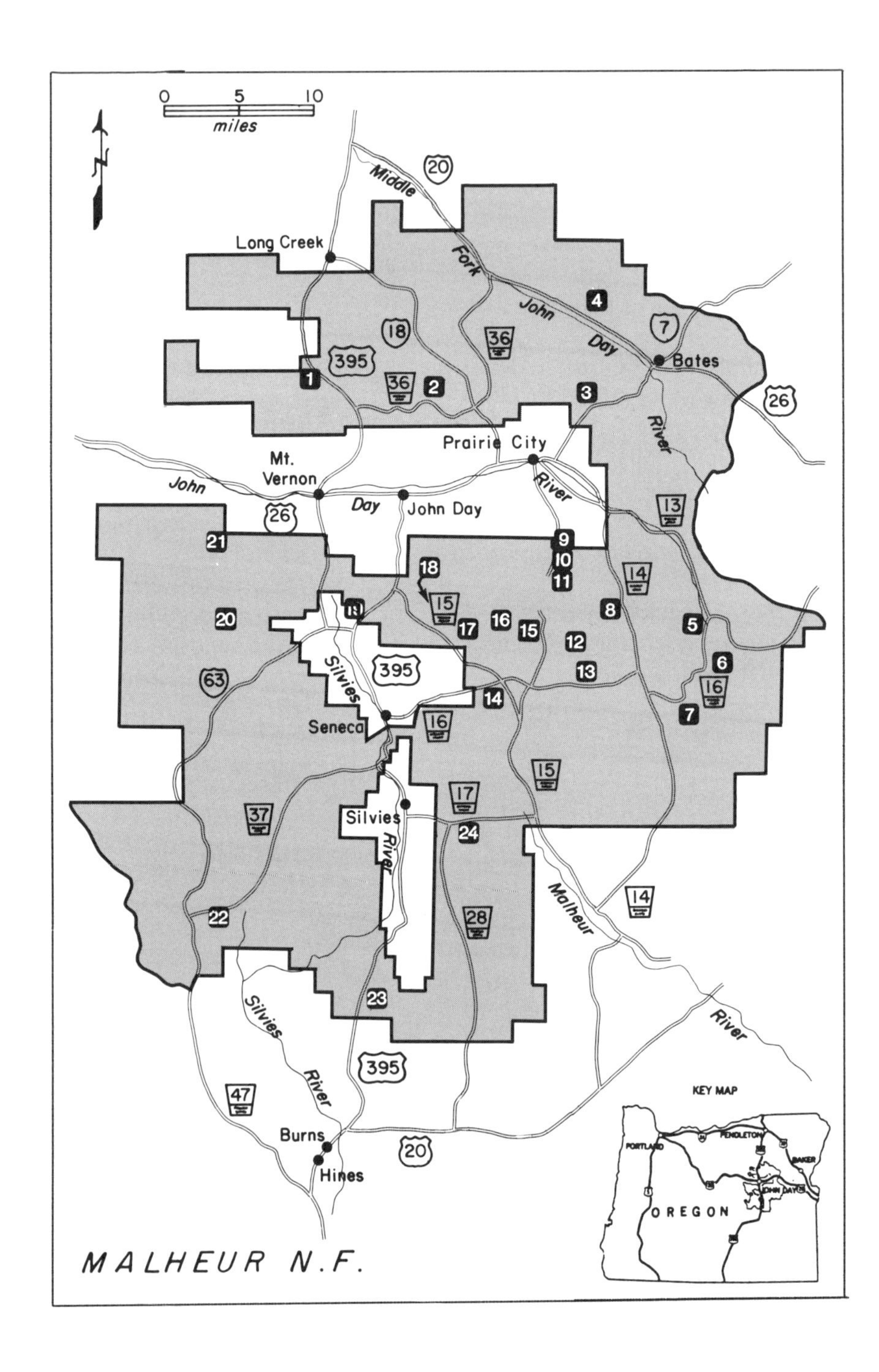

0
5
10
miles
Middle
Fork
John
Day
River
20
Long Creek
18
395
36
1
2
3
4
7
Bates
26
Prairie City
Mt.
Vernon
John
Day
John Day
River
26
13
21
9
10
11
18
15
14
19
20
17
16
15
8
5
12
6
13
16
7
Silvies
395
63
14
Seneca
16
15
17
37
Silvies
Silvies
River
24
Malheur
14
28
22
23
Silvies
River
Malheur
River
395
47
Burns
Hines
20
KEY MAP
PORTLAND
PENDLETON
BAKER
JOHN DAY
OREGON
MALHEUR N.F.

MALHEUR NATIONAL FOREST

Map Location	Elevation	Picnic Units	Tent Units	Tent-Trailer Units	Fee	Drinking Water

Long Creek Ranger District

Beech Creek

Access: Hwy. 395, 17 miles N of Mt. Vernon.
Special Activities & Facilities: Hunting, RVs under 16'.

Map Location	Elevation	Picnic Units	Tent Units	Tent-Trailer Units	Fee	Drinking Water
1	4500			8		

Magone Lake

Access: 20 miles NE Mt. Vernon via US 395, FRs 36, 3618.
Special Activities & Facilities: Boat launch, swimming, hiking, fishing, hunting.

Map Location	Elevation	Picnic Units	Tent Units	Tent-Trailer Units	Fee	Drinking Water
2	5000	19		22		x

Dixie

Access: 8 miles NE of Prairie City, just off US 26.
Special Activities & Facilities: Group picnic, berry picking, hunting.

Map Location	Elevation	Picnic Units	Tent Units	Tent-Trailer Units	Fee	Drinking Water
3	5000	4		11		x

Middlefork

Access: 19 miles NE of Prairie City via US 26, St. Hwy. 7, Cty. Rd. 20.
Special Activities & Facilities: On Middle Fork John Day River, lightly improved, fishing, hunting.

Map Location	Elevation	Picnic Units	Tent Units	Tent-Trailer Units	Fee	Drinking Water
4	4200			11		

Prairie City Ranger District

Elk Creek

Access: 25 miles SE of Prairie City via Cty. Rd. 62, FRs 13, 16, 1675.
Special Activities & Facilities: Stream fishing, hunting, lightly improved.

Map Location	Elevation	Picnic Units	Tent Units	Tent-Trailer Units	Fee	Drinking Water
5	5000			5		

North Fork Malheur

Access: 29 miles SE of Prairie City via Cty. Rd. 62, FRs 13, 16, 1675.
Special Activities & Facilities: Stream fishing, hunting, lightly improved.

Map Location	Elevation	Picnic Units	Tent Units	Tent-Trailer Units	Fee	Drinking Water
6	4700			5		

Little Crane

Access: 30 miles SE of Prairie City via Cty. Rd. 62, FRs 13, 16.
Special Activities & Facilities: Stream fishing, hunting, lightly improved.

Map Location	*Elevation*	*Picnic Units*	*Tent Units*	*Tent-Trailer Units*	*Fee*	*Drinking Water*
7	*5500*			*5*		

Crescent

Access: 17 mile SE of Prairie City via Cty. Rd. 62, FR 14.
Special Activities & Facilities: Stream fishing, hunting, RVs under 16'.

Map Location	*Elevation*	*Picnic Units*	*Tent Units*	*Tent-Trailer Units*	*Fee*	*Drinking Water*
*8**	*5200*			*4*		

Trout Farm

Access: 15 miles SE of Prairie City via Cty. Rd. 62, FR 14.
Special Activities & Facilities: Pond and stream fishing, group picnic, hunting.

Map Location	*Elevation*	*Picnic Units*	*Tent Units*	*Tent-Trailer Units*	*Fee*	*Drinking Water*
*8**	*4900*	*1*	*3*	*5*		*x*

McNaughton Springs

Access: 8 miles S of Prairie City via Cty. Rd. 60, FR 6001.
Special Activities & Facilities: Stream fishing, hunting, wilderness access, lightly improved.

Map Location	*Elevation*	*Picnic Units*	*Tent Units*	*Tent-Trailer Units*	*Fee*	*Drinking Water*
9	*4800*			*4*		

Slide Creek

Access: 9 miles S of Prairie City via Cty. Rd. 60, FR 6001.
Special Activities & Facilities: Fishing, corral, hiking, wilderness access, lightly improved.

Map Location	*Elevation*	*Picnic Units*	*Tent Units*	*Tent-Trailer Units*	*Fee*	*Drinking Water*
10	*4900*			*4*		

Strawberry

Access: 11 miles S of Prairie City via Cty. Rd. 60, FR 6001.
Special Activities & Facilities: Stream fishing, corrals, hiking, hunting, wilderness access.

Map Location	*Elevation*	*Picnic Units*	*Tent Units*	*Tent-Trailer Units*	*Fee*	*Drinking Water*
11	*5700*			*4*		*x*

Murray

Access: 21 miles E of Seneca via FRs 16, 924.
Special Activities & Facilities: Stream fishing, hiking, hunting, lightly improved.

Map Location	*Elevation*	*Picnic Units*	*Tent Units*	*Tent-Trailer Units*	*Fee*	*Drinking Water*
12	*5200*			*4*		

Meadow Mountain, Malheur National Forest

Map Location	Elevation	Picnic Units	Tent Units	Tent-Trailer Units	Fee	Drinking Water

Big Creek

Access: 21 miles E of Seneca via FR 16.
Special Activities & Facilities: Stream fishing, hunting.

13	5100			4		x

Bear Valley Ranger District

Parish Cabin

Access: 14 miles E of Seneca on FR 16.
Special Activities & Facilities: Group picnic, stream fishing, hunting.

14	4900	10		20		x

Indian Springs

Access: 25 miles NE of Seneca via FRs 16, 1640.
Special Activities & Facilities: Hunting, hiking, wilderness access.

15	6000			7		

Canyon Meadows

Access: 24 miles SE of John Day via US 395, Cty. Rd. 65, FRs 15, 1520.
Special Activities & Facilities: Hiking, hunting, fishing, picnic, wilderness access, RVs under 16'.

16	5100	32		15		x

Wickiup

Access: 18 miles SE of John Day via US 395, Cty. Rd. 65.
Special Activities & Facilities: Stream fishing, hunting, group picnic.

17	4300	10	2	7		x

Ray Cole

Access: 14 miles SE of John Day via US 395, Cty. Rd. 65, FR 6510.
Special Activities & Facilities: Stream fishing, hiking, hunting, wilderness access, lightly improved.

18	4300		2	2		

Starr

Access: 16 miles S of John Day via US 395.
Special Activities & Facilities: Snow play area, hunting.

Map Location	Elevation	Picnic Units	Tent Units	Tent-Trailer Units	Fee	Drinking Water
19	5100	21	5	9		

Oregon Mine

Access: 25 miles SW of Mt. Vernon via US 26W, FRs 21, 2170.
Special Activities & Facilities: Stream fishing, hunting.

Map Location	Elevation	Picnic Units	Tent Units	Tent-Trailer Units	Fee	Drinking Water
20	4300	3		4		

Billy Fields

Access: 17 miles SW of Mt. Vernon via US 26W, FR 21.
Special Activities & Facilities: Stream fishing, group picnic, hunting.

Map Location	Elevation	Picnic Units	Tent Units	Tent-Trailer Units	Fee	Drinking Water
21	4000	2		6		

Burns Ranger District

Yellowjacket

Access: 38 miles NW of Burns via US 20, Cty. Rd. 127, FRs 47, 37, 3745.
Special Activities & Facilities: Boating, lake fishing, hunting.

Map Location	Elevation	Picnic Units	Tent Units	Tent-Trailer Units	Fee	Drinking Water
22	4800			20		x

Idlewild

Access: 17 miles N of Burns on US 395.
Special Activities & Facilities: Group picnic, hunting.

Map Location	Elevation	Picnic Units	Tent Units	Tent-Trailer Units	Fee	Drinking Water
♿ 23	5300	3 ❶		24 ❸		x

Rock Springs

Access: 6 miles E of Silvies via US 395, Cty. Rd. 73, FRs 17, 17054.
Special Activities & Facilities: Hunting.

Map Location	Elevation	Picnic Units	Tent Units	Tent-Trailer Units	Fee	Drinking Water
24	5000			9		x

Handicapped Accessibility Codes
❶ Fully Accessible
❷ Usable
❸ Difficult
See page 7 for full description.

Mt. Baker-Snoqualmie National Forest

Mt. Baker, Mt. Baker-Snoqualmie National Forest. Photo by Jim Hughes.

On the western slopes of the Cascade Mountains, bordering Canada to the north and Mt. Rainier National Park on the south, this lush forest is thickly timbered with fir, spruce, hemlock, and cedar, and its picturesque beauty ranges from glacial-cut valley bottoms to rugged, glacial-capped mountains. The moderate climate provided abundant roots, berries and spawning salmon to generations of Pacific Northwest Indian tribes. Seven alpine ski areas and miles of nordic trails for cross-country skiing, snowshoeing and snowmobiling offer excellent winter recreation opportunities.

Special places of interest include Mt. Baker, a dormant volcano which still occasionally emits steam and sulfurous fumes; panoramic views of the North Cascades at Heather Meadows and Artist Point; spectacular Austin Pass; Baker Lake; white-water rafting on the Skagit Wild and Scenic River; Big Four ice caves; scenic driving on the Mountain Loop Highway; a new forest growing on the remains of an old forest at Youth on Age Trail; Deception Falls; Franklin Falls; the historic remnants of Snoqualmie Pass wagon road; the delightful forest walk at Asahel Curtis Nature Trail; the Dalles Nature Trail; Suntop Lookout; Crystal Mountain winter sports area; Naches Pass Trail; giant Douglas-firs along the Mather Memorial Parkway to Mt. Rainier National Park; Glacier Peak and Alpine Lakes wildernesses.

Further information about recreation opportunities, campground locations and facilities, as well as current maps of the area, are available at the following offices:

Mt. Baker-Snoqualmie National
Forest Supervisor's Office
Holyoke Building
1022 First Ave.
Seattle, WA 98104
(206) 442-0170

Darrington Ranger District
1405 Emmens St.
Darrington, WA 98241
(206) 436-1155

Glacier Public Service Center
(summer only) (206) 599-2714

Mt. Baker Ranger District
2105 Highway 20
Sedro Wooley, WA 98284
(206) 856-5700

North Bend Ranger District
42404 S.E. North Bend Way
North Bend, WA 98045
(206) 888-1421

Skykomish Ranger District
P.O. Box 305
Skykomish, WA 98288
(206) 677-2414

Verlot Public Service Center
(summer only)
(206) 691-7791

White River Ranger District
857 Roosevelt Ave., East
Enumclaw, WA 98022
(206) 825-6585

Snoqualmie Pass Visitor Information Center
(206) 434-6111

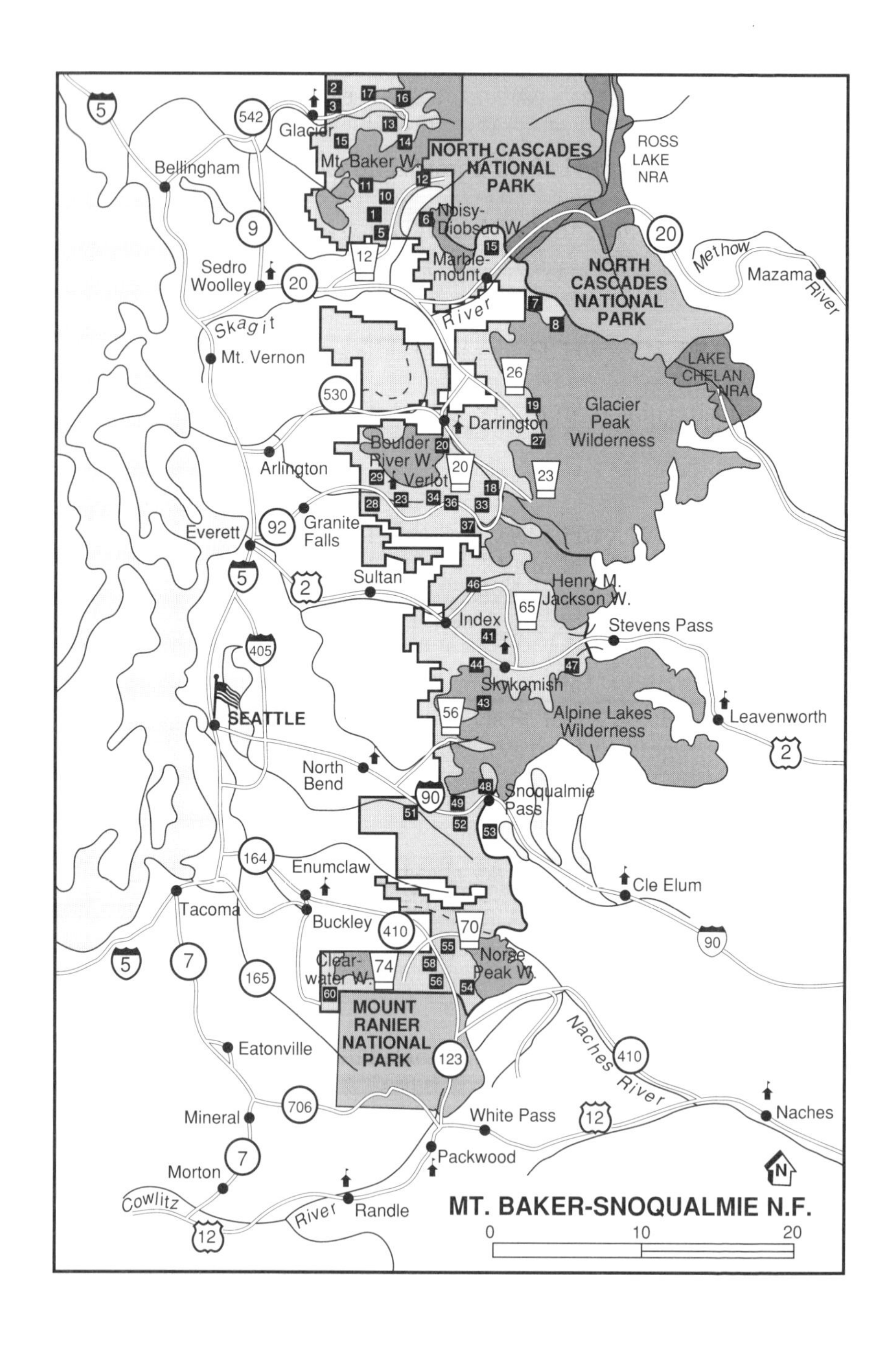

MT. BAKER-SNOQUALMIE N.F.
NORTH CASCADES NATIONAL PARK
ROSS LAKE NRA
LAKE CHELAN NRA
Mt. Baker W.
Noisy-Diobsud W.
Glacier Peak Wilderness
Boulder River W.
Henry M. Jackson W.
Alpine Lakes Wilderness
Norse Peak W.
Clear-water W.
MOUNT RANIER NATIONAL PARK
Glacier
Bellingham
Sedro Woolley
Marblemount
Mazama
Mt. Vernon
Darrington
Arlington
Verlot
Granite Falls
Everett
Sultan
Index
Stevens Pass
Skykomish
Leavenworth
SEATTLE
North Bend
Snoqualmie Pass
Enumclaw
Cle Elum
Tacoma
Buckley
Eatonville
Mineral
White Pass
Naches
Packwood
Morton
Randle
Skagit River
Methow River
Naches River
Cowlitz River
0
10
20

Map Location	*Elevation*	*Picnic Units*	*Tent Units*	*Tent-Trailer Units*	*Fee*	*Drinking Water*

Mt. Baker Ranger District

Campgrounds

Boulder Creek

Access: 32 miles NE of Sedro Woolley via St. Hwy. 20, FR 11.
Special Activities & Facilities: Fishing, berry picking, near Baker Lake..

Map Location	*Elevation*	*Picnic Units*	*Tent Units*	*Tent-Trailer Units*	*Fee*	*Drinking Water*
1	*1100*			*10*		

Douglas-Fir

Access: 2 miles E of Glacier via St. Hwy. 542.
Special Activities & Facilities: Nature trails, fishing.

Map Location	*Elevation*	*Picnic Units*	*Tent Units*	*Tent-Trailer Units*	*Fee*	*Drinking Water*
3	*1000*	*6*		*30*	*x*	*x*

Horseshoe Cove

Access: 30 miles NE of Sedro Woolley via St. Hwy. 20, FR 11.
Special Activities & Facilities: Boating, swimming, fishing, waterskiing, Baker Lake.

Map Location	*Elevation*	*Picnic Units*	*Tent Units*	*Tent-Trailer Units*	*Fee*	*Drinking Water*
5	*700*	*8*	*8*	*26*	*x*	*x*

Maple Grove

Access: (at Baker Lake via boat or trail) via St. Hwy. 20, FR 11.
Special Activities & Facilities: Boating, swimming, fishing, waterskiing, hiking.

Map Location	*Elevation*	*Picnic Units*	*Tent Units*	*Tent-Trailer Units*	*Fee*	*Drinking Water*
6	*700*		*6*			

Marble Creek

Access: 9 miles E of Marblemount.
Special Activities & Facilities: Fishing, mountain climbing, scenery.

Map Location	*Elevation*	*Picnic Units*	*Tent Units*	*Tent-Trailer Units*	*Fee*	*Drinking Water*
7	*900*	*6*		*24*		

Panorama Point

Access: 33 miles NE of Sedro Woolley via St. Hwy. 20, FR 11.
Special Activities & Facilities: Baker Lake, boating, fishing, sailing, waterskiing.

Map Location	*Elevation*	*Picnic Units*	*Tent Units*	*Tent-Trailer Units*	*Fee*	*Drinking Water*
10	*700*			*16*	*x*	*x*

Map Location	Elevation	Picnic Units	Tent Units	Tent-Trailer Units	Fee	Drinking Water

Park Creek

Access: 34 miles NE of Sedro Woolley via St. Hwy. 20, FR 11.
Special Activities & Facilities: Fishing, near Baker Lake.

Map Location	Elevation	Picnic Units	Tent Units	Tent-Trailer Units	Fee	Drinking Water
11	800			12		

Shannon Creek

Access: 37 miles NE of Sedro Woolley via St. Hwy. 20, FR 11.
Special Activities & Facilities: Boating, fishing, Baker Lake, waterskiing.

Map Location	Elevation	Picnic Units	Tent Units	Tent-Trailer Units	Fee	Drinking Water
12	800	2	2	18		

Silver Fir

Access: 14 miles E of Glacier via St. Hwy. 542.
Special Activities & Facilities: Fishing.

Map Location	Elevation	Picnic Units	Tent Units	Tent-Trailer Units	Fee	Drinking Water
13	2000	6	1	20	x	x

Day Use Sites

Austin Pass

Access: 23 miles E of Glacier via St. Hwy. 542.
Special Activities & Facilities: Mountain climbing, hiking, outstanding scenery.

Map Location	Elevation	Picnic Units	Tent Units	Tent-Trailer Units	Fee	Drinking Water
14	4600	42				

Shuksan Picnic Area

Access: 13-1/2 miles E of Glacier via St. Hwy. 542.
Special Activities & Facilities: Fishing.

Map Location	Elevation	Picnic Units	Tent Units	Tent-Trailer Units	Fee	Drinking Water
16	2000	5				

Group Reservation Camps

Excelsior

Access: 7 miles E of Glacier via St. Hwy. 542.
Special Activities & Facilities: Fishing, botanical, (capacity 40 people).

Map Location	Elevation	Picnic Units	Tent Units	Tent-Trailer Units	Fee	Drinking Water
17	1300		13			

	Map Location	Elevation	Picnic Units	Tent Units	Tent-Trailer Units	Fee	Drinking Water

Darrington Ranger District

Bedal

Access: 19 miles SE of Darrington via FR 20.
Special Activities & Facilities: Community, shelter, fishing, white-water rafting.

	Map Location	Elevation	Picnic Units	Tent Units	Tent-Trailer Units	Fee	Drinking Water
	18*	1250	2		16		

Buck Creek

Access: 24 miles E of Darrington on FR 26.
Special Activities & Facilities: Nature trails, fishing.

	Map Location	Elevation	Picnic Units	Tent Units	Tent-Trailer Units	Fee	Drinking Water
	19	1200	4	7	18		

Clear Creek

Access: 3 miles SE of Darrington on FR 20.
Special Activities & Facilities: Fishing, hiking.

	Map Location	Elevation	Picnic Units	Tent Units	Tent-Trailer Units	Fee	Drinking Water
	20	600	1		9		

Gold Basin

Access: 13 miles E of Granite Falls via Cty. Rd.
Special Activities & Facilities: Fishing.

	Map Location	Elevation	Picnic Units	Tent Units	Tent-Trailer Units	Fee	Drinking Water
♿	23*	1100		10	84 ❷	x	x

Red Bridge

Access: 18 miles E of Granite Falls via Cty. Rd..
Special Activities & Facilities: Fishing.

	Map Location	Elevation	Picnic Units	Tent Units	Tent-Trailer Units	Fee	Drinking Water
	36*	1300		2	14		

Sulphur Creek

Access: 30 miles E of Darrington on FR 26.
Special Activities & Facilities: Fishing, hiking, RVs under 16'.

	Map Location	Elevation	Picnic Units	Tent Units	Tent-Trailer Units	Fee	Drinking Water
	27	1500		1	19		

Turlo

Access: 11 miles E of Granite Falls via Cty. Rd.
Special Activities & Facilities: Fishing.

	Map Location	Elevation	Picnic Units	Tent Units	Tent-Trailer Units	Fee	Drinking Water
	28	900			19	x	x

Map Location	Elevation	Picnic Units	Tent Units	Tent-Trailer Units	Fee	Drinking Water

Verlot

Access: 11 miles E of Granite Falls via Cty. Rd.
Special Activities & Facilities: Hiking, fishing.

Map Location	Elevation	Picnic Units	Tent Units	Tent-Trailer Units	Fee	Drinking Water
29	900			26	x	x

White Chuck

Access: 11 miles SE of Darrington on FR 20.
Special Activities & Facilities: Fishing, hiking, river rafting.

Map Location	Elevation	Picnic Units	Tent Units	Tent-Trailer Units	Fee	Drinking Water
	900			5		

Day Use Sites

Big Four

Access: 25 miles E of Granite Falls via Cty. Rd.
Special Activities & Facilities: Handicapped facilities, scenery, mountain climbing, hiking.

Map Location	Elevation	Picnic Units	Tent Units	Tent-Trailer Units	Fee	Drinking Water
31*	1700	6				

Hemple Creek

Access: 13 miles E of Granite Falls via Cty. Rd.
Special Activities & Facilities: Fishing, hiking.

Map Location	Elevation	Picnic Units	Tent Units	Tent-Trailer Units	Fee	Drinking Water
23	1100	36 ❶				x

Group Reservation Camps

Beaver Creek

Access: 24 miles E of Granite Falls via Cty. Rd.
Special Activities & Facilities: Fishing, (capacity 20 persons).

Map Location	Elevation	Picnic Units	Tent Units	Tent-Trailer Units	Fee	Drinking Water
33	1600		4		x	

Esswine

Access: 16 miles E of Granite Falls via Cty. Rd.
Special Activities & Facilities: Fishing, reservations.

Map Location	Elevation	Picnic Units	Tent Units	Tent-Trailer Units	Fee	Drinking Water
34*	1200		5		x	

Marten Creek

Access: 21 miles E of Granite Falls via Cty. Rd.
Special Activities & Facilities: Fishing, hiking, reservations.

Map Location	Elevation	Picnic Units	Tent Units	Tent-Trailer Units	Fee	Drinking Water
36	1400		3	1	x	

Map Location	Elevation	Picnic Units	Tent Units	Tent-Trailer Units	Fee	Drinking Water

Boardman Creek

Access: 16.5 miles E of Granite Falls via Cty. Rd.
Special Activities & Facilities: Fishing, hiking.

Map Location	Elevation	Picnic Units	Tent Units	Tent-Trailer Units	Fee	Drinking Water
34	1200		4	4		

Coal Creek Bar

Access: 23 miles E of Granite Falls via Cty. Rd..
Special Activities & Facilities: Capacity 40, reservations.

Map Location	Elevation	Picnic Units	Tent Units	Tent-Trailer Units	Fee	Drinking Water
37	1600			5	x	

Gold Basin Group

Access: 13 miles E of Granite Falls via Cty. Rd.
Special Activities & Facilities: Capacity 150, reservations.

Map Location	Elevation	Picnic Units	Tent Units	Tent-Trailer Units	Fee	Drinking Water
23*	1100				x	x

Tulalip Millsite

Access: 19 miles E of Granite Falls via Cty. Rd.
Special Activities & Facilities: Group area suitable for recreation vehicles, reservations.

Map Location	Elevation	Picnic Units	Tent Units	Tent-Trailer Units	Fee	Drinking Water
36*	1400			12	x	

Wiley Creek

Access: 15 miles E of Granite Falls via Cty. Rd.
Special Activities & Facilities: Rustic shelters (capacity 50 persons), reservations, no RVs.

Map Location	Elevation	Picnic Units	Tent Units	Tent-Trailer Units	Fee	Drinking Water
34	1200				x	

North Bend Ranger District

Campgrounds

Commonwealth

Access: Exit 52 from I-90 to FS Road 58, 22 miles E of North Bend.
Special Activities & Facilities: Hiking, horse riding, scenery, mountain climbing.

Map Location	Elevation	Picnic Units	Tent Units	Tent-Trailer Units	Fee	Drinking Water
48	3000	3	6			

	Map Location	Elevation	Picnic Units	Tent Units	Tent-Trailer Units	Fee	Drinking Water

Denny Creek

Access: Exit 47 from I-90 to FR 58, 20 miles E of North Bend.
Special Activities & Facilities: Fishing, historic trail, scenery.

	49	2240		20	17	x	x

Tinkham

Access: Exit 42 from I-90 to FR 55, 12 miles E of North Bend.
Special Activities & Facilities: Fishing, scenery.

♿	51	1520		13	34❷	x	x

Day Use Sites

Asahel Curtis

Access: Exit 47 from I-90 to FR 55, 20 miles E of North Bend.
Special Activities & Facilities: Fishing, nature trail, memorial.

	52	2000	27				x

Lake Keechelus

Access: Exit 54 from I-90, on FR 2219, 27 miles E of North Bend.
Special Activities & Facilities: Boat launch, fishing, NW end of Lake Keechelus.

	53	2500	8				

Group Camp

Denny Creek

Access: Exit 47 from I-90 to FR 58, 20 miles E of North Bend.
Special Activities & Facilities: (Capacity 30 persons, reservations required).

	49	2240				x	x

Mt. Shuksan from Artists Point, Mt. Baker-Snoqualmie National Forest

Map Location	Elevation	Picnic Units	Tent Units	Tent-Trailer Units	Fee	Drinking Water

Skykomish Ranger District

Campgrounds

Beckler River

Access: 2 miles N of Skykomish via US 2, FR 65.

Special Activities & Facilities: Fishing.

Map Location	Elevation	Picnic Units	Tent Units	Tent-Trailer Units	Fee	Drinking Water
41	*900*	*3*	*7*	*20*	*x*	*x*

Money Creek

Access: 4 miles W of Skykomish, just off US 2.

Special Activities & Facilities: Swimming, fishing, hiking.

Map Location	Elevation	Picnic Units	Tent Units	Tent-Trailer Units	Fee	Drinking Water
44	*900*	*4*	*12*	*13*	*x*	*x*

San Juan

Access: 14 miles NE of Index on FR 63.

Special Activities & Facilities: Fishing, hiking.

Map Location	Elevation	Picnic Units	Tent Units	Tent-Trailer Units	Fee	Drinking Water
*46**	*1400*		*7*	*3*		

Troublesome Creek

Access: 12 miles NE of Index on FR 63.

Special Activities & Facilities: Fishing, hiking, nature trail.

Map Location	Elevation	Picnic Units	Tent Units	Tent-Trailer Units	Fee	Drinking Water
*46**	*1300*	*3*	*19*	*12*		

Day Use Sites

Deception Falls

Access: 8 miles E of Skykomish on US 2.

Special Activities & Facilities: Fishing, nature trail, hiking.

Map Location	Elevation	Picnic Units	Tent Units	Tent-Trailer Units	Fee	Drinking Water
47	*2200*	*5*				

Group Camps

Miller River

Access: 5.5 miles SW of Skykomish via Cty. Rd., on FR 6410.

Special Activities & Facilities: Fishing, swimming, parking for trailers. Reservations.

Map Location	Elevation	Picnic Units	Tent Units	Tent-Trailer Units	Fee	Drinking Water
43	*1000*			*22*	*x*	

Map Location	*Elevation*	*Picnic Units*	*Tent Units*	*Tent-Trailer Units*	*Fee*	*Drinking Water*

White River Ranger District

Campgrounds

Corral Pass

Access: 37 miles SE of Enumclaw via St. Hwy. 410, FR 7174.
Special Activities & Facilities: Horse riding, berry picking, hiking, scenery.

54	*5600*		*12*			

The Dalles

Access: 25 miles SE of Enumclaw via St. Hwy. 410.
Special Activities & Facilities: Fishing, nature trails, hiking.

55	*2165*	*10*	*19*	*26*	*x*	*x*

Silver Springs

Access: 31 miles SE of Enumclaw via St. Hwy. 410.
Special Activities & Facilities: Fishing, hiking.

56	*2600*	*10*	*16*	*40*	*x*	*x*

Evans Creek

Access: 35 miles S of Enumclaw via St. Hwy. 165.
Special Activities & Facilities: ORV park, picnic shelter, 40 miles of ORV trail.

60	*3400*	*1*		*20*		

Day Use Sites

Sun Top

Access: Via St. Hwy. 410, FRs 73, 7315, 35 miles SE of Enumclaw.
Special Activities & Facilities: Scenery, berry picking, fire lookout.

58	*5300*	*7*❶				

*Multiple sites in area

Handicapped Accessibility Codes
❶ Fully Accessible
❷ Usable
❸ Difficult
See page 7 for full description.

Mt. Hood National Forest

Mt. Hood from Burnt Lake, Mt. Hood National Forest. Photo by Jim Pollock.

Brightly colored wildflowers, cool alpine meadows, and breathtaking waterfalls along the Columbia River are a "must-see." Towering Mt. Hood is the central feature of the Mt. Hood Wilderness and of the forest. Other wildernesses include Badger Creek, Bull of the Woods, Columbia, and Salmon-Huckleberry.

Special places of interest include Columbia River Gorge National Scenic Area; Multnomah Falls and Lodge where the spectacular falls plunges 542 feet into a pristine pool before cascading another 69 feet; Wahkeena Falls; unique Oneonta Gorge; Horsetail Falls; waterfalls at Eagle Creek; Wahtum Lake; Larch Mountain for a scenic drive; Lost Lake with reflections of Mt. Hood; historic Timberline Lodge; Mt. Hood Meadows winter sports area; Trillium Lake with views of Mt. Hood; the Cloud Cap area on the north side of Mt. Hood; Clear Lake; Little Crater Lake; Timothy Lake; Clackamas River Drive; Olallie Lake Scenic Area; and a walk to Bagby Hot Springs.

Further information about recreation opportunities, campground locations and facilities, as well as current maps of the area, are available at the following offices:

Mt. Hood National Forest
Supervisor's Office
2955 N.W.Division
Gresham, OR 97030
(503) 666-0700

Barlow Ranger District
P.O. Box 67
Dufur, OR 97021
(503) 467-2291

Bear Springs Ranger District
Rt. 1 Box 222
Maupin, OR 97037
(503) 328-6211

Columbia Gorge Ranger District
31520 S.E. Woodard Rd.
Troutdale, OR 97060
(503) 695-2276

Estacada Ranger District
595 N.W. Industrial Way
Estacada, OR 97023
(503) 630-6861

Hood River Ranger District
6780 Highway 35
Mt. Hood-Parkdale, OR 97041
(503) 666-0701

(Clackamas) Ripplebrook Ranger Dist.
61431 East Hwy 224
Estacada, OR 97023
(503) 630-4256

Zigzag Ranger District
70220 East Hwy 26
Zigzag, OR 97049
(503) 666-0704

Columbia Gorge Nat'l Scenic Area
902 Wasco Ave. Suite 301
Hood River, OR 97031
(503) 386-2333

Other information sources

Timberline Lodge
Government Camp, OR 97028
Reservations: (503) 231-5400
General Info: (503) 226-7979

Multomah Falls Lodge
Bridal Veil, OR 97010
(503) 695-2376

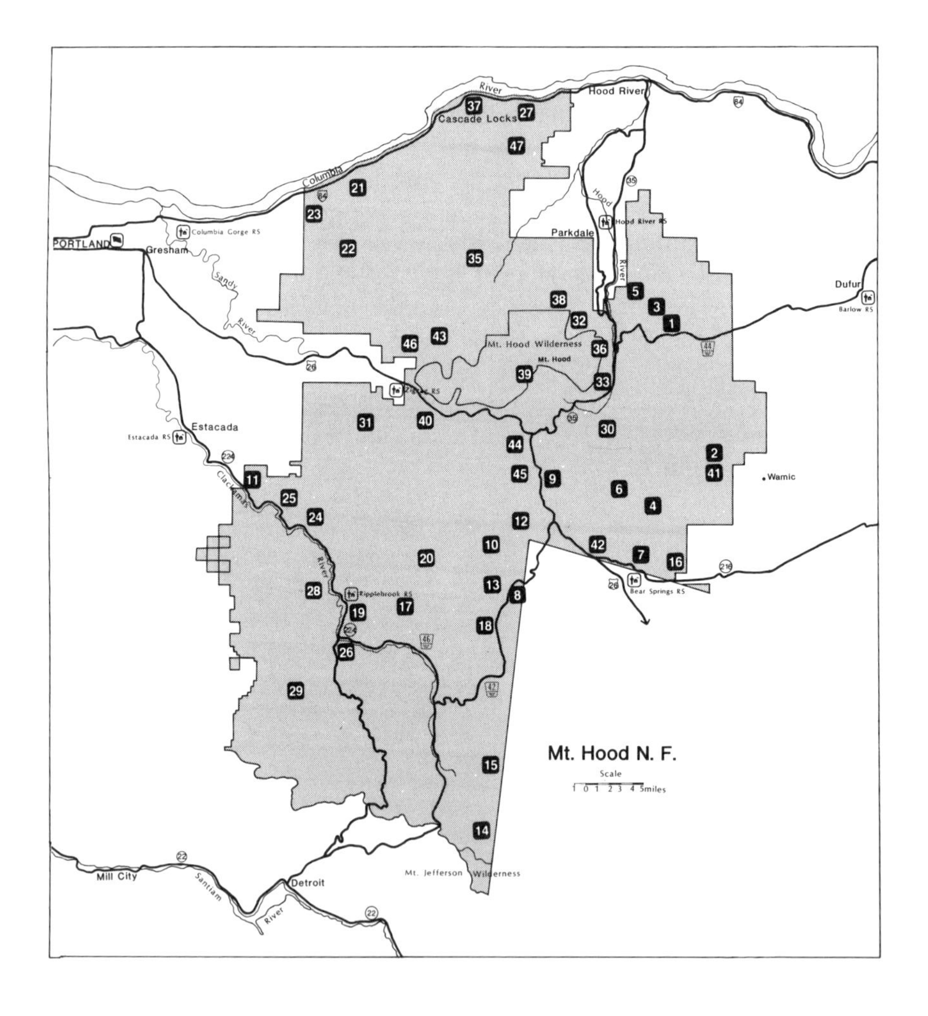
River
Hood River
Cascade Locks
Columbia
PORTLAND
Gresham
Columbia Gorge RS
Sandy
River
Hood
River
Hood River RS
Parkdale
Dufur
Barlow RS
Mt. Hood Wilderness
Mt. Hood
Estacada
Estacada RS
Clackamas
River
Ripplebrook RS
Wamic
Bear Springs RS
Mt. Hood N. F.
Scale
1 0 1 2 3 4 5miles
Mill City
Santiam
River
Detroit
Mt. Jefferson Wilderness
1
2
3
4
5
6
7
8
9
10
11
12
13
14
15
16
17
18
19
20
21
22
23
24
25
26
27
28
29
30
31
32
33
35
36
37
38
39
40
41
42
43
44
45
46
47

MT. HOOD NATIONAL FOREST

Map Location	Elevation	Picnic Units	Tent Units	Tent-Trailer Units	Fee	Drinking Water

Developed Sites

Pebble Ford

Access: 18 miles SW of Dufur via Cty. Rd. 1, on FR 44.

Special Activities & Facilities: RVs to 16', lightly improved site.

Map Location	Elevation	Picnic Units	Tent Units	Tent-Trailer Units	Fee	Drinking Water
1*	4100			4		

Eight Mile Crossing

Access: 17 miles SW of Dufur via Cty. Rd. 1, FR 44.

Special Activities & Facilities: RVs to 30', fishing.

Map Location	Elevation	Picnic Units	Tent Units	Tent-Trailer Units	Fee	Drinking Water
1*	3800			14		

Bonney Meadows

Access: 26 miles W of Wamic via Cty. Rd. 226, FRs 48, 4890, 4891. Or, 35 miles E of Government Camp via US 26, FRs 35, 48, 4890, 4891.

Special Activities & Facilities: Hiking trails, improved site.

Map Location	Elevation	Picnic Units	Tent Units	Tent-Trailer Units	Fee	Drinking Water
30	5300			5		

Bonney Crossing

Access: 10 miles NW of Wamic via Cty. Rd. 226, FRs 48, 4810, 4811, 2710.

Special Activities & Facilities: Lightly improved, horse facilities, hiking trails, wilderness.

Map Location	Elevation	Picnic Units	Tent Units	Tent-Trailer Units	Fee	Drinking Water
2	2200		8			

Rock Creek Reservoir

Access: 7.5 miles W of Wamic via Cty. Rd. 226, FR 48.

Special Activities & Facilities: Boating (no motor), barrier-free fishing, swimming.

Map Location	Elevation	Picnic Units	Tent Units	Tent-Trailer Units	Fee	Drinking Water
♿ 41	2200	13		33❷	x	x

Forest Creek

Access: 20 miles SW of Wamic via Cty. Rd. 226, FRs 48, 4885, 3530.

Special Activities & Facilities: Site is lightly improved.

Map Location	Elevation	Picnic Units	Tent Units	Tent-Trailer Units	Fee	Drinking Water
4	3000			5		

Knebal Springs

Access: 21 miles W of Dufur via Cty. Rd. 1, FRs 44, 4430, 1720.

Special Activities & Facilities: Lightly improved, horse facilities, spring water, trails.

Map Location	Elevation	Picnic Units	Tent Units	Tent-Trailer Units	Fee	Drinking Water
3	3800			4		

Map Location	Elevation	Picnic Units	Tent Units	Tent-Trailer Units	Fee	Drinking Water

Gibson Prairie Horse Camp

Access: 15 miles S of Hood River via St. Hwy. 35, FR 17.
Special Activities & Facilities: Lightly improved, horse facilities, trails.

Map Location	Elevation	Picnic Units	Tent Units	Tent-Trailer Units	Fee	Drinking Water
5	3900			4		

Clear Creek

Access: 30 miles W of Maupin via St. Hwy. 216, FR 2130.
Special Activities & Facilities: Fishing, RVs under 16'.

Map Location	Elevation	Picnic Units	Tent Units	Tent-Trailer Units	Fee	Drinking Water
42	3000			6		

Bear Springs

Access: 25 miles W of Maupin via St. Hwy. 216.
Special Activities & Facilities: Concessionaire operated. Reservations for picnic shelters.

Map Location	Elevation	Picnic Units	Tent Units	Tent-Trailer Units	Fee	Drinking Water
7	3200	6		21	x	x

McCubbins Gulch

Access: 25 miles NW of Maupin via St. Hwy. 216, FR 2110.
Special Activities & Facilities: Lightly improved, RVs under 16'.

Map Location	Elevation	Picnic Units	Tent Units	Tent-Trailer Units	Fee	Drinking Water
16	3000			5		

White River Station

Access: 14 miles SE of Gov't Camp via US 26, St. Hwy. 35, FRs 48, 3530.
Special Activities & Facilities: Fishing, RVs under 16'.

Map Location	Elevation	Picnic Units	Tent Units	Tent-Trailer Units	Fee	Drinking Water
6*	2800			5		

Herman Horse Camp

Access: 1.6 miles E of Cascade Locks via Cty. Rd.
Special Activities & Facilities: Designed for equestrians, horse handling facilities.

Map Location	Elevation	Picnic Units	Tent Units	Tent-Trailer Units	Fee	Drinking Water
37	200	5		7	x	x

Harriet Lake

Access: 34.7 miles SE Estacada via St. Hwy. 224, FR 57, W on 4630.
Special Activities & Facilities: Boating, swimming, fishing, barrier-free toilet.

Map Location	Elevation	Picnic Units	Tent Units	Tent-Trailer Units	Fee	Drinking Water
♿ 17*	2100			13	x	x

	Map Location	Elevation	Picnic Units	Tent Units	Tent-Trailer Units	Fee	Drinking Water

Hideaway Lake

Access: 43 miles SE Estacada via St. Hwy. 224, FRs 57, 58, 5830.
Special Activities & Facilities: Boating, swimming, fishing, hiking, RVs to 16'.

	Map Location	Elevation	Picnic Units	Tent Units	Tent-Trailer Units	Fee	Drinking Water
	*17**	*4600*		2	7	*x*	*x*

Olallie Meadow

Access: 58.4 miles SE Estacada via St. Hwy. 224, FRs 46, 4690, 4220.
Special Activities & Facilities: Hiking, RVs to 16'.

	Map Location	Elevation	Picnic Units	Tent Units	Tent-Trailer Units	Fee	Drinking Water
	*15**	*4500*			*7*		

Peninsula

Access: 63.6 miles SE Estacada via St. Hwy. 224, FRs 46, 4690, 4220.
Special Activities & Facilities: Boating, swimming, fishing, barrier-free fishing platform.

	Map Location	Elevation	Picnic Units	Tent Units	Tent-Trailer Units	Fee	Drinking Water
♿	*14**	*5000*		*16*	*18* ❶	*x*	*x*

Paul Dennis

Access: 63.3 miles SE Estacada via St. Hwy. 224, FRs 46, 4690, 4220.
Special Activities & Facilities: Boating, swimming, fishing, hiking, RVs to 16'.

	Map Location	Elevation	Picnic Units	Tent Units	Tent-Trailer Units	Fee	Drinking Water
	*14**	*5000*		*14*	*5*	*x*	*x*

Breitenbush Lake

Access: 64 miles SE Estacada via St. Hwy. 224, FRs 46, 4690, 4220.
Special Activities & Facilities: Primitive, difficult access road for cars and trailers, RVs to 16', boating, fishing, hiking.

	Map Location	Elevation	Picnic Units	Tent Units	Tent-Trailer Units	Fee	Drinking Water
	*14**	*1400*		*6*	*10*		

Riverside

Access: 29.7 miles SE Estacada via St. Hwy. 224.
Special Activities & Facilities: Fishing, hiking, barrier-free toilet.

	Map Location	Elevation	Picnic Units	Tent Units	Tent-Trailer Units	Fee	Drinking Water
♿	*26**	*1400*		*6*	*10*	*x*	*x*

Shellrock Creek

Access: 35 miles SE Estacada via St. Hwy. 224, FRs 57, 58.
Special Activities & Facilities: Fishing.

	Map Location	Elevation	Picnic Units	Tent Units	Tent-Trailer Units	Fee	Drinking Water
	*17**	*2300*		*5*			

Lower Lake

Access: 61.5 miles SE Estacada via St. Hwy. 224, FRs 46, 4690, 4220.

Special Activities & Facilities: RVs to 16', hiking.

Map Location	Elevation	Picnic Units	Tent Units	Tent-Trailer Units	Fee	Drinking Water
15*	4600			9		

Camp Ten

Access: 63.1 miles SE Estacada via St. Hwy. 224, FRs 46, 4690, 4220.

Special Activities & Facilities: RVs to 16', boating, fishing, hiking.

Map Location	Elevation	Picnic Units	Tent Units	Tent-Trailer Units	Fee	Drinking Water
14*	5000			6		

Ripplebrook

Access: 26.5 miles SE Estacada via St. Hwy. 224.

Special Activities & Facilities: RVs to 16', fishing, barrier-free toilet.

Map Location	Elevation	Picnic Units	Tent Units	Tent-Trailer Units	Fee	Drinking Water
19*	1500		4	10	x	x

Raab

Access: 32 miles SE Estacada via St. Hwy. 224, FRs 46, 63.

Special Activities & Facilities: RVs to 20', fishing.

Map Location	Elevation	Picnic Units	Tent Units	Tent-Trailer Units	Fee	Drinking Water
26*	1500		2	25		

Rainbow

Access: 27 miles SE Estacada via St. Hwy. 224, FR 46.

Special Activities & Facilities: Swimming, fishing, hiking, barrier-free toilet.

Map Location	Elevation	Picnic Units	Tent Units	Tent-Trailer Units	Fee	Drinking Water
19*	1400			17	x	x

Highrock Spring

Access: 46 miles SE Estacada via St. Hwy. 224, FRs 57, 58.

Special Activities & Facilities: Huckleberry fields in the fall.

Map Location	Elevation	Picnic Units	Tent Units	Tent-Trailer Units	Fee	Drinking Water
20	4400		7			

Riverford

Access: 31 miles SE Estacada via St. Hwy. 224.

Special Activities & Facilities: RVs to 16', swimming, fishing, hiking, barrier-free toilet.

Map Location	Elevation	Picnic Units	Tent Units	Tent-Trailer Units	Fee	Drinking Water
26*	1500		6	4		

Map Location	*Elevation*	*Picnic Units*	*Tent Units*	*Tent-Trailer Units*	*Fee*	*Drinking Water*
Lazy Bend Access: 10.7 miles SE Estacada via St. Hwy. 224. Special Activities & Facilities: Fishing.						
11	*800*		*9*	*13*	*x*	*x*
Roaring River Access: 18.2 miles SE Estacada via St. Hwy. 224. Special Activities & Facilities: Fishing, hiking, at junction of Roaring & Clackamas rivers.						
*24**	*1000*		*5*	*9*	*x*	*x*
Fish Creek Access: 15.6 miles SE Estacada via St. Hwy. 224. Special Activities & Facilities: Fishing, located on Clackamas River.						
*25**	*800*		*10*	*15*		
Carter Bridge Access: 15 miles SE Estacada via St. Hwy. 224. Special Activities & Facilities: Fishing.						
*25**	*800*	*5*	*4*	*13*	*x*	*x*
Armstrong Access: 15.4 miles SE Estacada via St. Hwy. 224. Special Activities & Facilities: Fishing, located on Clackamas River.						
*25**	*900*			*11*	*x*	*x*
Kingfisher Access: 35 miles SE Estacada via St. Hwy. 224, FRs 46, 63, 70. Special Activities & Facilities: Fishing, Hot Springs Fork of Collawash River.						
29	*1600*		*19*	*14*	*x*	*x*
Lockaby Access: 15.3 miles SE of Estacada via St. Hwy. 224. Special Activities & Facilities: Fishing, on Clackamas River.						
*25**	*900*		*22*	*8*	*x*	*x*

	Map Location	Elevation	Picnic Units	Tent Units	Tent-Trailer Units	Fee	Drinking Water

Indian Henry

Access: 23.5 miles SE of Estacada via St. Hwy. 224.
Special Activities & Facilities: Fishing, hiking.

	Map Location	Elevation	Picnic Units	Tent Units	Tent-Trailer Units	Fee	Drinking Water
♿	28	1200			86❷	x	x

Lost Lake (partially closed 1990, undergoing construciton)

Access: 28 miles SW Hood River via Cty. Rd. N22, FR 13.
Special Activities & Facilities: Boating, fishing, swimming, hiking, bicycling. Concessionaire operated site, heavily used, group facilities, barrier-free toilet.

	Map Location	Elevation	Picnic Units	Tent Units	Tent-Trailer Units	Fee	Drinking Water
♿	35	3200	26	14	77	x	x

Tilly Jane

Access: 19.7 miles SW Parkdale, via St. Hwy. 35, on FR 3512.
Special Activities & Facilities: Hiking, historic area, walk-in site, lightly improved.

	Map Location	Elevation	Picnic Units	Tent Units	Tent-Trailer Units	Fee	Drinking Water
	32	5700		14			

Cloud Cap Saddle

Access: 20 miles S Parkdale via St. Hwy. 35, FR 3512.
Special Activities & Facilities: On Timberline Trail, hiking, scenery.

	Map Location	Elevation	Picnic Units	Tent Units	Tent-Trailer Units	Fee	Drinking Water
	32	5900		3			x

Sherwood

Access: 11 miles SE Parkdale via St. Hwy. 35.
Special Activities & Facilities: Fishing, hiking, barrier-free toilet.

	Map Location	Elevation	Picnic Units	Tent Units	Tent-Trailer Units	Fee	Drinking Water
♿	36	3000	5		14	x	x

Robinhood

Access: 15 miles SE Parkdale via St. Hwy. 35.
Special Activities & Facilities: Fishing, hiking, RVs to 16', barrier-free toilet.

	Map Location	Elevation	Picnic Units	Tent Units	Tent-Trailer Units	Fee	Drinking Water
♿	33	3600	3		24	x	x

Wahtum Lake

Access: 28 miles SW Hood River via Dee, Or., FRs 13, 1310.
Special Activities & Facilities: 1/4 mile off lake shore, fishing, swimming, boating, hiking.

	Map Location	Elevation	Picnic Units	Tent Units	Tent-Trailer Units	Fee	Drinking Water
	34*	3900			5		

	Map Location	Elevation	Picnic Units	Tent Units	Tent-Trailer Units	Fee	Drinking Water

Indian Springs

Access: 30 miles SW Hood River via Dee, Or., FRs 13, 1310.
Special Activities & Facilities: Primitive camp on Pacific Crest National Scenic Trail.

	Map Location	Elevation	Picnic Units	Tent Units	Tent-Trailer Units	Fee	Drinking Water
	34*	4200		4			

Rainy Lake

Access: SW Hood River via Dee, Or., FRs 2810, 2820.
Special Activities & Facilities: 1/8 mile to lake, fishing, hiking.

	Map Location	Elevation	Picnic Units	Tent Units	Tent-Trailer Units	Fee	Drinking Water
	47	4100		4			

Green Canyon

Access: 5.6 miles S Welches on FR 2618.
Special Activities & Facilities: Fishing, hiking, barrier-free toilet.

	Map Location	Elevation	Picnic Units	Tent Units	Tent-Trailer Units	Fee	Drinking Water
♿	31	1600	6		15	x	x

McNeil

Access: 5 miles NE Zigzag on FR 18.
Special Activities & Facilities: Fishing, bicycling, near Sandy River, mushrooming, geologic features.

	Map Location	Elevation	Picnic Units	Tent Units	Tent-Trailer Units	Fee	Drinking Water
	43*	2000			34	x	x

Toll Gate

Access: .5 miles SE Rhododendron on US 26.
Special Activities & Facilities: Fishing, hiking, Barlow trail, barrier-free toilet.

	Map Location	Elevation	Picnic Units	Tent Units	Tent-Trailer Units	Fee	Drinking Water
♿	40*	1700	6	14	1	x	x

Camp Creek

Access: 2.9 miles SE Rhododendron on US 26.
Special Activities & Facilities: Fishing, hiking.

	Map Location	Elevation	Picnic Units	Tent Units	Tent-Trailer Units	Fee	Drinking Water
	40*	2200	4		24	x	x

Still Creek

Access: 1.7 miles SE Gov't Camp via US 26.
Special Activities & Facilities: Fishing, RVs to 16', hiking the Barlow trail.

	Map Location	Elevation	Picnic Units	Tent Units	Tent-Trailer Units	Fee	Drinking Water
	44	3700			27	x	x

Alpine

Access: 5.4 miles NE Gov't Camp on St. Hwy. 173.
Special Activities & Facilities: Near Timberline Lodge. Operated by concessionaire, wildflowers.

Map Location	*Elevation*	*Picnic Units*	*Tent Units*	*Tent-Trailer Units*	*Fee*	*Drinking Water*
39	*5400*		*16*		*x*	*x*

Trillium Lake (partially closed 1990, undergoing construction)

Access: 3.5 miles SE Gov't Camp via US 26, FR 2656.
Special Activities & Facilities: Boating, swimming, fishing, bicycling, barrier-free toilet.

Map Location	*Elevation*	*Picnic Units*	*Tent Units*	*Tent-Trailer Units*	*Fee*	*Drinking Water*
45	*3600*	*5*		*39*	*x*	*x*

Riley

Access: 6 miles NE Zigzag via FRs 18, 1825, 382.
Special Activities & Facilities: Fishing, trails, horse facilities.

Map Location	*Elevation*	*Picnic Units*	*Tent Units*	*Tent-Trailer Units*	*Fee*	*Drinking Water*
46	*2100*			*14*	*x*	*x*

Oak Fork

Access: 26.5 miles S Gov't Camp via US 26, FRs 42, 57.
Special Activities & Facilities: Concessionaire operated, boating, fishing, on Timothy Lake.

Map Location	*Elevation*	*Picnic Units*	*Tent Units*	*Tent-Trailer Units*	*Fee*	*Drinking Water*
*13**	*3200*			*47*	*x*	*x*

Pine Point

Access: 27 miles S Gov't Camp via US 26, FRs 42, 57.
Special Activities & Facilities: Concessionaire operated, boating, fishing, hiking, barrier-free fishing and toilets.

Map Location	*Elevation*	*Picnic Units*	*Tent Units*	*Tent-Trailer Units*	*Fee*	*Drinking Water*
*13**	*3200*	*10*		*25*	*x*	*x*

Clackamas Lake

Access: 23 miles SE Government Camp via US 26, FRs 42, 4270.
Special Activities & Facilities: Horse facilities, barrier-free toilet.

Map Location	*Elevation*	*Picnic Units*	*Tent Units*	*Tent-Trailer Units*	*Fee*	*Drinking Water*
*8**				*47*	*x*	*x*

Little Crater

Access: 24 miles SE Govt Camp via US 26, FRs 42, 4280, 58.
Special Activities & Facilities: Barrier-free toilet.

Map Location	*Elevation*	*Picnic Units*	*Tent Units*	*Tent-Trailer Units*	*Fee*	*Drinking Water*
10			*2*	*16*	*x*	*x*

	Map Location	Elevation	Picnic Units	Tent Units	Tent-Trailer Units	Fee	Drinking Water
Clear Lake Access: 11 miles SE Govt Camp via US 26. Special Activities & Facilities: Boating, swimming, fishing, waterskiing.							
♿	*12*	*3600*			*28❸*	*x*	*x*
Frog Lake Access: 8.5 miles SE Govt Camp via US 26. Special Activities & Facilities: Boating, fishing, swimming, barrier-free toilet.							
♿	*9*	*3800*			*33*	*x*	*x*
Joe Graham Horse Camp Access: 23 miles SE Govt Camp via US 26, FR 42. Special Activities & Facilities: Horse facilities.							
	*8**	*3400*			*14*	*x*	*x*
Hood View Access: 27 miles S Govt Camp via US 26, FRs 42, 57. Special Activities & Facilities: Boating, swimming, fishing, on Timothy Lake, barrier-free toilet.							
♿	*13**	*3200*			*43*	*x*	*x*
Barlow Crossing Access: 12 miles SE Govt Camp via US 26, FR 43. Special Activities & Facilities: Fishing, RVs under 16'.							
	*6**	*3100*			*5*		
Gone Creek Access: 26.5 miles S Govt Camp via US 26, FRs 42, 57. Special Activities & Facilities: Boating, swimming, fishing, barrier-free toilet.							
♿	*13**				*50*	*x*	*x*
Kinnikinnick Access: 10 miles S Parkdale via Cty. Rd. 32, FR 2810. Special Activities & Facilities: Laurance Lake Reservoir, boating, swimming, fishing.							
	38	*3000*	*8*	*4*			

Map Location	Elevation	Picnic Units	Tent Units	Tent-Trailer Units	Fee	Drinking Water

Summit Lake

Access: 29 miles SE Govt Camp via US 26, FRs 42, 141.
Special Activities & Facilities: Boating.

18	*4000*		*6*			

Barlow Creek

Access: 12 Miles SE Govt Camp via US 26, St. Hwy. 35, FR 3530.
Special Activities & Facilities: Fishing, RVs under 16'.

*6**	*3100*			*5*		

Wyeth

Access: 7 miles E Cascade Locks via I-84, exit 51.
Special Activities & Facilities: Swimming, fishing, hiking.

27	*200*			*17*❷	*x*	*x*

Eagle Creek

Access: West of Cascade Locks via I-84, exit 41, turn right.
Special Activities & Facilities: Swimming, fishing, hiking, biking.

*21**	*200*	*50*		*19*	*x*	*x*

Overlook

Access: West of Cascade Locks via I-84, exit 41, turn right.
Special Activities & Facilities: Group picnicking, camping for groups with reservations only.

*21**		*28*	*40*		*x*	*x*

Sunstrip

Access: 19 miles SE Estacada via St. Hwy. 224.
Special Activities & Facilities: Fishing.

*24**	*1000*		*2*	*7*	*x*	*x*

Day Use Sites

Pegleg Falls

Access: 36 miles S Estacada via St. Hwy. 224, FRs 46, 63, 70.
Special Activities & Facilities: Fishing, Hot Springs Fk. Collowash River.

*29**	*2000*	*5*				

<table>
<tr><th></th><th>Map Location</th><th>Elevation</th><th>Picnic Units</th><th>Tent Units</th><th>Tent-Trailer Units</th><th>Fee</th><th>Drinking Water</th></tr>
<tr><td colspan="8">Olallie Lake
Access: 63 miles SE Estacada via St. Hwy. 224, FRs 46, 4690, 4220.
Special Activities & Facilities: Boating, fishing.</td></tr>
<tr><td></td><td>14*</td><td>4900</td><td>5</td><td></td><td></td><td></td><td>x</td></tr>
<tr><td colspan="8">Two Rivers
Access: 30 miles SE Estacada via St. Hwy. 224, FR 46.
Special Activities & Facilities: Swimming, barrier-free fishing, toilet.</td></tr>
<tr><td></td><td>26*</td><td>1400</td><td>7</td><td></td><td></td><td></td><td>x</td></tr>
<tr><td colspan="8">Larch Mountain
Access: 19 miles E of Corbett. From I-84 take exit 18, US 30 E, to signed intersection for Larch Mtn.
Special Activities & Facilities: Hiking, biking, scenery.</td></tr>
<tr><td></td><td>22</td><td>4000</td><td>49</td><td></td><td></td><td></td><td></td></tr>
<tr><td colspan="8">Wahkeena Falls
Access: 3 miles E of Bridal Veil.
Special Activities & Facilities: Fishing, hiking, biking, waterfall.</td></tr>
<tr><td></td><td>23</td><td>100</td><td>56</td><td></td><td></td><td></td><td>x</td></tr>
<tr><td colspan="8">Big Eddy
Access: 14 miles SE Estacada via St. Hwy. 224.
Special Activities & Facilities: Swimming, fishing, Clackamas River.</td></tr>
<tr><td></td><td>25</td><td>800</td><td></td><td></td><td></td><td></td><td></td></tr>
<tr><td colspan="8">Lost Creek (Under construction 1990)
Access: 7 miles NE Zigzag via FRs 18, 1825.
Special Activities & Facilities: Handicapped accessible trail, fishing. Units are constructed to provide various levels of challange for users. Tent units are pack in sites.</td></tr>
<tr><td>♿</td><td>43*</td><td>2400</td><td>4❶</td><td>5❶</td><td>11❶</td><td></td><td></td></tr>
</table>

Handicapped Accessibility Codes
❶ Fully Accessible
❷ Usable
❸ Difficult
See page 7 for full description.

*Sites in close proximity to others

Columbia River Gorge National Scenic Area

Tanner Creek, Columbia River National Scenic Area. Photo by Jim Pollock.

The Columbia River Gorge is a spectacular river canyon cutting through the volcanic rock of the Cascade Mountain Range and is the only sea-level river flowing through the Cascades. In addition to being a natural wonder, the gorge contains cities, farms, and industries, and is home to 50,000 people. It serves as an important water, rail, and highway transportation corridor.

In 1986 Congress created the 292,000-acre Columbia River Gorge National Scenic Area, forming a partnership between the US Forest Service, the Gorge Commission with appointees from the states of Washington and Oregon, and six local counties to manage the gorge, protecting and enhancing scenic, cultural, recreational, and natural resources while encouraging compatible economic growth and development.

A few of the special points and activities of interest to the visitor are the historic Columbia River Scenic Highway; Crown Point's 30-mile vista of the gorge; Multnomah Falls and Lodge; many waterfalls; Beacon Rock; and windsurfing at Hood River and Home Valley.

For further information about recreation opportunities, campground locations and facilities, refer to the sections on the Gifford Pinchot and Mt. Hood National Forests. Information and maps of the Columbia River Gorge National Scenic Area are available at the following areas.

Columbia River Gorge
National Scenic Area
Wacoma Center
902 Wasco Avenue
Hood River, OR 97301
(503) 386-2333

Mt. Hood National Forest
2955 NW Division Street
Gresham, OR 97030
(503) 667-0511

Columbia Gorge Ranger District
31520 SE Woodard Road
Troutdale, OR 97230
(503) 695-2276

Wind River Ranger District
Carson, WA 98610
(509) 427-5171

Oregon State Parks
525 Trade St. SE, Suite 301
Salem, OR 97301

The Columbia River Gorge
Commission
P.O. Box 730
White Salmon, WA 98672
(509) 493-3323

Gifford Pinchot National Forest
500 West 12th Street
Vancouver, WA 98660
(206) 696-7500

Hood River Ranger District
6780 Highway 35
Mt. Hood-Parkdale, OR 97041
(503) 352-6002

Mt. Adams Ranger District
Trout Lake, WA 98650
(509) 395-2501

Washington State Parks
7155 Clearwater Lane, KY-11
Olympia, Wa 98504
(206) 753-2027

Ochoco National Forest and Crooked River National Grassland

Ochoco National Forest. Photo by Jim Pollock.

Deep canyons, picturesque rimrocks, and ancient landforms are major features of this forest. Visitors are drawn to the unique geologic sites where thunder eggs, agates, sagemite, jasper, limb casts, and petrified wood reward rock enthusiasts. A diversity of wildlife includes mule deer, elk, antelope, a herd of wild horses, even an occasional wildcat; and, at rare and special times, a cougar can be sighted. Often referred to as "high desert," the Crooked River National Grassland is characterized by grasslands dotted with sagebrush and juniper and is home to a small herd of antelope as well as numerous mule deer, quail and chukars. Three wildernesses, Black Canyon, Bridge Creek, and Mill Creek, offer beauty and solitude.

Special places of interest include 350-feet-tall Steins Pillar which protrudes above the forest; two large geologic formations called Twin Pillars; a full circle view from Spanish Peak Vista; Lookout Mountain; Lake Billy Chinook with its steep grand-canyon-like walls, Round Butte vista point, the Deschutes River gorge; historic Cyrus Homesteads; Cow Camp Cabin, an old ranger station; Mayflower mining settlement ruins; Walton Lake; Wild Horse Range and its bands of wild horses; and Mt. Pisgah observation point.

Further information about recreation opportunities, campground locations and facilities, as well as current maps of the area, are available at the following offices:

Ochoco National Forest
Supervisor's Office
Federal Building
155 North Court St.
P.O. Box 490
Prineville, OR 97754
(503) 447-6247

Big Summit Ranger District
348855 Ochoco Ranger District
Prineville, OR 97754-9612
(503) 447-9645

Paulina Ranger District (Rager)
HC-68, Box 6015
Paulina, OR 97751-9706
(503) 477-3713

Prineville Ranger District
2321 East Third
Prineville, OR 97754-9117
(503) 447-3826

Snow Mountain Ranger District
HC-74 Box 12870
Hines, OR 97738-9401
(503) 573-7292

Crooked River National Grassland
2321 East Third
Prinevillle, OR 97754-9117
(503) 447-4120

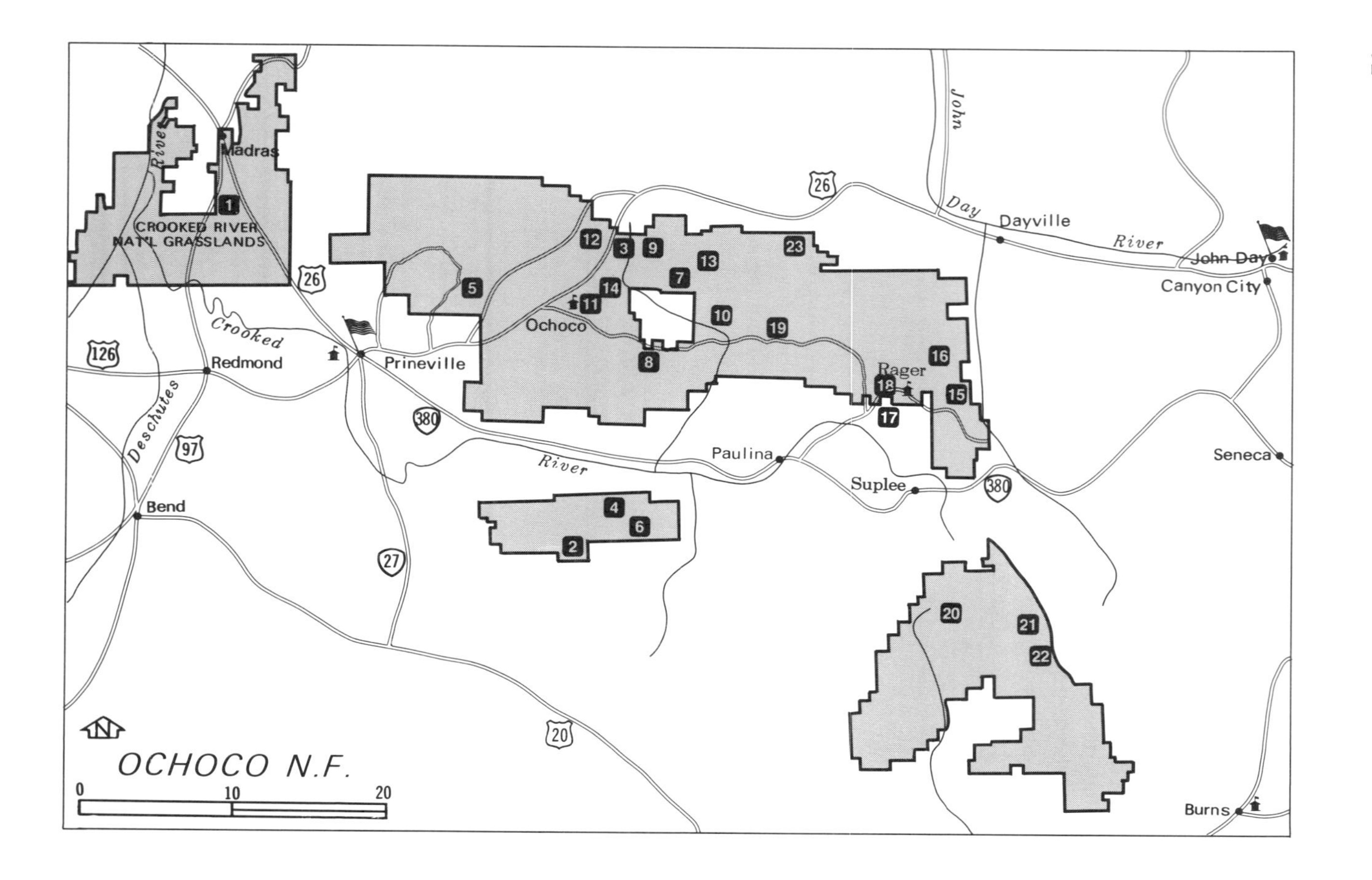
Madras
1
CROOKED RIVER
NAT'L GRASSLANDS
River
26
126
Crooked
Redmond
Prineville
Deschutes
97
Bend
380
River
27
20
OCHOCO N.F.
0
10
20
5
12
3
9
13
23
7
14
11
Ochoco
10
19
8
16
Rager
18
15
17
Paulina
Suplee
380
4
6
2
20
21
22
John
Day
Dayville
River
John Day
Canyon City
Seneca
Burns

OCHOCO NATIONAL FOREST

Map Location	Elevation	Picnic Units	Tent Units	Tent-Trailer Units	Fee	Drinking Water

Crooked River National Grassland

Haystack Reservoir

Access: 14 miles S Madras via US 97, Cty. Rd. 6, FR 1130.
Special Activities & Facilities: Boat launch, swimming, fishing.

	Map Location	Elevation	Picnic Units	Tent Units	Tent-Trailer Units	Fee	Drinking Water
♿	1	2900	2❸		24 ❸	x	x

Prineville Ranger District

Antelope Reservoir

Access: 43 miles SE Prineville via Cty. Rd. 380, FR 17.
Special Activities & Facilities: Boat launch, swimming, fishing.

Map Location	Elevation	Picnic Units	Tent Units	Tent-Trailer Units	Fee	Drinking Water
2	4600	1		25	x	x

Elkhorn

Access: 37 miles SE Prineville via Cty. Rd. 380, FR 16.
Special Activities & Facilities:

Map Location	Elevation	Picnic Units	Tent Units	Tent-Trailer Units	Fee	Drinking Water
4	4500			4		x

Wildcat

Access: 20 miles NE Prineville via US 26, Cty. Rd. 122, FR 33.
Special Activities & Facilities: Hiking, access to Mill Creek Wilderness.

Map Location	Elevation	Picnic Units	Tent Units	Tent-Trailer Units	Fee	Drinking Water
5	3700	3		17	x	x

Wiley Flat

Access: 47 miles SE Prineville via Cty. Rd. 380, FRs 16, 400.
Special Activities & Facilities: Lightly improved.

Map Location	Elevation	Picnic Units	Tent Units	Tent-Trailer Units	Fee	Drinking Water
6	5000			5		x

Big Summit Ranger District

Allen Creek

Access: NE edge of Big Summit Prairie via US 26, FR 22.
Special Activities & Facilities: Corrals for horses.

Map Location	Elevation	Picnic Units	Tent Units	Tent-Trailer Units	Fee	Drinking Water
7	4800			6		

Biggs

Access: 45 miles E of Prineville via US 26, Cty. Rd. 23, FRs 42, 4215.
Special Activities & Facilities:

Map Location	Elevation	Picnic Units	Tent Units	Tent-Trailer Units	Fee	Drinking Water
8	4800			3		

Deep Creek

Access: 49 miles E Prineville via US 26, Cty. Rd. 23, FR 42.
Special Activities & Facilities: Creek fishing.

Map Location	Elevation	Picnic Units	Tent Units	Tent-Trailer Units	Fee	Drinking Water
10	4400			8		x

Ochoco Forest Camp (closed summer 1990 for reconstruction)

Access: 25 miles NE Prineville at Ochoco Ranger Station via US 26, Cty. Rd. 23.
Special Activities & Facilities: Hiking, fishing.

Map Location	Elevation	Picnic Units	Tent Units	Tent-Trailer Units	Fee	Drinking Water
11	4000	1		6		x

Ochoco Divide

Access: 31 miles NE Prineville via US 26.
Special Activities & Facilities:

Map Location	Elevation	Picnic Units	Tent Units	Tent-Trailer Units	Fee	Drinking Water
12	4700			28	x	x

Scotts' Camp

Access: NE of Prineville via US 26, Cty. Rd. 23, FR 22.
Special Activities & Facilities:

Map Location	Elevation	Picnic Units	Tent Units	Tent-Trailer Units	Fee	Drinking Water
13	5300			3		x

Walton Lake

Access: 32 miles NE Prineville via US 26, Cty. Rd. 23, FR 22.
Special Activities & Facilities: Boat ramp (no motors), hiking, fishing, barrier-free fishing, trails.

Map Location	Elevation	Picnic Units	Tent Units	Tent-Trailer Units	Fee	Drinking Water
♿ 14	5200	3 ❸	6	25❷	x	x

White Rock

Acess: 29 miles NE of Prineville via US 26, FRs 3350, 3350-301.
Special Activities & Facilities:

Map Location	Elevation	Picnic Units	Tent Units	Tent-Trailer Units	Fee	Drinking Water
	5400			5		x

Blue Mountains, Ochoco National Forest

Map Location	Elevation	Picnic Units	Tent Units	Tent-Trailer Units	Fee	Drinking Water

Wildwood

Access: 30 miles E of Prineville via US 26, Cty. Rd. 23, FRs 22, 2210.

Special Activities & Facilities:

Map Location	Elevation	Picnic Units	Tent Units	Tent-Trailer Units	Fee	Drinking Water
3	4800			5		x

Paulina Ranger District

Barnhouse

Access: 18 miles SE of Mitchell via US 26, FR 12.

Special Activities & Facilities:

Map Location	Elevation	Picnic Units	Tent Units	Tent-Trailer Units	Fee	Drinking Water
23	5100			5		

Big Spring

Access: 55 miles E of Prineville via US 26, Cty. Rd. 23, FRs 42, 4270.

Special Activities & Facilities:

Map Location	Elevation	Picnic Units	Tent Units	Tent-Trailer Units	Fee	Drinking Water
19	5000			2		

Frazier

Access: 24 miles NE Paulina via Cty. Rds. 113, 135, FRs 58, 500.

Special Activities & Facilities:

Map Location	Elevation	Picnic Units	Tent Units	Tent-Trailer Units	Fee	Drinking Water
15	5000			5		

Mud Springs

Access: 24 miles NE of Paulina via Cty. Rds. 113, 135, FRs 58, 5840.

Special Activities & Facilities:

Map Location	Elevation	Picnic Units	Tent Units	Tent-Trailer Units	Fee	Drinking Water
16	5000			4		

Sugar Creek

Access: 12 miles N Paulina via Cty. Rd. 113, FR 58.

Special Activities & Facilities: Fishing, swimming.

Map Location	Elevation	Picnic Units	Tent Units	Tent-Trailer Units	Fee	Drinking Water
17	4000	3		10	x	x

Wolf Creek

Access: 12 miles NE Paulina via Cty. Rd. 113, FR 42.

Special Activities & Facilities: Fishing.

Map Location	Elevation	Picnic Units	Tent Units	Tent-Trailer Units	Fee	Drinking Water
18	4100			17		

Map Location	Elevation	Picnic Units	Tent Units	Tent-Trailer Units	Fee	Drinking Water

Snow Mountain Ranger District

Delintment Lake

Access: 43 miles NW Burns via US 20, FRs 47, 41.
Special Activities & Facilities: Boat launch, fishing.

Map Location	Elevation	Picnic Units	Tent Units	Tent-Trailer Units	Fee	Drinking Water
20	5600	2 ❸		24	x	x

Emigrant

Access: 36 miles NW Burns via FRs 47, 43, 4340.
Special Activities & Facilities: Fishing.

Map Location	Elevation	Picnic Units	Tent Units	Tent-Trailer Units	Fee	Drinking Water
21	5100	1		6	x	x

Falls

Access: 35 miles NW Burns via FRs 47, 43.
Special Activities & Facilities: Fishing.

Map Location	Elevation	Picnic Units	Tent Units	Tent-Trailer Units	Fee	Drinking Water
22	5000	2		5	x	x

Handicapped Accessibility Codes
- ❶ Fully Accessible
- ❷ Usable
- ❸ Difficult

See page 7 for full description.

Okanogan National Forest

Liberty Bell Mountain, Okanogan National Forest. Photo by Ross Files.

From the Columbia River to mountains at subalpine levels exceeding 9,000 feet, the 1.7 million-acre Okanogan National Forest has a feeling of orderliness. The beautiful Pasayten and portions of the Lake Chelan/ Sawtooth wildernesses comprise approximately 37 percent of the forest. The North Cascades Scenic Highway winds through spectacular scenery, offering one of the best views of the impressive high mountain landscape which includes the majestic Sawtooth Mountain Range. With numerous scenic drives available, a visit to the Okanogan National Forest is rewarding in its gentle beauty, magnificent vistas and historic appeal.

Special places of interest to the visitor include the spectacular North Cascades Scenic Highway; jagged mountain peaks and information at Washington Pass Overlook (with handicapped trail access); Cedar Creek Falls; exhibits and information at the Early Winters Visitor Center; the Goat Wall rising 2,000 feet above the Methow Valley; handicapped trail access through high alpine country to Rainy Lake; Slate Peak Vista, at 7,500 feet, which offers views of high mountain peaks including Mt. Baker; Buttermilk Butte, with a scenic view of mountain peaks and the Methow Valley; old mining towns and the community of Winthrop with its early western storefronts; the North Cascades Smokejumper Base where visitors are welcome; the Big Tree Botanical Area; and the scenic Five-Lakes area.

Further information about recreation opportunities, campground locations and facilities, as well as current maps of the area, are available at the following offices:

Okanogan National Forest
Supervisor's Office:
1240 Second Ave. South
Okanogan, WA 98840
P.O. Box 950
(509) 422-2704

Twisp Ranger District
502 Glover
P.O. Box 188
Twisp, WA 98856
(509) 997-2131

Tonasket Ranger District
1 West Winesap
P.O. Box 466
Tonasket, WA 98855
(509) 486-2186

Winthrop Ranger District
West Chewuch Rd.
P.O. Box 579
Winthrop, WA 98862
(509) 996-2266

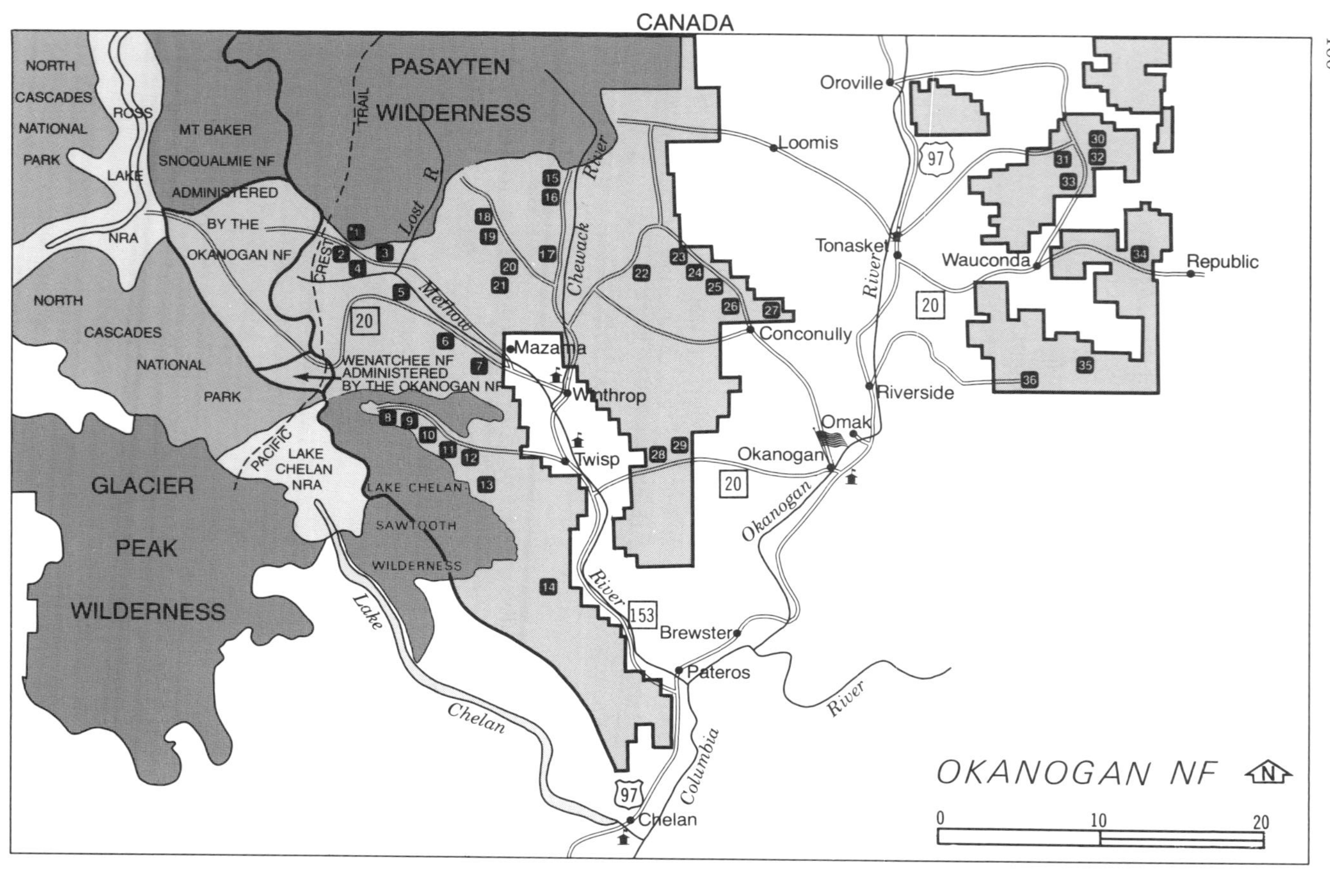

CANADA
NORTH CASCADES NATIONAL PARK
ROSS LAKE NRA
MT BAKER SNOQUALMIE NF ADMINISTERED BY THE OKANOGAN NF
PASAYTEN WILDERNESS
PACIFIC CREST TRAIL
Lost R
Chewack River
Methow
WENATCHEE NF ADMINISTERED BY THE OKANOGAN NF
NORTH CASCADES NATIONAL PARK
GLACIER PEAK WILDERNESS
LAKE CHELAN NRA
LAKE CHELAN-SAWTOOTH WILDERNESS
Lake Chelan
Mazama
Winthrop
Twisp
River
Oroville
Loomis
Tonasket
River
Wauconda
Republic
Conconully
Riverside
Omak
Okanogan
Okanogan
Brewster
Pateros
River
Columbia
Chelan
OKANOGAN NF
N
0
10
20

OKANOGAN NATIONAL FOREST

Map Location	*Elevation*	*Picnic Units*	*Tent Units*	*Tent-Trailer Units*	*Fee*	*Drinking Water*

Developed Sites

Tonasket Ranger District

Beaver Lake

Access: 32 miles NE Tonasket via St. Hwy. 20, Cty. Rd. 4953, FR 32.
Special Activities & Facilities: Boating, fishing, swimming, hiking.

Map Location	Elevation	Picnic Units	Tent Units	Tent-Trailer Units	Fee	Drinking Water
32	*3000*			*13*	*x*	*x*

Beth Lake

Access: 34 miles NE Tonasket via St. Hwy. 20, Cty. Rd. 4953, FR 32, Cty. Rd. 9480.
Special Activities & Facilities: Boating, fishing, swimming, hiking.

Map Location	Elevation	Picnic Units	Tent Units	Tent-Trailer Units	Fee	Drinking Water
30	*2900*	*3*		*14*	*x*	*x*

Bonaparte Lake

Access: 26 miles NE Tonasket via St. Hwy. 20, Cty. Rd. 4953, FR 32.
Special Activities & Facilities: Boating, fishing, swimming, hiking, group picnic area.

Map Location	Elevation	Picnic Units	Tent Units	Tent-Trailer Units	Fee	Drinking Water
33	*3600*	*8*		*29*	*x*	*x*

Cottonwood

Access: 2 miles N Conconully via FR 38.
Special Activities & Facilities: Fishing.

Map Location	Elevation	Picnic Units	Tent Units	Tent-Trailer Units	Fee	Drinking Water
26	*2700*		*1*	*4*	*x*	*x*

Crawfish Lake

Access: 19 miles E Riverside via Cty. Rd. 9320, FRs 30 and 30100.
Special Activities & Facilities: Boating, fishing.

Map Location	Elevation	Picnic Units	Tent Units	Tent-Trailer Units	Fee	Drinking Water
36	*4500*	*5*		*17*		

Kerr

Access: 4 miles NW Conconully via FR 38.
Special Activities & Facilities: Fishing.

Map Location	Elevation	Picnic Units	Tent Units	Tent-Trailer Units	Fee	Drinking Water
24	*3100*			*13*		

Lost Lake

Access: 35 miles NE Tonasket via St. Hwy. 20, Cty. Rd. 4953, FRs 32, 33, 33050.
Special Activities & Facilities: Boating, fishing, swimming, hiking, group picnic area, group reservation unit, barrier-free toilet.

Map Location	Elevation	Picnic Units	Tent Units	Tent-Trailer Units	Fee	Drinking Water
31	3800	13		18	x	x

Lyman Lake

Access: 28 miles SE Tonasket via St. Hwy. 20, Cty. Rds. 9455 and 3785.
Special Activities & Facilities: Fishing, swimming.

Map Location	Elevation	Picnic Units	Tent Units	Tent-Trailer Units	Fee	Drinking Water
35	2900			4		

Oriole

Access: 3 miles NW Conconully via FRs 38 and 38025.
Special Activities & Facilities: Fishing.

Map Location	Elevation	Picnic Units	Tent Units	Tent-Trailer Units	Fee	Drinking Water
25	2900			10	x	x

Salmon Meadows

Access: 9 miles NW Conconully via FR 38.
Special Activities & Facilities: Hiking, community kitchen.

Map Location	Elevation	Picnic Units	Tent Units	Tent-Trailer Units	Fee	Drinking Water
23	4500	3	9		x	x

Sugarloaf

Access: 5 miles NE Conconully via Cty. Rd. 4015.
Special Activities & Facilities: Boating, swimming, fishing.

Map Location	Elevation	Picnic Units	Tent Units	Tent-Trailer Units	Fee	Drinking Water
27	2400		4	1		

Sweat Creek

Access: 31 miles E Tonasket on St. Hwy. 20.
Special Activities & Facilities:

Map Location	Elevation	Picnic Units	Tent Units	Tent-Trailer Units	Fee	Drinking Water
34	3500	6		8	x	x

Tiffany Springs

Access: 31 miles NW Conconully via Cty. Rd. 2017 and FRs 37 and 39.
Special Activities & Facilities: Hiking, RVs to 16'.

Map Location	Elevation	Picnic Units	Tent Units	Tent-Trailer Units	Fee	Drinking Water
22	6800			6		

	Map Location	Elevation	Picnic Units	Tent Units	Tent-Trailer Units	Fee	Drinking Water

Twisp Ranger District

Black Pine Lake

Access: 19 miles SW Twisp via Cty. Rd. 9114, FR 43.
Special Activities & Facilities: Boating, fishing, hiking.

	Map Location	Elevation	Picnic Units	Tent Units	Tent-Trailer Units	Fee	Drinking Water
	13	4200	1	3	20	x	x

Foggy Dew

Access: 9 miles SW Carlton via Cty. Rds. 1029, 1034 and FR 4340.
Special Activities & Facilities: Community kitchen.

	Map Location	Elevation	Picnic Units	Tent Units	Tent-Trailer Units	Fee	Drinking Water
	14	2400			13		

JR

Access: 12 miles E Twisp on St. Hwy. 20.
Special Activities & Facilities: Barrier-free toilet.

	Map Location	Elevation	Picnic Units	Tent Units	Tent-Trailer Units	Fee	Drinking Water
♿	28	3900			6	x	x

Loup Loup

Access: 13 miles E Twisp via St. Hwy. 20, FR 42.
Special Activities & Facilities: Group picnic area.

	Map Location	Elevation	Picnic Units	Tent Units	Tent-Trailer Units	Fee	Drinking Water
	29	4200	1	4	20	x	x

Mystery

Access: 18 miles W Twisp via Cty. Rd. 9114, FR 44.
Special Activities & Facilities: Fishing, hiking.

	Map Location	Elevation	Picnic Units	Tent Units	Tent-Trailer Units	Fee	Drinking Water
	11	2800			4		

Poplar Flat

Access: 20 miles W Twisp via Cty. Rd. 9114, FRs 44 and 4440.
Special Activities & Facilities: Fishing, hiking, community kitchen.

	Map Location	Elevation	Picnic Units	Tent Units	Tent-Trailer Units	Fee	Drinking Water
♿	10	2900	3 ❸		15	x	x

Roads End

Access: 25 miles W Twisp via Cty. Rd. 9114, FRs 44 and 4440.
Special Activities & Facilities: RVs under 16', fishing, hiking.

	Map Location	Elevation	Picnic Units	Tent Units	Tent-Trailer Units	Fee	Drinking Water
	8	3600			4		

Harts Pass, Silver Star Mountain, Okanogan National Forest. Photo by Jim Hughes.

Map Location	Elevation	Picnic Units	Tent Units	Tent-Trailer Units	Fee	Drinking Water

South Creek

Access: 22 miles W Twisp via Cty. Rd. 9114, FRs 44 and 4440.
Special Activities & Facilities: RVs under 16', fishing, hiking.

9	3100			4		

Twisp River Horse Camp

Access: 22 miles W Twisp via Cty. Rds. 9114, 1090, FRs 4430 and 4435.
Special Activities & Facilities: Barrier-free toilet.

9	3100	1		12		

War Creek

Access: 14 miles W Twisp via Cty. Rd. 9114, FR 44.
Special Activities & Facilities: Fishing, hiking.

12	2400			11	x	x

Winthrop Ranger Distirct

Ballard

Access: 22 miles NW Winthrop via St. Hwy. 20, Cty. Rd. 1163, FR 5400.
Special Activities & Facilities: Fishing.

3	2600		6	1		

Buck Lake

Access: 12 miles N Winthrop via Cty. Rd. 9137 and FRs 51, 5130, 100, and 5130100.
Special Activities & Facilities: RVs to 16', boating.

21	3200		9			

Camp 4

Access: 18 miles NE Winthrop via Cty. Rd. 9137 and FR 51.
Special Activities & Facilities: Fishing.

15	2400		5			

Chewuch

Access: 15 miles NE Winthrop via Cty. Rd. 9137 and FR 51.
Special Activities & Facilities: RVs to 16', fishing.

16	2200		4			

Map Location	*Elevation*	*Picnic Units*	*Tent Units*	*Tent-Trailer Units*	*Fee*	*Drinking Water*

Early Winters

Access: 16 miles NW Winthrop via St. Hwy. 20.
Special Activities & Facilities: RVs to 16', fishing.

7	*2400*		*7*	*6*	*x*	*x*

Falls Creek

Access: 12 miles N Winthrop via Cty. Rd. 9137 and FR 51.
Special Activities & Facilities: RVs to 16', fishing, waterfall.

17	*2300*		*4*	*3*	*x*	*x*

Flat

Access: 11 miles N Winthrop via Cty. Rd. 9137 and FRs 51 and 5130.
Special Activities & Facilities: RVs to 16', fishing.

*20**	*2600*		*9*	*3*		

Hart's Pass

Access: 33 miles NW Winthrop via St. Hwy. 20, Cty. Rd. 1163, FR 5400. NOTE: Trailers prohibited on FR 5400 500.
Special Activities & Facilities: Alpine meadows, access to Pacific Crest National Scenic Trail.

1	*6200*		*5*			

Honeymoon

Access: 18 miles NW Winthrop via Cty. Rd. 9137 and FRs 51 and 5130.
Special Activities & Facilities: Fishing.

18	*3300*			*5*		

Klipchuck

Access: 18 miles NW Winthrop on St. Hwy. 20.
Special Activities & Facilities: Fishing, hiking.

6	*3000*		*6*	*40*	*x*	*x*

Lone Fir

Access: 27 miles NW Winthrop on St. Hwy. 20.
Special Activities & Facilities: Fishing, hiking.

5	*3800*		*21*	*6*	*x*	*x*

Meadows

Access: 34 miles NW Winthrop via St. Hwy. 20, Cty. Rd. 1163, FRs 5400, 5400500. NOTE: Trailers prohibited on FR 5400 500.
Special Activities & Facilities: Alpine meadows, access to Pacific Crest National Scenic Trail.

Map Location	*Elevation*	*Picnic Units*	*Tent Units*	*Tent-Trailer Units*	*Fee*	*Drinking Water*
2	*6200*		*14*			

Nice

Access: 13 miles N Winthrop via Cty. Rd. 9137 and FRs 51 and 5130.
Special Activities & Facilities: Fishing.

Map Location	*Elevation*	*Picnic Units*	*Tent Units*	*Tent-Trailer Units*	*Fee*	*Drinking Water*
*20**	*2700*		*4*			

River Bend

Access: 23 miles NW Winthrop via St. Hwy. 20, Cty. Rd. 1163 and FR 5400.
Special Activities & Facilities: Fishing, hiking.

Map Location	*Elevation*	*Picnic Units*	*Tent Units*	*Tent-Trailer Units*	*Fee*	*Drinking Water*
4	*2700*		*3*	*3*	*x*	*x*

Ruffed Grouse

Access: 17 miles NW Winthrop via Cty. Rd. 9137, FRs 51, 5130.
Special Activities & Facilities: Fishing.

Map Location	*Elevation*	*Picnic Units*	*Tent Units*	*Tent-Trailer Units*	*Fee*	*Drinking Water*
19	*3200*		*4*			

* Indicates more than one site in area.

Handicapped Accessibility Codes
❶ Fully Accessible
❷ Usable
❸ Difficult
See page 7 for full description.

Olympic National Forest

Rhododendron, Olympic National Forest

The Olympic National Forest, surrounded on three sides by salt water, is noted for its variety of environments within short distances. Synonymous with the Olympic Peninsula, the forest is a unique blend of marine climate, lush vegetation, wildlife, and mountainous terrain. A walk in the Quinault Rain Forest reveals giant moss-covered trees and emerald foliage covering the forest floor. Ancient Douglas-fir and western redcedar trees stand over 200 feet tall. Sitka spruce, western hemlock and Pacific silver fir are other native tree species common to the Olympic. The majestic Roosevelt elk thrives in this environment, providing the forest with the largest population of its kind anywhere. Spectacular views of valleys and mountains, rivers, lakes, waterfalls, and Puget Sound beaches combine with the rain forest to create an unusual and exciting National Forest experience.

Special places of interest to the visitor include the Hamma Hamma River; a unique marine environment at Seal Rock Campground on Hood Canal; the Dosewallips River; views of the Olympic Peninsula and Puget Sound from Mount Walker Viewpoint; Pioneer's Path nature trail in Klahowya Campground on the Soleduck River; Quinault Lake set in the rain forest, and the ferns, moss, and immense trees of the Quinault Rain Forest Trail; Wynoochee Reservoir; historic Interrorum Guard Station; and the nature trail near the Duckabush River.

Further information about recreation opportunities, campground locations and facilities, as well as current maps of the area, are available at the following offices:

Olympic National Forest
Supervisor's Office
P.O. Box 2288
801 Capitol Way
Olympia, WA 98507
(206) 753-9534

Hood Canal Ranger District
P.O. Box 68
Hoodsport, WA 98548
(206) 877-5254

Quilcene Ranger District
P.O. Box 280
Quilcene, WA 98376
(206) 765-3368

Quinault Ranger District
Quinault, WA 98575
(206) 288-2525

Soleduck Ranger District
R.R. 1,Box 5750
Forks, WA 98331
(206) 374-6522

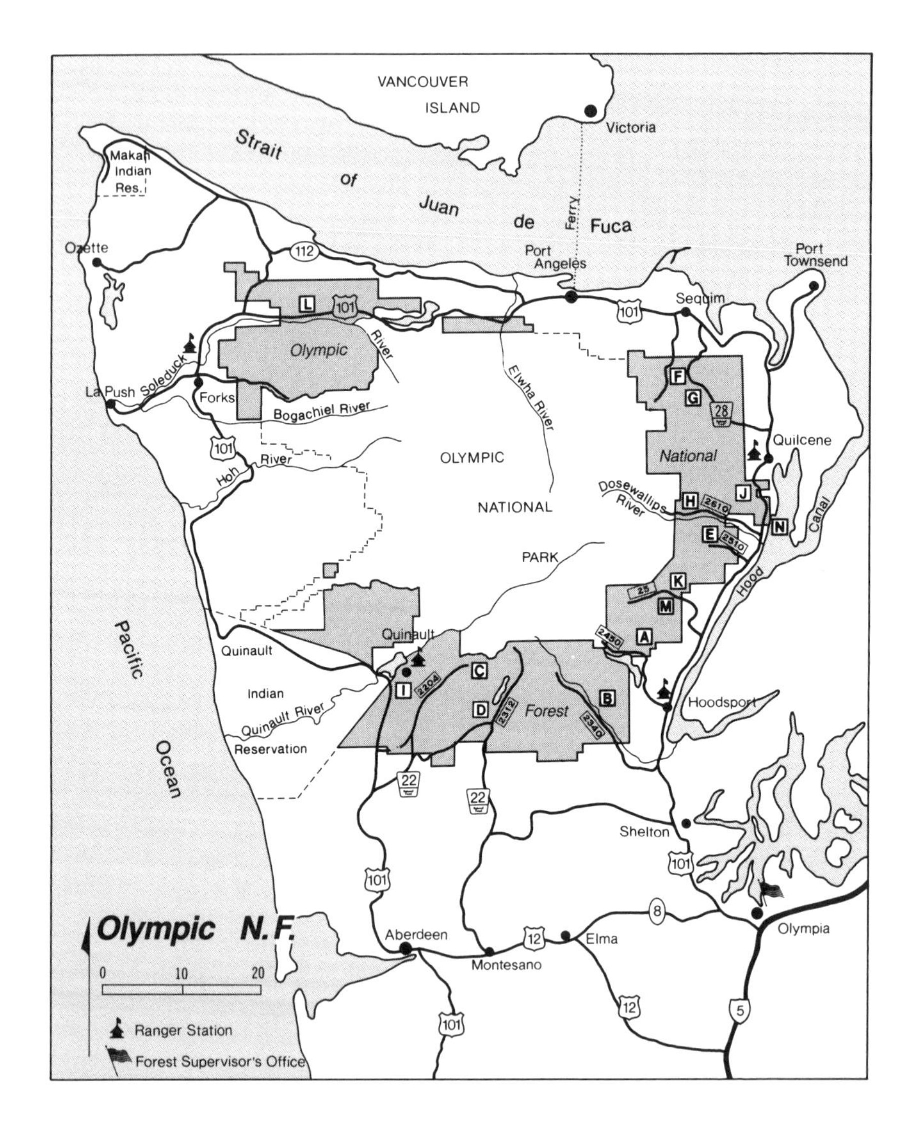
VANCOUVER
ISLAND
Victoria
Strait
of
Juan
de
Ferry
Fuca
Makah
Indian
Res.
Ozette
112
Port
Angeles
Port
Townsend
Sequim
L
101
101
Olympic
River
Elwha River
La Push
Soleduck
Forks
Bogachiel River
F
G
28
Quilcene
National
101
Hoh
River
OLYMPIC
NATIONAL
PARK
Dosewallips
River
H
2610
J
E
2510
N
Canal
Hood
K
25
M
Pacific
Quinault
Quinault
2450
A
C
I
2204
Indian
D
2312
Forest
B
2340
Hoodsport
Quinault River
Reservation
Ocean
22
22
Shelton
101
101
Olympic N.F.
0
10
20
Aberdeen
8
12
Elma
Olympia
Montesano
12
5
101
Ranger Station
Forest Supervisor's Office

OLYMPIC NATIONAL FOREST

Map Location	Elevation	Picnic Units	Tent Units	Tent-Trailer Units	Fee	Drinking Water

Developed Sites

Big Creek

Access: 10 miles NW of Hoodsport via Cty. Rd. 44.
Special Activities & Facilities: Fishing, hunting, trails, mountain climbing, creek.

A	*700*			*23*	*x*	*x*

Brown Creek

Access: 22 miles NW of Shelton via US 101, FRs 23, 2353, 2346.
Special Activities & Facilities: Fishing, hunting, hiking, swimming, berry picking.

B	*600*		*7*	*12*	*x*	*x*

Campbell Tree Grove

Access: 25.5 miles NE of Humptulips via FRs 22, 2204.
Special Activities & Facilities: Fishing, hunting, hiking, river, lightly improved.

C	*1100*		*3*	*8*		*x*

Chetwoot

Access: 39 miles N Montesano via FRs 22, 2294.
Special Activities & Facilities: Hike-in, boat-in, fishing, hiking, swimming, boating, lake.

*D**	*800*		*8*			

Coho

Access: 38 miles N Montesano via FRs 22, 2294.
Special Activities & Facilities: Nature trail, fishing, swimming, boat ramp, group picnic area, lake.

♿ *D**	*900*	*12* ❸	*10*	*46* ❷	*x*	*x*

Collins

Access: 8 miles W Brinnon via US 101S, Cty. Rd. 3, FR 2510.
Special Activities & Facilities: Fishing, hunting, hiking, near river.

E	*200*		*6*	*10*	*x*	*x*

	Map Location	Elevation	Picnic Units	Tent Units	Tent-Trailer Units	Fee	Drinking Water

Dungeness Forks

Access: 11.5 miles S Sequim via US 101E, FRs 28, 2880.
Special Activities & Facilities: Fishing, hunting, hiking, river.

	Map Location	Elevation	Picnic Units	Tent Units	Tent-Trailer Units	Fee	Drinking Water
	F	*1000*		*10*			*x*

East Crossing

Access: 13 miles S Sequim via US 101E, FRs 28, 2860.
Special Activities & Facilities: Fishing, hunting, hiking, river, RVs to 16', barrier-free trail and fishing.

	Map Location	Elevation	Picnic Units	Tent Units	Tent-Trailer Units	Fee	Drinking Water
♿	*G*	*1200*			*10*		*x*

Elkhorn

Access: 11 miles NW Brinnon via US 101N, Cty. Rd. 10, FR 2610.
Special Activities & Facilities: Fishing, hunting, hiking, scenery, river, RVs to 21'.

	Map Location	Elevation	Picnic Units	Tent Units	Tent-Trailer Units	Fee	Drinking Water
	H	*600*		*16*	*4*	*x*	*x*

Falls Creek

Access: .2 miles NE Quinault via S Shore Quinault Lake Rd.
Special Activities & Facilities: Boat ramp, nature trail, hiking, fishing, swimming, RVs to 16', lake.

	Map Location	Elevation	Picnic Units	Tent Units	Tent-Trailer Units	Fee	Drinking Water
♿	*I**	*200*	*4*[1]	*10*	*21*	*x*	*x*

Falls View

Access: 3.5 miles SW of Quilcene via US 101.
Special Activities & Facilities: Hiking, scenery. Short trail to river.

	Map Location	Elevation	Picnic Units	Tent Units	Tent-Trailer Units	Fee	Drinking Water
♿	*J**	*500*	*4*	*16*	*14*[3]	*x*	*x*

Gatton Creek

Access: .5 miles NE Quinault via S Shore Quinault Lake Road.
Special Activities & Facilities: Swimming, hiking, fishing, lake and creek, RV camping in parking area only.

	Map Location	Elevation	Picnic Units	Tent Units	Tent-Trailer Units	Fee	Drinking Water
	*I**	*200*	*3*	*5*	*8*	*x*	

Hamma Hamma

Access: 7 miles NW Eldon via US 101, FR 25.
Special Activities & Facilities: Fishing, hiking, scenery, mountain climbing, river.

	Map Location	Elevation	Picnic Units	Tent Units	Tent-Trailer Units	Fee	Drinking Water
	K	*600*			*15*	*x*	*x*

<table>
<tr><th></th><th>Map Location</th><th>Elevation</th><th>Picnic Units</th><th>Tent Units</th><th>Tent-Trailer Units</th><th>Fee</th><th>Drinking Water</th></tr>
<tr><td colspan="8">Klahowya
Access: 8 miles E of Sappho via US 101.
Special Activities & Facilities: Fishing, hunting, nature trail, boat ramp for winter use, river.</td></tr>
<tr><td>♿</td><td>L</td><td>800</td><td>3</td><td>15</td><td>40❸</td><td>x</td><td>x</td></tr>
<tr><td colspan="8">Lena Creek
Access: 9 miles NW Eldon via US 101, FR 25.
Special Activities & Facilities: Fishing, hunting, hiking, scenery, river.</td></tr>
<tr><td></td><td>M</td><td>700</td><td></td><td></td><td>12</td><td>x</td><td>x</td></tr>
<tr><td colspan="8">Mt. Walker Viewpoint
Access: 10 miles SW Quilcene via US 101S, FR 2730.
Special Activities & Facilities: Scenery (views of Olympics & Puget Sound; rhododendrons in June).</td></tr>
<tr><td></td><td>J*</td><td>2800</td><td></td><td></td><td></td><td></td><td></td></tr>
<tr><td colspan="8">Rainbow
Access: 5 miles S of Quilcene via US 101.
Special Activities and Facilities: Fishing, hiking, hunting, short trail to river.</td></tr>
<tr><td></td><td>J*</td><td>800</td><td></td><td>9</td><td></td><td>x</td><td>x</td></tr>
<tr><td colspan="8">Seal Rock
Access: 2 miles N of Brinnon via US 101.
Special Activities & Facilities: Fishing, beachcombing, boating (no ramp), swimming, Hood Canal.</td></tr>
<tr><td>♿</td><td>N</td><td>100</td><td>9❸</td><td>19</td><td>42❷</td><td>x</td><td>x</td></tr>
<tr><td colspan="8">Willaby
Access: .5 miles SW Quinault via S. Shore Quinault Lake Rd.
Special Activities & Facilities: Hiking, swimming, scenery, boat ramp, nature trail, lake, fishing.</td></tr>
<tr><td></td><td>I*</td><td>200</td><td>5</td><td>7</td><td>15</td><td>x</td><td>x</td></tr>
</table>

*Indicates more than one site in area.

Handicapped Accessibility Codes

❶ Fully Accessible
❷ Usable
❸ Difficult

See page 7 for full description.

Rogue River National Forest

Sky Lakes Wilderness, Rogue River National Forest

Beginning in the northeast corner of the Rogue River National Forest, the Rogue River winds its ageless journey, dramatically carving and forming the river gorge to its own purpose. The forest, which surrounds the Rogue valley, has a rich geological history. To the west are the narrow canyons and steep ridges of the Siskiyou Mountain Range and the headwaters of the Applegate River. Once home to several Indian tribes, the area became "gold country" during the late 1800s, and remnants of mining activities can be seen even today. The forest's elevations peak at 9,495 feet on Mt. McLoughlin, one of the major volcanic cones in the Oregon Cascades. For the hiker, trails abound in the Sky Lakes Wilderness Area, an enchanting region of 200 lakes shared with the Winema National Forest.

Special places of interest to the visitor include the raging narrows of the Rogue River Gorge; Natural Bridge, where the river disappears into a volcanic hole; rustic Union Creek Historic District; the fallen giant at the Mammoth Pines Nature Trail; seven sky-blue lakes clustered together in the Seven Lakes Basin; Applegate Valley and reservoir; the Gin Lin Interpretive Trail, where one can explore gold mining history; Squaw Lakes; Dutchman Peak Lookout; Meridan Overlook; Mount Ashland; J. Herbert Stone Forest Nursery, where visitors are welcome to see the fields of tree seedlings; the old military wagon road over the Cascades; and the historic Klamath Indian berry-gathering area at Huckleberry Mountain.

Further information about recreation opportunities, campground locations and facilities, as well as current maps of the area, are available at the following offices:

Rogue River National Forest
Supervisor's Office
333 West 8th Street
P.O. Box 520
Medford, OR 97501
(503) 776-3600

Applegate Ranger District
6941 Upper Applegate Rd.
Jacksonville, OR 97530
(503) 899-1812

Ashland Ranger District
645 Washington St.
Ashland, OR 97520
(503) 482-3333

Butte Falls Ranger District
Butte Falls, OR 97522
(503) 865-3581

Prospect Ranger District
47201 Hwy. 62
Prospect, OR 97536
(503) 560-3623

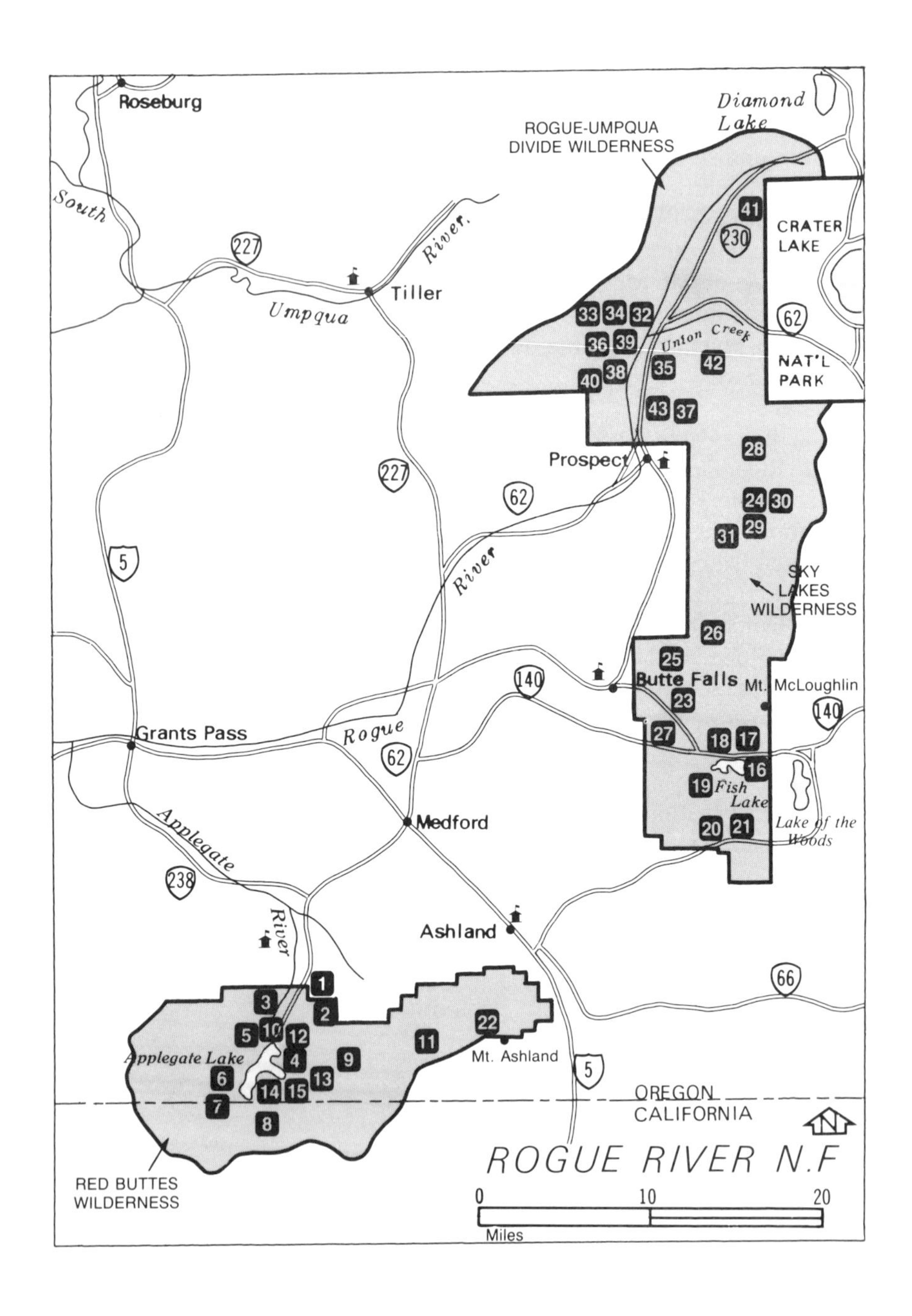

Roseburg
Diamond Lake
ROGUE-UMPQUA DIVIDE WILDERNESS
South
River
227
Tiller
Umpqua
CRATER LAKE
NAT'L PARK
230
62
Union Creek
Prospect
227
62
5
River
SKY LAKES WILDERNESS
140
Butte Falls
Mt. McLoughlin
140
Grants Pass
Rogue
62
Fish Lake
Medford
Lake of the Woods
Applegate
238
River
Ashland
66
Applegate Lake
Mt. Ashland
5
OREGON
CALIFORNIA
N
ROGUE RIVER N.F
RED BUTTES WILDERNESS
0
10
20
Miles

ROGUE RIVER NATIONAL FOREST

Map Location	Elevation	Picnic Units	Tent Units	Tent-Trailer Units	Fee	Drinking Water

Developed Sites

Prospect Ranger District

Farewell Bend

Access: 12 miles N of Prospect on Hwy. 62.
Special Activities & Facilities: Fishing, hiking, near Union Creek Resort.

Map Location	Elevation	Picnic Units	Tent Units	Tent-Trailer Units	Fee	Drinking Water
34	*3400*			*61*	*x*	*x*

Union Creek

Access: 11 miles N of Prospect on Hwy. 62.
Special Activities & Facilities: Fishing, hiking, community kitchen, near Union Creek Resort.

Map Location	Elevation	Picnic Units	Tent Units	Tent-Trailer Units	Fee	Drinking Water
35	*3200*	*7*		*72*	*x*	*x*

Abbott Creek

Access: 10 miles N of Prospect via Hwy. 62, FR 68.
Special Activities & Facilities: Fishing.

Map Location	Elevation	Picnic Units	Tent Units	Tent-Trailer Units	Fee	Drinking Water
36	*3100*	*1*	*11*	*12*	*x*	*x*

Mill Creek

Access: 3 miles NE of Prospect via Hwy. 62, FR 030.
Special Activities & Facilities: Fishing.

Map Location	Elevation	Picnic Units	Tent Units	Tent-Trailer Units	Fee	Drinking Water
37	*2800*		*8*			

River Bridge

Access: 5 miles N of Prospect via Hwy. 62, FR 6210.
Special Activities & Facilities: Fishing, hiking.

Map Location	Elevation	Picnic Units	Tent Units	Tent-Trailer Units	Fee	Drinking Water
38	*2900*		*6*			

Natural Bridge

Access: 10 miles N of Prospect via Hwy. 62, FR 300.
Special Activities & Facilities: Hiking, geologic point of interest, camping.

Map Location	Elevation	Picnic Units	Tent Units	Tent-Trailer Units	Fee	Drinking Water
39	*3200*			*16*		

Woodruff Bridge

Access: 8 miles N of Prospect via Hwy. 62, FR 68.
Special Activities & Facilities: Fishing, hiking.

Map Location	Elevation	Picnic Units	Tent Units	Tent-Trailer Units	Fee	Drinking Water
40	*2900*	*4*				*x*

Map Location	Elevation	Picnic Units	Tent Units	Tent-Trailer Units	Fee	Drinking Water

Hamaker

Access: 23 miles N of Prospect via Hwys. 62, 230, FR 900.
Special Activities & Facilities: Fishing, hiking.

41	*4000*			*10*	*x*	*x*

Huckleberry Mountain

Access: 22 miles NE of Prospect via Hwy. 62, FR 60.
Special Activities & Facilities: Hiking, berry picking.

42	*5400*		*15*	*4*		*x*

Mammoth Pines

Access: 5 miles N of Prospect on Hwy. 62.
Special Activities & Facilities: Interpretive nature trail.

43	*2900*	*3*				

Applegate Ranger District

Wrangle

Access: 29 miles SE of Star RS, Cty. Rd. 10, FR 20, FR 2030.
Special Activities & Facilities: Hiking.

11	*5000*	*5*				

McKee Bridge

Access: 2 miles S of Star RS on Cty. Rd. 10.
Special Activities & Facilities: Swimming, fishing, group site, community kitchen, reservation & fee for groups.

1	*1600*	*40*				*x*

Beaver-Sulpher

Access: 5 miles SE of Star RS via Cty. Rd. 10 and FR 20.
Special Activities & Facilities: Stream.

2	*2100*			*10*	*x*	*x*

Flumet Flat

Access: 3 miles S of Star RS off Cty. Rd. 10.
Special Activities & Facilities: Historic interpretive trail, group reservation.

Map Location	*Elevation*	*Picnic Units*	*Tent Units*	*Tent-Trailer Units*	*Fee*	*Drinking Water*
3	*1700*		*4*	*23*	*x*	*x*

Hart-tish Park

Access: 9 miles S of Star RS on Cty. Rd. 10.
Special Activities & Facilities: Swimming, boating, hiking.

Map Location	*Elevation*	*Picnic Units*	*Tent Units*	*Tent-Trailer Units*	*Fee*	*Drinking Water*
5	*2000*	*24*			*x*	*x*

Carberry

Access: 14 miles S of Star RS on Cty. Rd. 10.
Special Activities & Facilities: Fishing, hiking.

Map Location	*Elevation*	*Picnic Units*	*Tent Units*	*Tent-Trailer Units*	*Fee*	*Drinking Water*
6	*2000*		*10*		*x*	*x*

Watkins

Access: 12 miles S of Star RS on Cty. Rd. 10.
Special Activities & Facilities: Fishing, hiking.

Map Location	*Elevation*	*Picnic Units*	*Tent Units*	*Tent-Trailer Units*	*Fee*	*Drinking Water*
7	*2000*		*14*		*x*	*x*

Seattle Bar

Access: 14 miles S of Star RS on Cty. Rd. 10, FR 1040.
Special Activities & Facilities: Fishing, boating, swimming, horse ramp, hiking.

Map Location	*Elevation*	*Picnic Units*	*Tent Units*	*Tent-Trailer Units*	*Fee*	*Drinking Water*
8	*2000*	*5*				*x*

Squaw Lakes

Access: 17 miles SE of Star RS via Cty. Rd. 10 and FR 1075.
Special Activities & Facilities: Swimming, fishing, hiking, walking.

Map Location	*Elevation*	*Picnic Units*	*Tent Units*	*Tent-Trailer Units*	*Fee*	*Drinking Water*
9	*3000*	*6*	*14*		*x*	*x*

French Gulch

Access: 10 miles S of Star RS via Cty. Rd. 10, FR 1075.
Special Activities & Facilities: Hiking, fishing.

Map Location	*Elevation*	*Picnic Units*	*Tent Units*	*Tent-Trailer Units*	*Fee*	*Drinking Water*
12	*2000*		*9*		*x*	*x*

Map Location	Elevation	Picnic Units	Tent Units	Tent-Trailer Units	Fee	Drinking Water

Stringtown

Access: 12 miles S of Star RS via Cty. Rd. 10, FR 1075.
Special Activities & Facilities: Hiking, fishing.

Map Location	Elevation	Picnic Units	Tent Units	Tent-Trailer Units	Fee	Drinking Water
13	*2000*		*5*		*x*	*x*

Ashland Ranger District

Fish Lake

Access: 32 miles E White City via St. Hwy. 140.
Special Activities& Facilities: Fishing, boating, hiking, community kitchen.

Map Location	Elevation	Picnic Units	Tent Units	Tent-Trailer Units	Fee	Drinking Water
17	*4600*	*9*		*17*	*x*	*x*

Doe Point

Access: 32 miles E of White City via St. Hwy. 140.
Special Activities & Facilities: Fishing, boating, hiking.

Map Location	Elevation	Picnic Units	Tent Units	Tent-Trailer Units	Fee	Drinking Water
18	*4600*	*17*		*25*	*x*	*x*

North Fork

Access: 29 miles NE White City via St. Hwy. 140, FR 37.
Special Activities & Facilities: Fishing, hiking.

Map Location	Elevation	Picnic Units	Tent Units	Tent-Trailer Units	Fee	Drinking Water
19	*4500*		*1*	*6*		*x*

Beaver Dam

Access: 26 miles NE of Ashland via St. Hwy. 140, FR 37.
Special Activities & Facilities: Fishing.

Map Location	Elevation	Picnic Units	Tent Units	Tent-Trailer Units	Fee	Drinking Water
20	*4500*		*1*	*3*		

Daley Creek

Access: 26 miles NE of Ashland via St. Hwy. 62, FR 37.
Special Activities & Facilities: Fishing.

Map Location	Elevation	Picnic Units	Tent Units	Tent-Trailer Units	Fee	Drinking Water
21	*4500*		*5*			

Butte Falls Ranger District

Whiskey Springs

Access: 10 miles SE of Butte Falls via Cty. Rd. 965, FR 30.
Special Activities & Facilities: Nature trail, fishing.

Map Location	Elevation	Picnic Units	Tent Units	Tent-Trailer Units	Fee	Drinking Water
23	*3200*	*4*	*17*	*19*	*x*	*x*

Map Location	*Elevation*	*Picnic Units*	*Tent Units*	*Tent-Trailer Units*	*Fee*	*Drinking Water*

Fourbit Ford

Access: 10 miles E of Butte Falls via Cty. Rd. 965, FRs 30, 3065.
Special Activities & Facilities: Fishing.

25	*3200*		*3*	*4*	*x*	*x*

Snowshoe

Access: 14 miles E of Butte Falls via Cty. Rd. 965, FRs 30, 3065.
Special Activities & Facilities:

26	*4000*		*5*			*x*

Willow Prairie Horse Camp

Access: 30 miles E of White City via St. Hwy. 140, FRs 37, 3735.
Special Activities & Facilities: Horse facilities, trails.

27	*4400*			*10*	*x*	*x*

Imnaha

Access: 11 miles SE Prospect via St. Hwy. 62, Butte Falls-Prospect Hwy.,FR 37.
Special Activities & Facilities: Fishing, hiking.

28	*3800*		*2*	*2*		

South Fork

Access: 20 miles NE Butte Falls, via Butte Falls-Prospect Hwy., FRs 34, 37.
Special Activities & Facilities: Fishing, hiking.

29	*4000*		*1*	*5*		

Parker Meadows

Access: 21 miles NE of Butte Falls via Butte Falls-Prospect Hwy., FRs 34, 37.
Special Activities & Facilities: Hiking, berry picking, RVs to 16'.

31	*5000*		*4*	*5*	*x*	*x*

Big Ben

Access: 17 miles SE of Prospect St. Hwy. 62, FRs 34, 37.
Special Activities & Facilities: Hiking, fishing.

30	*4000*			*2*		

Nichols Creek

Access: 21 miles NE of Butte Falls via Butte Falls-Prospect Hwy., FRs 34, 3775.
Special Activities & Facilities:

24	*4000*	*4*				

Siskiyou National Forest

Mule Creek Canyon, Rogue National Wild and Scenic River, Siskiyou National Forest. Photo by Jim Hughes.

Rare plants, delicate flowers, and a random mixture of sedimentary and volcanic rock that has been pushed, shoved, lifted, and scrambled through the ages, offer the visitor to the Siskiyou National Forest a fascinating study. A botanist's paradise, the forest contains an unusual number of rare plants, including a unique shrub called Kalmiopsis, the rare Port-Orford-cedar, Brewer weeping spruce, and the carnivorous cobra plant which resembles the shape of a cobra ready to strike. Cedar groves contain 175-foot Port-Orford-cedars, as well as 200-foot Douglas-firs. Peridotite, a strange and ancient type of volcanic rock, is found in parts of the forest and is easily identified by its vivid red color. Portions of the rugged Rogue and Illinois rivers are classified as National Wild and Scenic Rivers. One can experience a white-water rafting adventure or take a commercial jetboat ride to view a gentler river segment. The forest contains five wilderness areas: Grassy Knob, Red Buttes, Siskiyou, Kalmiopsis, and the Wild Rogue, which straddles the Wild and Scenic Rogue River.

Special places and activites of interest include rafting on the Rogue and Illinois rivers; hiking and exploring the Rogue River Trail; Brewer weeping spruce in the Baby Foot Lake Botanical Area; the Kalmiopsis Wilderness; the rare plants of the York Creek Botanical Area; Wheeler Creek's stand of giant redwoods topping 200 feet in height; and the Redwood Nature Trail with giant redwoods and Douglas-firs.

Further information about recreation opportunities, campground locations and facilities, as well as current maps of the area, are available at the following offices:

Siskiyou National Forest
Supervisor's Office
200 N.E. Greenfield Rd.
P.O. Box 440
Grants Pass, OR 97526
(503) 479-5301

Chetco Ranger District
555 5th Street
Brookings, OR 97415
(503) 469-2196

Galice Ranger District
1465 NE 7th St.
Grants Pass, OR 97526
(503) 476-3830

Gold Beach Ranger District
1225 South Ellensburg
P.O. Box 7
Gold Beach, OR 97444
(503)247-6651

Illinois Valley Ranger District
26568 Redwood Highway
Cave Junction, OR 97523
(503) 592-2166

Powers Ranger District
Powers, OR 97466
(503) 439-3011

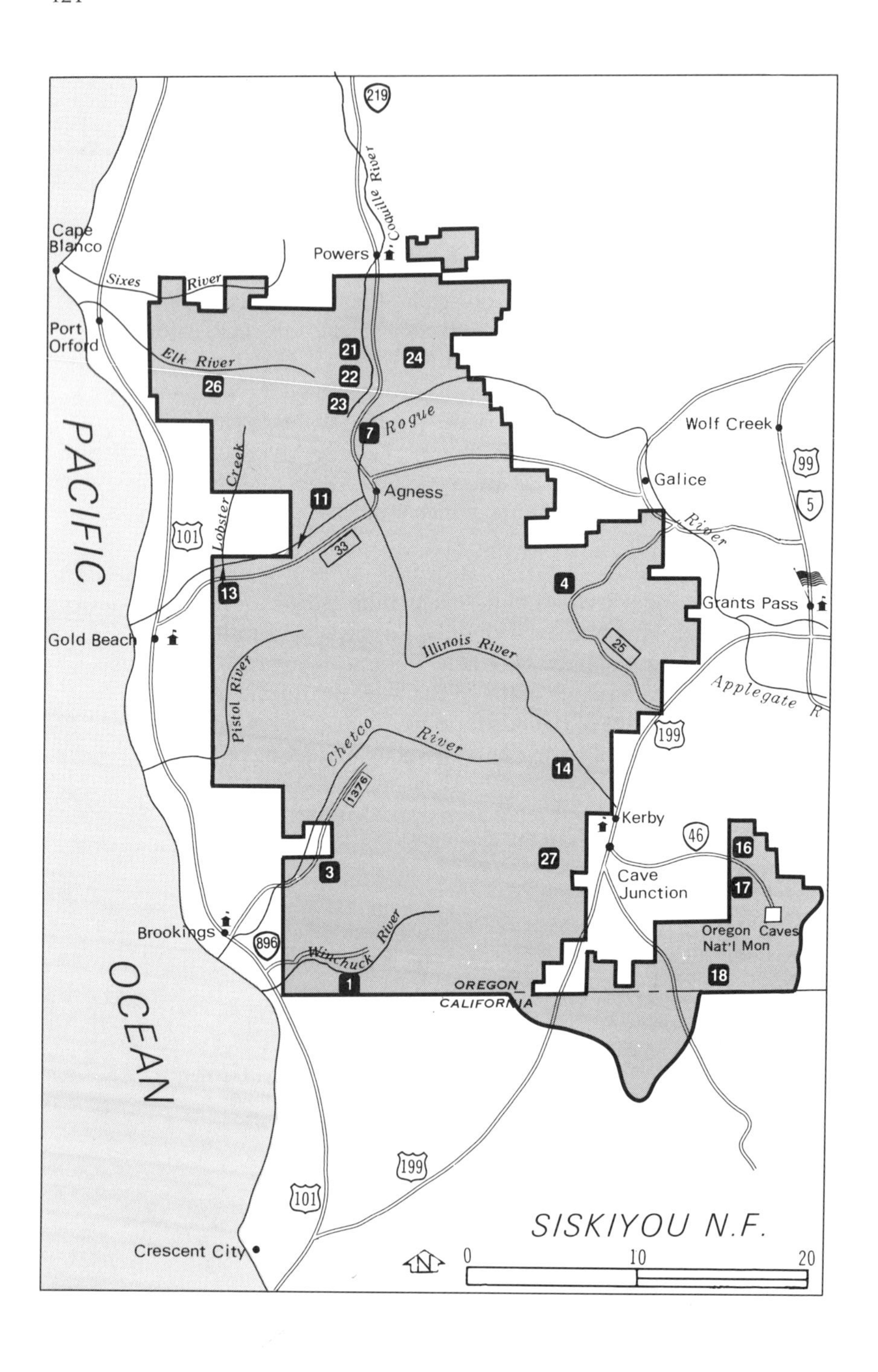

219
Coquille River
Cape Blanco
Powers
Sixes
River
Port Orford
Elk River
21
22
23
24
26
7
Rogue
Wolf Creek
99
Lobster Creek
PACIFIC
Agness
Galice
11
5
River
101
33
4
Grants Pass
13
Gold Beach
25
Illinois River
Pistol River
Applegate R
199
Chetco
River
14
1376
Kerby
46
16
27
3
Cave Junction
17
Brookings
Oregon Caves Nat'l Mon
896
Winchuck River
18
1
OREGON
CALIFORNIA
OCEAN
199
101
SISKIYOU N.F.
Crescent City
N
0
10
20

SISKIYOU NATIONAL FOREST

	Map Location	Elevation	Picnic Units	Tent Units	Tent-Trailer Units	Fee	Drinking Water

Chetco Ranger District

Winchuck

Access: 13 miles SE of Brookings via US 101, Cty. Rd. 896; FR 1107.

Special Activities & Facilities: Swimming, fishing, RVs to 16'.

	Map Location	Elevation	Picnic Units	Tent Units	Tent-Trailer Units	Fee	Drinking Water
	1	100	3 ❸	5	8 ❸	x	x

Little Redwood

Access: 14 miles NE of Brookings, via Cty. Rd. 784, FR 1376.

Special Activities & Facilities: Swimming, fishing, nature trail, RVs to 16'.

	Map Location	Elevation	Picnic Units	Tent Units	Tent-Trailer Units	Fee	Drinking Water
	3	100	3 ❸	5	7 ❸	x	x

Galice Ranger District

Big Pine

Access: 29 miles W of Grants Pass via I-5 to Merlin exit, Cty. Rd. #2-6, FR 25.

Special Activities & Facilities: Playfield, hiking, dump station.

	Map Location	Elevation	Picnic Units	Tent Units	Tent-Trailer Units	Fee	Drinking Water
	4	2300	10 ❷	6	8 ❸	x	x

Sam Brown

Access: 30 miles W of Grants Pass via I-5 to Merlin exit, Cty. Rd. 2-6, FR 25

Special Activities & Facilities: Group camping, hiking, fishing, wildlife viewing.

	Map Location	Elevation	Picnic Units	Tent Units	Tent-Trailer Units	Fee	Drinking Water
	4	2300			6		x

Gold Beach Ranger District

Quosatana

Access: 14 miles NE of Gold Beach via US 101, Cty. Rd. 595, FR 33.

Special Activities & Facilities: Boating, fishing, trailer dump station, Rogue National Wild and Scenic River.

	Map Location	Elevation	Picnic Units	Tent Units	Tent-Trailer Units	Fee	Drinking Water
♿	11	100			44 ❷	x	x

Map Location	*Elevation*	*Picnic Units*	*Tent Units*	*Tent-Trailer Units*	*Fee*	*Drinking Water*

Illahe

Access: 4.9 miles N of Agness via Cty. Rd. 375.
Special Activities & Facilities: Boating, fishing, hiking nearby, Rogue National Wild and Scenic River.

Map Location	*Elevation*	*Picnic Units*	*Tent Units*	*Tent-Trailer Units*	*Fee*	*Drinking Water*
7	*300*	*1*		*20*		*x*

Lobster Creek

Access: 10 miles NE of Gold Beach via US 101, Cty. Rd. 595.
Special Activities & Facilities: Boating, swimming, fishing, boat ramp.

Map Location	*Elevation*	*Picnic Units*	*Tent Units*	*Tent-Trailer Units*	*Fee*	*Drinking Water*
13	*100*	*5*	*3*	*5*		

Illinois Valley Ranger District

Grayback

Access: 12 miles E of Cave Junction via St. Hwy. 46.
Special Activities & Facilities: Swimming, fishing, picnic shelter, barrier-free facilities, RVs to 30', berry picking. Visit Oregon Caves.

Map Location	*Elevation*	*Picnic Units*	*Tent Units*	*Tent-Trailer Units*	*Fee*	*Drinking Water*
16	*1800*	*8* ❷		*35* ❷	*x*	*x*

Cave Creek

Access: 17 miles E of Cave Junction via St. Hwy. 46.
Special Activities & Facilities: Berry picking, fishing. Visit Oregon Caves.

Map Location	*Elevation*	*Picnic Units*	*Tent Units*	*Tent-Trailer Units*	*Fee*	*Drinking Water*
17	*2900*		*18*		*x*	*x*

Bolan Lake

Access: 28.5 miles SE of Cave Junction, via US 199, Cty. Rds. 5560, 5828, FRs 48, 4812.
Special Activities & Facilities: Swimming, fishing, hiking, fire lookout.

Map Location	*Elevation*	*Picnic Units*	*Tent Units*	*Tent-Trailer Units*	*Fee*	*Drinking Water*
18	*5400*		*12*			

Map Location	Elevation	Picnic Units	Tent Units	Tent-Trailer Units	Fee	Drinking Water

Powers Ranger District

Myrtle Grove

Access: 9 miles SE of Powers, Cty. Rd. 219, FR 33.
Special Activities & Facilities: Fishing, swimming.

Map Location	Elevation	Picnic Units	Tent Units	Tent-Trailer Units	Fee	Drinking Water
21	600	1	4			

Daphne Grove

Access: 15 miles S of Powers, Cty. Rd. 219, FR 33.
Special Activities & Facilities: Fishing, swimming, hiking trails, RVs to 16'.

Map Location	Elevation	Picnic Units	Tent Units	Tent-Trailer Units	Fee	Drinking Water
22	800		13	4	x	x

Rock Creek

Access: 18 miles S of Powers, via Cty. Rd. 219, FRs 33, 3347.
Special Activities & Facilities: Fishing, hiking trails, swimming.

Map Location	Elevation	Picnic Units	Tent Units	Tent-Trailer Units	Fee	Drinking Water
23	1200		4	3		

Squaw Lake

Access: 22.4 miles SE of Powers via Cty. Rd. 219, FRs 33, 3348, 3348.080.
Special Activities & Facilities: Fishing, hiking trails.

Map Location	Elevation	Picnic Units	Tent Units	Tent-Trailer Units	Fee	Drinking Water
24	2200		3	5		

Butler Bar

Access: 22 miles E of Port Orford via Cty. Rd. 208, FR 5325.
Special Activities & Facilities: Swimming, fishing.

Map Location	Elevation	Picnic Units	Tent Units	Tent-Trailer Units	Fee	Drinking Water
26	600	2	3	5		

Handicapped Accessibility Codes
❶ Fully Accessible
❷ Usable
❸ Difficult
See page 7 for full description.

Siuslaw National Forest

Oregon Dunes National Recreation Area, Siuslaw National Forest

This is one of the two forests in the continental United States bordering the Pacific Ocean. Thick Douglas-fir forests contrast sharply with miles of open sand dunes, beaches, and freshwater lakes. Coastal weather is characterized by continually changing moods; a winter day may bring a violent rain storm, yet the following day may be clear, calm, and sunny. Summer fog is common and temperatures remain mild year-round. The Cape Perpetua Scenic Area and the Oregon Dunes National Recreation Area are the main scenic attractions on the coast; while the inland area of the forest, including three wilderness areas, offers additional scenic and recreational opportunities.

Special places and activities of interest include the Oregon Dunes overlook; whale watching; riding dune buggies; the highest of the sand dunes at Umpqua Dunes; the Horsfall area; Three Mile Lake Trail; Cape Perpetua Visitor Center; tidepools at Cape Perpetua; geyser-like Spouting Horn; crashing waves in the Devils Churn; Cape Cove Beach; Heceta Head Lighthouse; rugged Cascade Head Scenic Area; Holman vista; the archeological site at Tahkenitch Lake; Mary's Peak hiking trails and views; Mt. Hebo Meadows and trails; and beautiful Kentucky Falls.

Further information about recreation opportunities, campground locations and facilities, as well as current maps of the area, are available at the following offices:

Siuslaw National Forest
Supervisor's Office
4077 Research Way
P.O. Box 1148
Corvallis, Or 97339
(503) 750-7000

Alsea Ranger District
18591 Alsea Highway
Alsea, OR 97324
(503) 487-5811

Hebo Ranger District
Hebo, OR 97122
(503) 392-3161

Waldport Ranger District
Waldport, OR 97394
(503) 563-3211

Cape Perpetua Visitor Center
P.O. Box 274
Yachats, OR 97498
(503) 547-3289

Oregon Dunes National
Recreation Area
855 Highway Ave.
Reedsport, OR 97467
(503) 271-3611

Mapleton Ranger District
Mapleton, OR 97453
(503) 268-4473

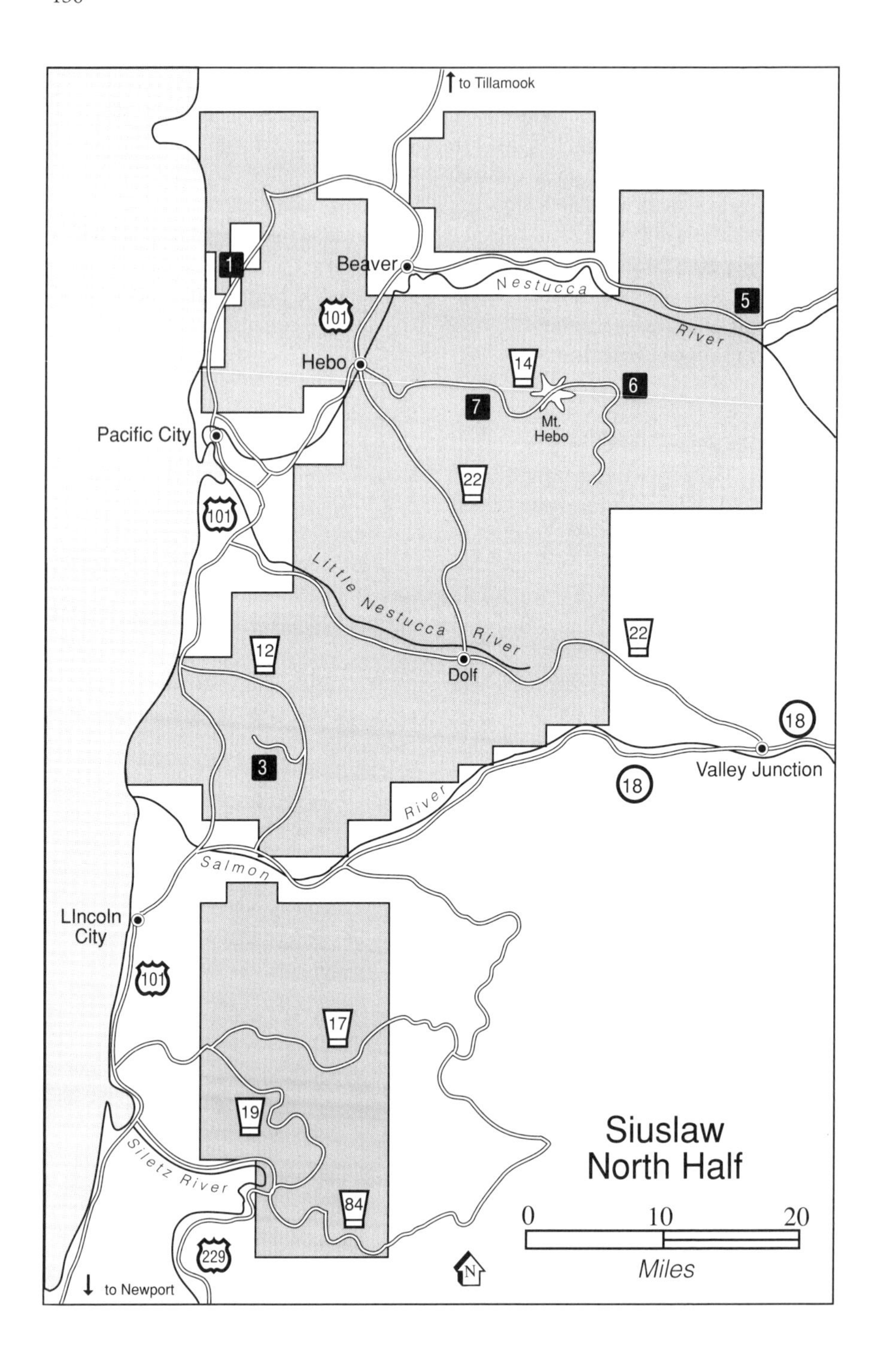

to Tillamook
Beaver
Nestucca
River
5
101
14
Hebo
6
7
Mt.
Hebo
Pacific City
22
101
Little Nestucca River
22
12
Dolf
18
Valley Junction
18
3
River
Salmon
Lincoln
City
101
17
19
Siletz River
84
229
to Newport
N
Siuslaw
North Half
0
10
20
Miles

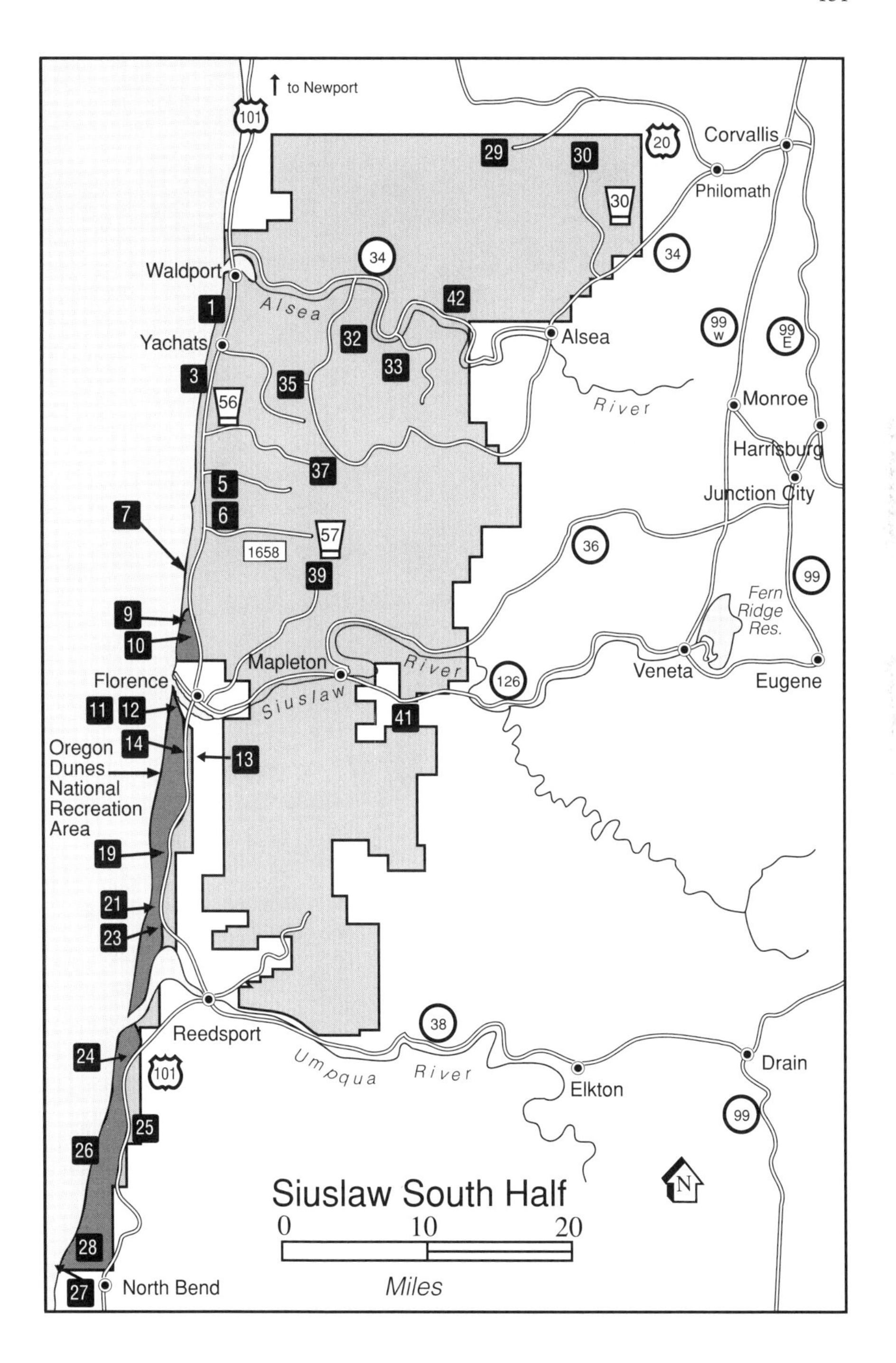

to Newport
101
20
Corvallis
29
30
30
Philomath
34
34
Waldport
1
Alsea
42
Alsea
Yachats
32
99 W
99 E
33
3
35
56
River
Monroe
Harrisburg
37
5
Junction City
7
6
36
57
1658
39
99
Fern Ridge Res.
9
10
Veneta
Eugene
Mapleton
River
Florence
126
Siuslaw
11
12
41
Oregon Dunes National Recreation Area
14
13
19
21
23
Reedsport
38
24
101
Umpqua
River
Elkton
Drain
99
25
26
28
27
North Bend
Siuslaw South Half
0
10
20
Miles

Map Location	Elevation	Picnic Units	Tent Units	Tent-Trailer Units	Fee	Drinking Water

South Half Recreation Sites

Tillcum Beach

Access: 4.7 miles S of Waldport via US 101.

Special Activities & Facilities: Adjacent to shore of Pacific Ocean.

Map Location	Elevation	Picnic Units	Tent Units	Tent-Trailer Units	Fee	Drinking Water
1	100			60	x	x

Cape Perpetua

Access: 2.7 miles S of Yachats via US 101.

Special Activities & Facilities: Visitor center, Cape Perpetua Scenic Area, auto tour, trails, Pacific Ocean, group camping.

Map Location	Elevation	Picnic Units	Tent Units	Tent-Trailer Units	Fee	Drinking Water
♿ 3	100			38❸	x	x

Ocean Beach

Access: 9 miles S of Yachats via US 101.

Special Activities & Facilities: Ocean beach access.

Map Location	Elevation	Picnic Units	Tent Units	Tent-Trailer Units	Fee	Drinking Water
5	100	4				

Rock Creek

Access: 10 miles S of Yachats via US 101.

Special Activities & Facilities: Ocean 1/4 mile west.

Map Location	Elevation	Picnic Units	Tent Units	Tent-Trailer Units	Fee	Drinking Water
5	100			16	x	x

Lanham Bike & Hike

Access: 10 miles S of Yachats via US 101.

Special Activities & Facilities: Developed for hikers and bicyclists only.

Map Location	Elevation	Picnic Units	Tent Units	Tent-Trailer Units	Fee	Drinking Water
6	100		8			

Alder Dune

Access: 10 miles N of Florence via US 101.

Special Activities & Facilities: Campsites on lake shore, fishing, trails.

Map Location	Elevation	Picnic Units	Tent Units	Tent-Trailer Units	Fee	Drinking Water
7	100	4		39	x	x

<table>
<tr><th></th><th>Map Location</th><th>Elevation</th><th>Picnic Units</th><th>Tent Units</th><th>Tent-Trailer Units</th><th>Fee</th><th>Drinking Water</th></tr>
<tr><td colspan="8">Sutton</td></tr>
<tr><td></td><td colspan="7">Access: 7 miles N of Florence via US 101 on Sutton Beach Road.
Special Activities & Facilities: Boat launching available at Sutton Lake, group picnic site w/shelter, reservations for group camping, loop trail to sand dunes and stream.</td></tr>
<tr><td></td><td>9</td><td>100</td><td>4</td><td></td><td>79</td><td>x</td><td>x</td></tr>
<tr><td colspan="8">Holman Vista</td></tr>
<tr><td></td><td colspan="7">Access: 7 miles N of Florence via US 101 on Sutton Beach Road.
Special Activities & Facilities: Group picnic shelter, 150' barrier-free trail to ocean vista, loop trails to sand dunes and stream.</td></tr>
<tr><td></td><td>10</td><td>100</td><td>2</td><td></td><td></td><td></td><td>x</td></tr>
<tr><td colspan="8">South Jetty</td></tr>
<tr><td></td><td colspan="7">Access: 1 mile S of Florence via US 101 on S. Jetty Road.
Special Activities & Facilities: Series of 10 parking lots, hiking, day use only, ORV access to sand dunes, crabbing/fishing pier, ocean beach access.</td></tr>
<tr><td></td><td>11</td><td>100</td><td></td><td></td><td></td><td></td><td></td></tr>
<tr><td colspan="8">Tyee</td></tr>
<tr><td></td><td colspan="7">Access: 6 miles S of Florence via US 101.
Special Activities & Facilities: Boat ramp to Siltcoos River, fishing.</td></tr>
<tr><td></td><td>13</td><td>100</td><td></td><td></td><td>15</td><td>x</td><td>x</td></tr>
<tr><td colspan="8">Lagoon (Siltcoos)</td></tr>
<tr><td></td><td colspan="7">Access: 7 miles S of Florence via US 101 on Siltcoos Dune & Beach Access Road.
Special Activities & Facilities: Ocean beach access, boardwalk trail, ORV access to sand dunes.</td></tr>
<tr><td></td><td>14*</td><td>100</td><td></td><td></td><td>40</td><td>x</td><td>x</td></tr>
<tr><td colspan="8">Waxmyrtle (Siltcoos)</td></tr>
<tr><td></td><td colspan="7">Access: 7 miles S of Florence via US 101 on Siltcoos Dune and Beach Access Road.
Special Activities & Facilities: Ocean beach access, trails, ORV access to sand dunes.</td></tr>
<tr><td></td><td>14*</td><td>100</td><td></td><td></td><td>56</td><td>x</td><td>x</td></tr>
</table>

Lodgepole (Siltcoos)

Access: 7 miles S of Florence via US 101 on Siltcoos Dune and Access Road.
Special Activities & Facilities: Located along Siltcoos River, fishing, ORV access to sand dunes.

Map Location	*Elevation*	*Picnic Units*	*Tent Units*	*Tent-Trailer Units*	*Fee*	*Drinking Water*
*14**	*100*			*3*	*x*	*x*

Driftwood II (Siltcoos)

Access: 7 miles S of Florence via US 101 on Siltcoos Dune and Access Road.
Special Activities & Facilities: Ocean beach access, ORV access to sand dunes. Large asphalt parking lot with individual campsites.

Map Location	*Elevation*	*Picnic Units*	*Tent Units*	*Tent-Trailer Units*	*Fee*	*Drinking Water*
*14**	*100*			*70*	*x*	*x*

Siltcoos Beach Parking (Siltcoos)

Access: 7 miles SW of Florence via US 101 on Siltcoos Dune and Access Road.
Special Activities & Facilities: Ocean beach access, day use only.

Map Location	*Elevation*	*Picnic Units*	*Tent Units*	*Tent-Trailer Units*	*Fee*	*Drinking Water*
*14**	*100*	*3*				

Carter Lake

Access: 8.5 miles S of Florence via US 101.
Special Activities & Facilities: Lakeshore camping, hiking trail to sand dunes, fishing.

Map Location	*Elevation*	*Picnic Units*	*Tent Units*	*Tent-Trailer Units*	*Fee*	*Drinking Water*
*19 **	*100*			*24*	*x*	*x*

Carter Lake Boat Ramp

Access: 8.6 miles S of Florence via US 101.
Special Activities & Facilities: Boat launching, fishing, day use only.

Map Location	*Elevation*	*Picnic Units*	*Tent Units*	*Tent-Trailer Units*	*Fee*	*Drinking Water*
*19**	*100*					

Oregon Dunes Overlook

Access: 9 miles S of Florence via US 101.
Special Activities & Facilities: Hiking/viewing, access to sand dunes/ocean, day use only, barrier-free facility.

Map Location	*Elevation*	*Picnic Units*	*Tent Units*	*Tent-Trailer Units*	*Fee*	*Drinking Water*
21	*100*	*4*				*x*

Map Location	Elevation	Picnic Units	Tent Units	Tent-Trailer Units	Fee	Drinking Water

Tahkenitch

Access: 7 miles N of Reedsport via US 101.
Special Activities & Facilities: Hiking trail to sand dunes, ocean and lake.

*23**	*100*			*35*	*x*	*x*

Tahkenitch Landing

Access: 7.5 miles N of Reedsport via US 101.
Special Activities & Facilities: Boat launching, fishing.

*23**	*100*			*26*	*x*	*x*

Umpqua Dunes

Access: 2 miles S of Winchester Bay on Cty. Rd. 251.
Special Activities & Facilities: Ocean beach access, ORV access to sand dunes, day use only.

24	*100*					

North Eel Creek

Access: 12 miles S of Reedsport via US 101.
Special Activities & Facilities: Hiking trail to sand dunes.

25	*100*			*52*	*x*	*x*

Mid-Eel

Access: 12 miles S of Reedsport via US 101.
Special Activities & Facilities: Adjacent to Eel Creek/scenic dunes, open intermittently.

25	*100*			*27*	*x*	*x*

Spinreel

Access: 8 miles N of North Bend via US 101.
Special Activities & Facilities: ORV access to sand dunes, trail, fishing.

26	*100*			*37*	*x*	*x*

Bluebill Lake

Access: 4 miles N of N Bend via US 101 on Horsfall Dune and Beach Access Rd.
Special Activities & Facilities: Ocean beach access, trail, ORV access to sand dunes.

28	*100*			*19*	*x*	*x*

Map Location	Elevation	Picnic Units	Tent Units	Tent-Trailer Units	Fee	Drinking Water

Horsfall Beach

Access: 4 miles N of N Bend via US 101 on Horsfall Dune and Beach Access Rd.

Special Activities & Facilities: Ocean beach access: ORV access to sand dunes, day use and camping on paved parking area.

*28 **	*100*			*34*	*x*	*x*

Horsfall

Access: 4 miles N of N Bend via US 101 on Horsfall Dune and Beach Access Road.

Special Activities & Facilities: ORV access to sand dunes. Large asphalt parking lot with individual campsites, barrier-free restrooms and showers.

*28 **	*100*			*70*	*x*	*x*

Wild Mare Horse Camp

Access: 4 miles N of N Bend via US 101 on Horsfall Dune and Beach Access Rd.

Special Activities & Facilities: Horse corrals provided, no ORVs.

*28**	*100*			*12*	*x*	*x*

Inland/Developed Sites

Big Elk

Access: 9 miles SW of Burnt Woods on Cty. Rd. 547.

Special Activities & Facilities: Fishing.

29	*200*			*10*	*x*	*x*

Marys Peak

Access: 20 miles SW of Philomath via St. Hwy. 34, Marys Peak Rd.

Special Activities & Facilities: Marys Peak scenic viewpoint, hiking.

30	*3600*	*5*			*x*	*x*

Blackberry

Access: 18 miles E of Waldport via St. Hwy. 34.

Special Activities & Facilities: On Alsea River, boat launching, fishing.

32	*100*	*3*		*31*	*x*	*x*

Map Location	Elevation	Picnic Units	Tent Units	Tent-Trailer Units	Fee	Drinking Water

Launching

Access: 19 miles E of Waldport via St. Hwy. 34.
Special Activities & Facilities: On Alsea River, boat launching, fishing. Mike Baur boat launching site is 2 miles west.

Map Location	Elevation	Picnic Units	Tent Units	Tent-Trailer Units	Fee	Drinking Water
33	100	6				

Canal Creek

Access: 11 miles SE of Waldport via St. Hwy. 34, FR 3462.
Special Activities & Facilities: Picnic shelter and playfield, trailers discouraged.

Map Location	Elevation	Picnic Units	Tent Units	Tent-Trailer Units	Fee	Drinking Water
35	200	3	12			x

Tenmile Creek

Access: 13 miles SE of Yachats via US 101, FR 56.
Special Activities & Facilities: Road 56 is narrow and winding, RVs to 16'.

Map Location	Elevation	Picnic Units	Tent Units	Tent-Trailer Units	Fee	Drinking Water
37	400			6		

North Fork Siuslaw

Access: 14 miles NE of Florence on N Fork Rd. via St. Hwy. 126, Cty. Rds. 5070, 5084.
Special Activities & Facilities: Located on N Fork Siuslaw River, fishing, hunting, group use.

Map Location	Elevation	Picnic Units	Tent Units	Tent-Trailer Units	Fee	Drinking Water
39	400		5			

Archie Knowles

Access: 3 miles E of Mapleton via St. Hwy. 126.
Special Activities & Facilities: Located on Knowles Ck, picnic area.

Map Location	Elevation	Picnic Units	Tent Units	Tent-Trailer Units	Fee	Drinking Water
41	200	1		9	x	x

Riveredge Group Camp

Access: 11 miles W of Alsea via St. Hwy. 34.
Special Activities & Facilities: Picnic shelters, fishing, boating access, barrier-free, field sports, group camp for up to 200 people, reservations required.

Map Location	Elevation	Picnic Units	Tent Units	Tent-Trailer Units	Fee	Drinking Water
 42	100	10 ❸			x	x

Map Location	Elevation	Picnic Units	Tent Units	Tent-Trailer Units	Fee	Drinking Water

North Half Recreation Sites

Sand Beach

Access: 10 miles N of Pacific City via Cty. Rds. 871, 872.
Special Activities & Facilities: ORV play area, sand dunes, beachcombing, area entry reservation required on summer holiday weekends, dump station.

Map Location	Elevation	Picnic Units	Tent Units	Tent-Trailer Units	Fee	Drinking Water
1*	50	5		101 ❷	x	x

Sand Beach East Parking

Access: 10 miles N of Pacific City.
Special Activities & Facilities: Fee is per vehicle. Area entry reservations required on summer holiday weekends, ORV, play area.

Map Location	Elevation	Picnic Units	Tent Units	Tent-Trailer Units	Fee	Drinking Water
1*	50			100 ❷	x	x

Sand Beach West Parking

Access: 10 miles N of Pacific City.
Special Activities & Facilities: Fee is per vehicle. Area entry reservations required on summer holiday weekends, ORV, play area.

Map Location	Elevation	Picnic Units	Tent Units	Tent-Trailer Units	Fee	Drinking Water
1*	50			75 ❷	x	x

Neskowin Creek

Access: 6 miles SE of Neskowin via US 101, Slab Cr. Rd., FR 12.
Special Activities & Facilities: Within Cascade Head Experimental Forest.

Map Location	Elevation	Picnic Units	Tent Units	Tent-Trailer Units	Fee	Drinking Water
3	200			12		

Castle Rock

Access: 5 miles SE of Hebo via St. Hwy. 22.
Special Activities & Facilities: Fishing.

Map Location	Elevation	Picnic Units	Tent Units	Tent-Trailer Units	Fee	Drinking Water
4	200		4			

Rocky Bend

Access: 13 miles SE of Beaver via Cty. Rd. 858, FR 85.
Special Activities & Facilities: On Nestucca River, fishing.

Map Location	Elevation	Picnic Units	Tent Units	Tent-Trailer Units	Fee	Drinking Water
5	600		7			

Map Location	Elevation	Picnic Units	Tent Units	Tent-Trailer Units	Fee	Drinking Water

Mt. Hebo

Access: 10 miles E of Hebo via St. Hwy. 22, FR 14.
Special Activities & Facilities: Approximately 2 miles E of Mt. Hebo viewpoint, hiking.

6	3000		4			

Hebo Lake

Access: 5 miles E of Hebo via St. Hwy. 22, FR 14.
Special Activities & Facilities: Picnic shelter, small lake, fishing, hiking.

7	1600		10		x	x

* indicates that several sites are in the area

Handicapped Accessibility Codes
❶ Fully Accessible
❷ Usable
❸ Difficult
See page 7 for full description.

Cape Perpetua and Visitor Center, Siuslaw National Forest

Umatilla National Forest

Kelly Prairie, Umatilla National Forest

The forest takes its name from the Indian word meaning "water rippling over sand"; and early-day Indians once peered through the trees as Lewis and Clark passed this way on their journey to the Pacific Ocean. The Wenaha River carves its way through the Wenaha-Tucannon Wilderness, forming a deep canyon with vertical cliffs topped with plateaus. Ghost towns and old mines tell the story of a once flourishing industry where the cry of "gold!" echoed through the Greenhorn Mountains as prospectors found over $10 million in gold and silver. Three wildernesses, abundant wildlife and dense timber stands add to the remote experience of this scenic forest.

Special places of interest include vistas into the Wenaha-Tucannon from Sunset Point, Table Rock and Big Hole viewpoints; the high alpine country of Vinegar Hill-Indian Rock Scenic Area; white-water rafting through the Grande Ronde scenic area; Fremont Powerhouse Historic District; the coolness of Olive and Jubilee lakes on a hot summer day; Bull Prairie Lake campground; lava outflows in 2,000 vertical feet of rimrock at Potamus Point; fishing and kayaking in the North Fork John Day River; Target Meadows Historic Site; the rugged Umatilla River Canyon seen from the Umatilla Breaks viewpoint; the Marcus Whitman Trail trail markers; snowmobiling in the Tollgate, Summit, Shaw Creek, Touchet, and Mountain Road snowmobile areas; and Spout Springs and Bluewood for downhill and cross-country skiing.

Further information about recreation opportunities, campground locations and facilities, as well as current maps of the area, are available at the following offices:

Umatilla National Forest
Supervisor's Office
2517 S.W. Hailey Ave.
Pendleton, OR 97801
(503) 276-3811

Heppner Ranger District
P.O. Box 7
Heppner, OR 97836
(503) 676-9187

North Fork John Day Ranger District
P.O. Box 158
Ukiah, OR 97880
(503) 427-3231

Pomeroy Ranger District
Rt. 1, Box 53-F
Pomeroy, WA 99347
(509) 843-1891

Walla Walla Ranger District
1415 West Rose
Walla Walla, WA 99362
(509) 522-6290

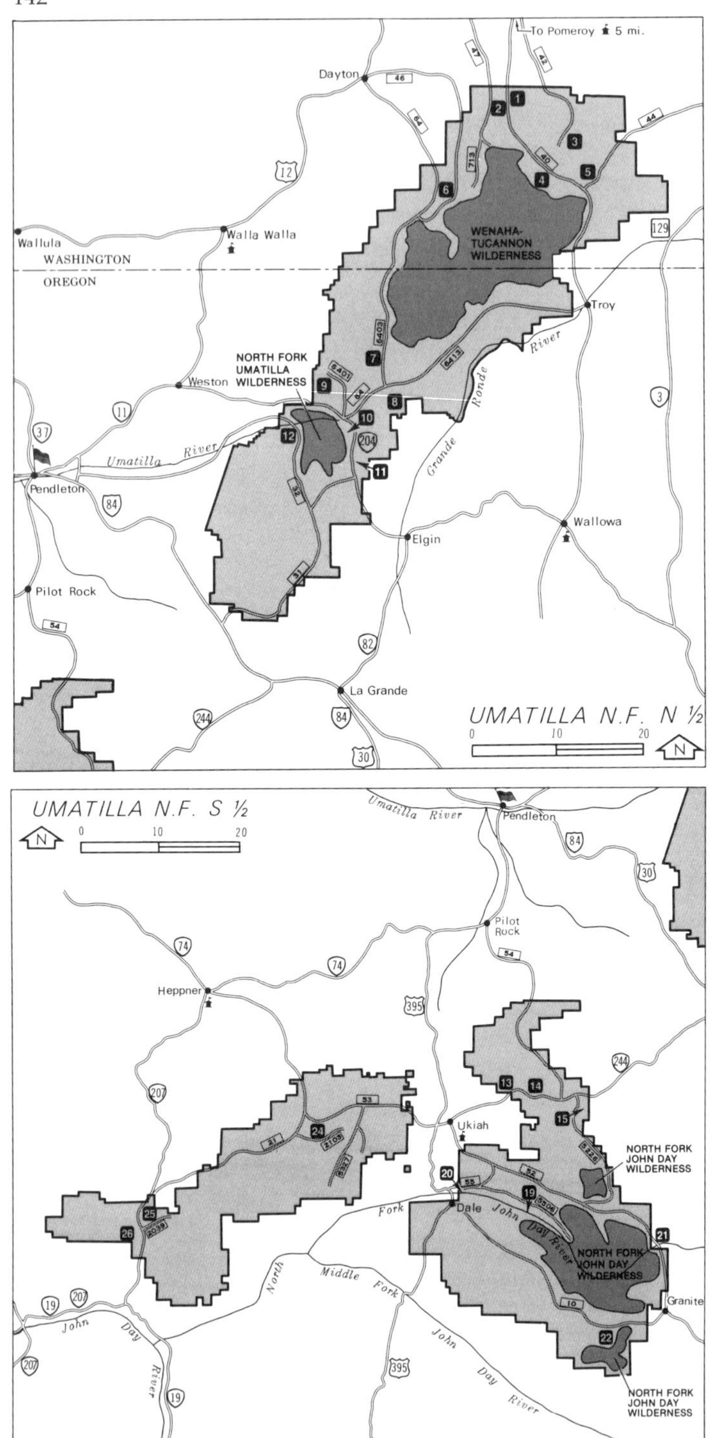
To Pomeroy 5 mi.
Dayton
Wallula
Walla Walla
WASHINGTON
OREGON
WENAHA-TUCANNON WILDERNESS
Troy
River
Ronde
Grande
NORTH FORK UMATILLA WILDERNESS
Weston
Umatilla River
Pendleton
Elgin
Wallowa
Pilot Rock
La Grande
UMATILLA N.F. N ½
0 10 20
N
UMATILLA N.F. S ½
0 10 20
N
Umatilla River
Pendleton
Pilot Rock
Heppner
Ukiah
NORTH FORK JOHN DAY WILDERNESS
Dale
North Fork John Day River
Middle Fork
John Day River
Granite
NORTH FORK JOHN DAY WILDERNESS
NORTH FORK JOHN DAY WILDERNESS

UMATILLA NATIONAL FOREST

Map Location	Elevation	Picnic Units	Tent Units	Tent-Trailer Units	Fee	Drinking Water

Heppner Ranger District

Bull Prairie Lake

Access: 36 miles S of Heppner via St. Hwy. 207, FR 2039.
Special Activities & Facilities: Hunting, fishing, nonmotorized boating, barrier-free facilities.

Map Location	Elevation	Picnic Units	Tent Units	Tent-Trailer Units	Fee	Drinking Water
25	4900	40		26	x	x

Fairview

Access: 34 miles S of Heppner on St. Hwy. 207.
Special Activities & Facilities: Hunting, RVs to 16'.

Map Location	Elevation	Picnic Units	Tent Units	Tent-Trailer Units	Fee	Drinking Water
26	4300	2		3		x

Penland Lake

Access: 26 miles SE of Heppner via FRs 53, 21, 2103.
Special Activities & Facilities: Hunting, fishing, nonmotorized boating.

Map Location	Elevation	Picnic Units	Tent Units	Tent-Trailer Units	Fee	Drinking Water
24	4950	10				

Pomeroy Ranger District

Alder Thicket

Access: 20 miles S of Pomeroy via St. Hwy. 128, Cty. Rd. 107, FR 40.
Special Activities & Facilities: Hunting, RVs to 16'.

Map Location	Elevation	Picnic Units	Tent Units	Tent-Trailer Units	Fee	Drinking Water
1	5100		2	4		

Big Springs

Access: 23 miles S of Pomeroy via St. Hwy. 128, Iron Spring Rd., FR 42.
Special Activities & Facilities: Hunting.

Map Location	Elevation	Picnic Units	Tent Units	Tent-Trailer Units	Fee	Drinking Water
3	5000	5	6			

Godman

Access: 25 miles SE of Dayton via Cty. Rds. 1240, 14240, FR 46.
Special Activities & Facilities: Hunting, trailhead, horse facilities, RVs to 16'.

Map Location	Elevation	Picnic Units	Tent Units	Tent-Trailer Units	Fee	Drinking Water
6	6050	1	3	4		

Map Location	Elevation	Picnic Units	Tent Units	Tent-Trailer Units	Fee	Drinking Water

Teal Spring

Access: 26 miles S of Pomeroy via St. Hwy. 128, Cty. Rd. 107, FR 40.
Special Activities & Facilities: Hunting, view.

4	5600	5	5	3		

Tucannon

Access: 25 miles S of Pomeroy via US 12, Tucannon Rd., FR 47.
Special Activities & Facilities: Hunting, fishing, hiking, RVs to 16'.

2	2600	6	10	5		

Wickiup

Access: 34 miles S of Pomeroy via St. Hwy. 128, Cty. Rd. 128, FRs 40 and 44.
Special Activities & Facilities: Hunting, view, RVs to 16'.

5	5800	6	1	5		

North Fork John Day Ranger District

Bear Wallow Creek

Access: 10 miles E of Ukiah on St. Hwy. 244.
Special Activities & Facilities: Hunting, hot springs, interpretive trail.

14	3900		2	5		

Frazier

Access: 19 miles E of Ukiah via St. Hwy. 244, FR 5226.
Special Activities & Facilities: Hunting, trail biking,hot springs.

15	4300	3	5	27		

Lane Creek

Access: 9 miles E of Ukiah on St. Hwy. 244.
Special Activities & Facilities: Hunting, hot springs.

13	3850		2	5		

North Fork

Access: 38 miles SE of Ukiah on FR 52.
Special Activities & Facilities: Hunting, fishing, wilderness access, trailhead facility.

21	5200		2	7		

Bull Prairie Lake Campground, Umatilla National Forest

Map Location	Elevation	Picnic Units	Tent Units	Tent-Trailer Units	Fee	Drinking Water

Olive Lake

Access: 26 miles SE of Dale on FR 10.
Special Activities & Facilities: Fishing, boating, hiking.

Map Location	Elevation	Picnic Units	Tent Units	Tent-Trailer Units	Fee	Drinking Water
22	6000	5	8	4		

Oriental Creek

Access: 12 miles E of Dale via FRs 55, 5506.
Special Activities & Facilities: Hunting, fishing, wilderness access, Wild and Scenic river.

Map Location	Elevation	Picnic Units	Tent Units	Tent-Trailer Units	Fee	Drinking Water
19	3500		5			

Tollbridge

Access: 1/2 miles NE of Dale on FR 55.
Special Activities & Facilities: Hunting, fishing, floating (April-June), Wild and Scenic river.

Map Location	Elevation	Picnic Units	Tent Units	Tent-Trailer Units	Fee	Drinking Water
20	3800			7	x	x

Walla Walla Ranger District

Jubilee Lake

Access: 12 miles NE of Tollgate on FR 64 (Tollgate is on St. Hwy. 204, E of Weston).
Special Activities & Facilities: Hunting, fishing, nonmotorized boating, swimming, hiking, barrier-free fishing and trails.

Map Location	Elevation	Picnic Units	Tent Units	Tent-Trailer Units	Fee	Drinking Water
♿ 8	4800	39 ❷	4	47❷	x	x

Mottet

Access: 14 miles NE of Tollgate via FRs 64, 6411, 6403 (Tollgate is on St. Hwy. 204, E of Weston).
Special Activities & Facilities: Hunting, hiking, trail biking.

Map Location	Elevation	Picnic Units	Tent Units	Tent-Trailer Units	Fee	Drinking Water
7	5200	3		7		x

Target Meadows

Access: 2 miles N of Tollgate via FRs 64, 6401 (Tollgate is on St. Hwy. 204, E of Weston).
Special Activities & Facilities: Hunting, hiking.

Map Location	Elevation	Picnic Units	Tent Units	Tent-Trailer Units	Fee	Drinking Water
9	4800	6	4	16	x	x

Map Location	Elevation	Picnic Units	Tent Units	Tent-Trailer Units	Fee	Drinking Water

Umatilla Forks

Access: 33 miles E of Pendleton on FR 32.
Special Activities & Facilities: Hunting, fishing, hiking, horse trail, trail biking, wilderness access.

Map Location	Elevation	Picnic Units	Tent Units	Tent-Trailer Units	Fee	Drinking Water
12	2400	16	7	13		x

Woodland

Access: 23 miles E of Weston on St. Hwy. 204.
Special Activities & Facilities: Hunting, mountain biking.

Map Location	Elevation	Picnic Units	Tent Units	Tent-Trailer Units	Fee	Drinking Water
11	5200	2		7		

Woodward

Access: 18 miles E of Weston on St. Hwy. 204.
Special Activities & Facilities: Hunting.

Map Location	Elevation	Picnic Units	Tent Units	Tent-Trailer Units	Fee	Drinking Water
10	4950	14		18		

Handicapped Accessibility Codes
- ❶ Fully Accessible
- ❷ Usable
- ❸ Difficult

See page 7 for full description.

Umpqua National Forest

Diamond Lake and Mt. Thielsen, Umpqua National Forest

The Umpqua National Forest extends from the summit of the Cascade Mountain range to the western lowlands in southwestern Oregon. The forest is named for the Umpqua Indians who once fished its rivers and roamed its green, timbered slopes. Boulder Creek Wilderness and the Rogue-Umpqua Divide Wilderness offer spectacular scenic beauty, while the Mt. Thielsen Wilderness features the prominent spire-like peak of the same name. Forest visitors will delight in the many summer and winter recreation opportunities, scenic landscapes, and many waterfalls of this forest. Miles of forest roads and many hiking trails meander through the forest for those seeking peace and solitude, with a new sight and experience awaiting visitors around every bend.

Special places of interest to the visitor include the North Umpqua River where an unusual geologic formation of perpendicular pillars of volcanic rock rises above the river's edge; the Colliding Rivers viewpoint on the scenic North Umpqua River Drive; picturesque Lemolo Lake and Diamond Lake, summer gateways to nearby Crater Lake National Park; Emile Grove of giant Douglas-fir; numerous beautiful waterfalls including Toketee, Lemolo, Clearwater, Watson, White Horse and Grotto falls; a lookout from the late 1920s on permanent display at the Tiller Ranger District; and tours of the Dorena Tree Improvement Center which plays a key role in the Pacific Northwest Region's genetic tree improvement program.

Further information about recreation opportunities, campground locations and facilities, as well as current maps of the area, are available at the following offices:

Umpqua National Forest
Supervisor's Office
P.O. Box 1008
2900 Stewart Parkway
Roseburg, OR 97470
(503) 672-6601

Cottage Grove Ranger District
78405 Cedar Parks Rd.
P.O. Box 38
Cottage Grove, OR 97424
(503) 942-5591

Diamond Lake Ranger District
HC-60, Box 101
Idleyld Park, OR 97447
(503) 498-2531

North Umpqua Ranger District
18772 N. Umpqua Hwy
Glide, OR 97443
(503) 496-3532

Tiller Ranger District
27812 Tiller Trail Hwy.
Tiller, OR 97484
(503) 825-3201

Other sources for Tiller Ranger District Info.
Millsite Park
2nd and Millsite Park Rd.
Myrtle Creek, OR 97457
(503) 863-3171

Canyonville City Hall
250 W. Main
Canyonville, OR 97417
(503) 839-4258

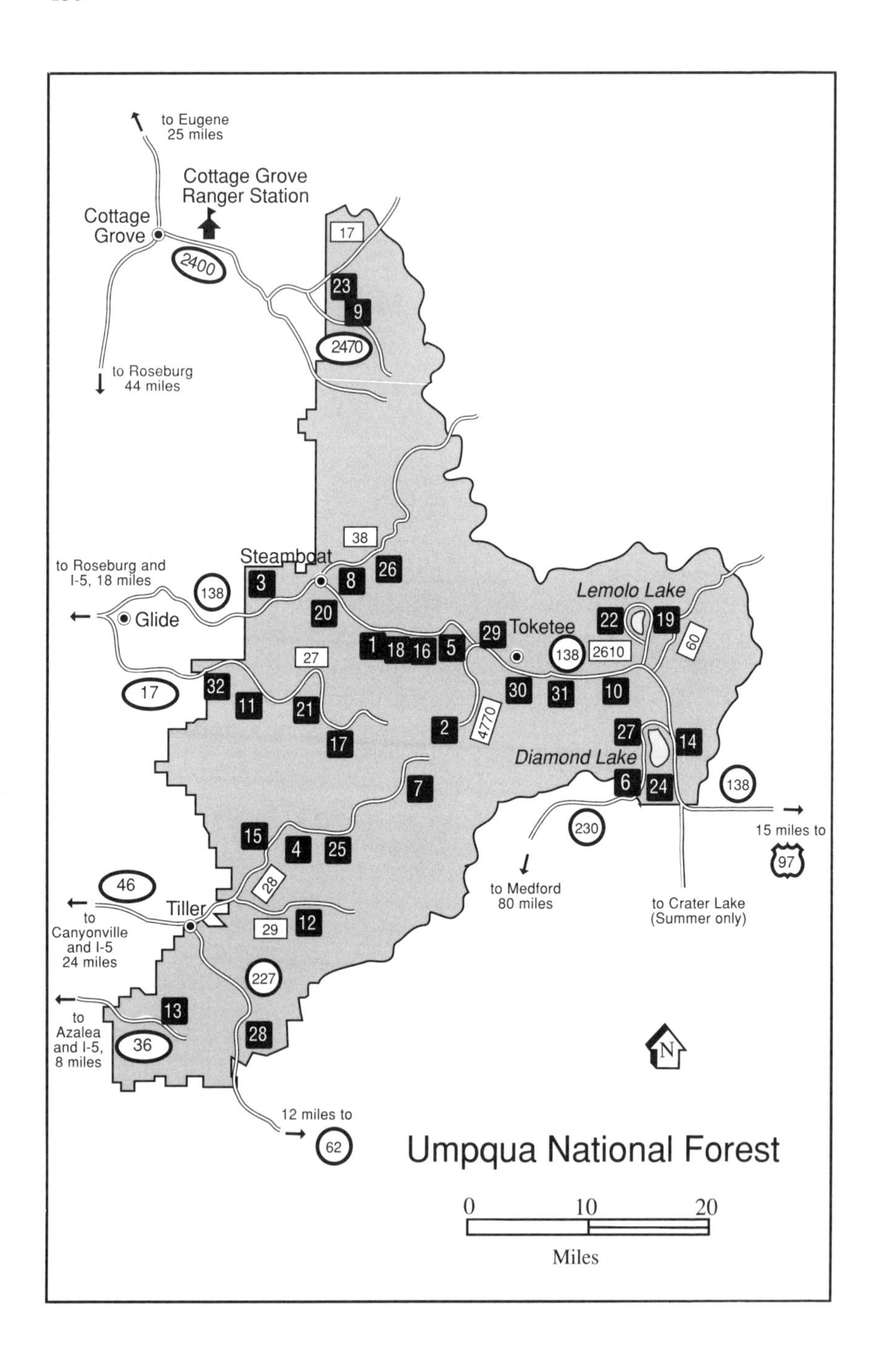

to Eugene
25 miles
Cottage Grove
Ranger Station
Cottage
Grove
2400
17
23
9
2470
to Roseburg
44 miles
38
Steamboat
to Roseburg and
I-5, 18 miles
138
3
8
26
Glide
20
Lemolo Lake
22
19
29
Toketee
1
18
16
5
138
2610
60
27
17
32
11
21
30
31
10
2
4770
17
27
14
Diamond Lake
7
6
24
138
15 miles to
97
230
15
4
25
to Medford
80 miles
46
28
to Crater Lake
(Summer only)
to
Canyonville
and I-5
24 miles
Tiller
29
12
227
to
Azalea
and I-5,
8 miles
13
36
28
N
12 miles to
62
Umpqua National Forest
0
10
20
Miles

UMPQUA NATIONAL FOREST

Map Location	Elevation	Picnic Units	Tent Units	Tent-Trailer Units	Fee	Drinking Water

Developed Sites

Apple Creek

Access: 6 miles E of Steamboat via St. Hwy. 138.
Special Activities & Facilities: Stream, fishing, on N. Umpqua River.

Map Location	Elevation	Picnic Units	Tent Units	Tent-Trailer Units	Fee	Drinking Water
1	1200			8		

Big Twin Lakes

Access: SE of Steamboat via St. Hwy. 138, FR 4770, 1/2-mile trail.
Special Activities & Facilities: Fishing, hiking, scenery, riding.

Map Location	Elevation	Picnic Units	Tent Units	Tent-Trailer Units	Fee	Drinking Water
2	5100		6			

Bogus Creek

Access: 36 miles NE Roseburg via St. Hwy. 138.
Special Activities & Facilities: Fishing.

Map Location	Elevation	Picnic Units	Tent Units	Tent-Trailer Units	Fee	Drinking Water
3	1100	5		15	x	x

Boulder Creek

Access: 14 miles NE Tiller, via Cty. Rd. 46, FR 28.
Special Activities & Facilities: Fishing, RVs to 16'.

Map Location	Elevation	Picnic Units	Tent Units	Tent-Trailer Units	Fee	Drinking Water
4	1400			8		

Boulder Flat

Access: 15 miles E of Steamboat via St. Hwy. 138.
Special Activities & Facilities: Fishing, hiking, scenery, N. Umpqua River.

Map Location	Elevation	Picnic Units	Tent Units	Tent-Trailer Units	Fee	Drinking Water
5	1600			11		

Broken Arrow

Access: at S end of Diamond Lake off St. Hwy. 138.
Special Activities & Facilities: Fishing, hiking, scenery, group camping.

Map Location	Elevation	Picnic Units	Tent Units	Tent-Trailer Units	Fee	Drinking Water
♿ 6	5200			148 ❶	x	x

Camp Comfort

Access: 26 miles NE Tiller, via Cty. Rd. 46, FR 28.
Special Activities & Facilities: Fishing, hiking, scenery, shelter.

Map Location	Elevation	Picnic Units	Tent Units	Tent-Trailer Units	Fee	Drinking Water
7	2000		1	4		

Canton Creek

Access: 1 mile N of Steamboat on FR 38.
Special Activities & Facilities: Group picnicking, shelter.

Map Location	Elevation	Picnic Units	Tent Units	Tent-Trailer Units	Fee	Drinking Water
8	1200		1	4	x	x

Cedar Creek

Access: 24 miles SE Cottage Grove via Cty. Rds. 2400, 2470.
Special Activities & Facilities: Fishing, hiking, RVs under 16'.

Map Location	Elevation	Picnic Units	Tent Units	Tent-Trailer Units	Fee	Drinking Water
9	1600		8			

Clearwater Falls

Access: 12 miles NW Diamond Lake via St. Hwy. 138, FR 4785.
Special Activities & Facilities: Fishing, scenery.

Map Location	Elevation	Picnic Units	Tent Units	Tent-Trailer Units	Fee	Drinking Water
10	4200	9	5			

Coolwater

Access: 16 miles E of Glide on Cty. Rd. 17.
Special Activities & Facilities: Fishing, hiking.

Map Location	Elevation	Picnic Units	Tent Units	Tent-Trailer Units	Fee	Drinking Water
11	1300			7		x

Cover

Access: 17 miles NE of Tiller, via Cty. Rd. 46, FR 29.
Special Activities & Facilities: Fishing.

Map Location	Elevation	Picnic Units	Tent Units	Tent-Trailer Units	Fee	Drinking Water
12	1700			7		

Devils Flat

Access: 18 miles E of Azalea on Cty. Rd. 36.
Special Activities & Facilities: Fishing, hiking.

Map Location	Elevation	Picnic Units	Tent Units	Tent-Trailer Units	Fee	Drinking Water
13	2100			3		

Diamond Lake

Access: On E shore of Diamond Lake off St. Hwy. 138.
Special Activities & Facilities: Boat launch, fishing, hiking, biking, bicycling, barrier-free trail.

Map Location	Elevation	Picnic Units	Tent Units	Tent-Trailer Units	Fee	Drinking Water
[wheelchair symbol] 14	5200		50	210 [1]	x	x

Dumont Creek

Access: 12 miles NE of Tiller, via Cty. Rd. 46, FR 28.
Special Activities & Facilities: Fishing, stream.

Map Location	Elevation	Picnic Units	Tent Units	Tent-Trailer Units	Fee	Drinking Water
15	1300			5		

Map Location	Elevation	Picnic Units	Tent Units	Tent-Trailer Units	Fee	Drinking Water

Eagle Rock

Access: 13 miles E of Steamboat on St. Hwy. 138.
Special Activities & Facilities: Trail, rafting, fishing on N Umpqua River.

16	*1600*			*27*	*x*	*x*

Hemlock Lake

Access: 32 miles SE of Glide via Cty. Rd. 17, FR 27.
Special Activities & Facilities: Hunting, trail, fishing, non-motorized boating.

17	*4400*	*1*		*13*		

Horseshoe Bend

Access: 9 miles E of Steamboat via St. Hwy. 138.
Special Activities & Facilities: Fishing, trail, rafting, group-use reservation.

18	*1300*		*16*	*18* ❷	*x*	*x*

Inlet

Access: 15 miles N of Diamond Lake via St. Hwy. 138, FRs 2610, 400.
Special Activities & Facilities: On Lemolo Lake, fishing, hiking, water sports.

19	*4200*		*3*	*10*		

Island

Access: 2 miles E of Steamboat via St. Hwy. 138.
Special Activities & Facilities: Hunting, fishing, rafting, N Umpqua River.

20	*1200*			*7*		

Lake-in-the-Woods

Access: 20 miles E of Glide, via Cty. Rd. 17, FR 27.
Special Activities & Facilities: Fishing, trail, scenery, RVs to 16'.

21	*3000*	*1*		*11*	*x*	*x*

	Map Location	Elevation	Picnic Units	Tent Units	Tent-Trailer Units	Fee	Drinking Water

Poole Creek

Access: 14 miles N of Diamond Lake via St. Hwy. 138, FR 2610.
Special Activities & Facilities: Lemolo Lake, boat launching, fishing, hiking, water sports, barrier-free toilets, swimming.

	Map Location	Elevation	Picnic Units	Tent Units	Tent-Trailer Units	Fee	Drinking Water
♿	22	4200			60	x	x

Rujada

Access: 21 miles SE Cottage Grove via Cty. Rd. 2400, FR 17.
Special Activities & Facilities: Fishing, group picnicking, stream, hiking, playfield.

	Map Location	Elevation	Picnic Units	Tent Units	Tent-Trailer Units	Fee	Drinking Water
	23	1200	10		10		x

South Shore

Access: S end of Diamond Lake off St. Hwy. 138 on FR 4795.
Special Activities & Facilities: Boating, fishing, group picnicking, shelter, bicycle, hiker camping only.

	Map Location	Elevation	Picnic Units	Tent Units	Tent-Trailer Units	Fee	Drinking Water
♿	24	5200	36❶	5			x

South Umpqua Falls

Access: 21 miles NE Tiller via Cty. Rd. 46, FR 28.
Special Activities & Facilities: Fishing, scenic waterfalls.

	Map Location	Elevation	Picnic Units	Tent Units	Tent-Trailer Units	Fee	Drinking Water
♿	25	1600	7❶				

Steamboat Falls

Access: 7 miles NE of Steamboat on FRs 38, 3810.
Special Activities & Facilities: Hiking, scenery, stream.

	Map Location	Elevation	Picnic Units	Tent Units	Tent-Trailer Units	Fee	Drinking Water
	26	1400		1	10		

Thielsen View

Access: W side of Diamond Lake on FR 4795.
Special Activities & Facilities: Boat launching, fishing, bicycling, barrier-free toilets and trails.

	Map Location	Elevation	Picnic Units	Tent Units	Tent-Trailer Units	Fee	Drinking Water
♿	27	5200			60 ❸	x	x

Threehorn

Access: 13 miles SE of Tiller via Cty. Rd. 1.
Special Activities & Facilities: Scenery.

	Map Location	Elevation	Picnic Units	Tent Units	Tent-Trailer Units	Fee	Drinking Water
	28	2600	1		5		

Toketee Lake

Access: 2 miles N of Toketee Ranger Station on FR 34.
Special Activities & Facilities: Boating, fishing, scenery, hiking.

Map Location	*Elevation*	*Picnic Units*	*Tent Units*	*Tent-Trailer Units*	*Fee*	*Drinking Water*
29	*2600*			*33*		

Watson Falls

Access: 1.5 miles E of Toketee Ranger Station via St. Hwy. 138.
Special Activities & Facilities: Scenery, hiking, waterfall.

Map Location	*Elevation*	*Picnic Units*	*Tent Units*	*Tent-Trailer Units*	*Fee*	*Drinking Water*
30	*2700*	*12*				

Whitehorse Falls

Access: 6 miles E of Toketee Ranger Station via St. Hwy. 138.
Special Activities & Facilities: Fishing, waterfall.

Map Location	*Elevation*	*Picnic Units*	*Tent Units*	*Tent-Trailer Units*	*Fee*	*Drinking Water*
31	*3800*	*4*	*5*			

Wolf Creek

Access: 12 miles SE Glide on Cty. Rd. 17.
Special Activities & Facilities: Fishing, playfield, reservations for group picnicking, trail, shelter.

Map Location	*Elevation*	*Picnic Units*	*Tent Units*	*Tent-Trailer Units*	*Fee*	*Drinking Water*
32	*1100*	*17*	*3*	*6*	*x*	*x*

Handicapped Accessibility Codes
- ❶ Fully Accessible
- ❷ Usable
- ❸ Difficult

See page 7 for full description.

Wallowa-Whitman National Forest

Fishing below Wildsheep Rapids on the Snake River,
Hells Canyon National Recreation Area,
Wallowa-Whitman National Forest. Photo by Jim Hughes.

The "must-see" attraction of this forest is the spectacular, rugged beauty of the Hells Canyon National Recreation Area. From this arid desert-like canyon, the deepest river gorge in North America, to the splendor of Oregon's Blue and Wallowa mountains and Idaho's Seven Devils mountains, the forest offers an array of impressive scenes. Remnants of gold mining and early-day logging activities can still be seen, along with the diverse scenery of four wildernesses.

Special places of interest include Hat Point viewpoint, 6,982 feet above the canyon; Pittsburgh Landing petroglyphs site; Elkhorn Drive; Anthony Lake; Trail Of Alpine Glacier; Mason Dam viewpoint; Phillips Lake; Stud Creek Trail; Buck Point overlook; Tipton, Granite, and Greenhorn mining towns; Starkey Forest Experiment Station; Mt. Emily and Indian Rock overlook; Lostine River Road; Wallowa Lake; Mt. Howard tramway; Buckhorn viewpoint, Hells Canyon dam; and, for river runners and Hells Canyon hikers, the Kirkwood Living History Ranch and the Mountain Chief mine.

Further information about recreation opportunities, campground locations and facilities, as well as current maps of the area, are available at the following offices:

Wallowa-Whitman National Forest
Supervisor's Office
1550 Dewey Ave.
P.O. Box 907
Baker, OR 97814
(503) 523-6391

Baker Ranger District
Route 1, Box 1
Pocahontas Rd.
Baker OR 97814
(503) 523-4476

Eagle Cap Ranger District
Rt. 1, Box 270A
Enterprise, OR 97828
(503) 426-3104

LaGrande Ranger District
3502 Highway 30
LaGrande, OR 97850
(503) 963-7186

Pine Ranger District
General Delivery
Halfway, OR 97834
(503) 742-7511

Unity Ranger District
P.O. Box 38
Unity, OR 97884
(503) 446-3351

Wallowa Valley Ranger District
Route 1, Box 270A
Enterprise, OR 97828
(503) 432-2171

Hells Canyon National Rec. Area
(Headquarters)
Rt. 1, Box 270A
Enterprise, OR 97828
(503) 426-3151

Hells Canyon National Recreation
Area
3620 B Snake River Ave.
Lewiston, ID 83501
(208) 743-3648

Hells Canyon National
Recreation Area
Box 832
Riggins, ID 83549
(208) 628-3916

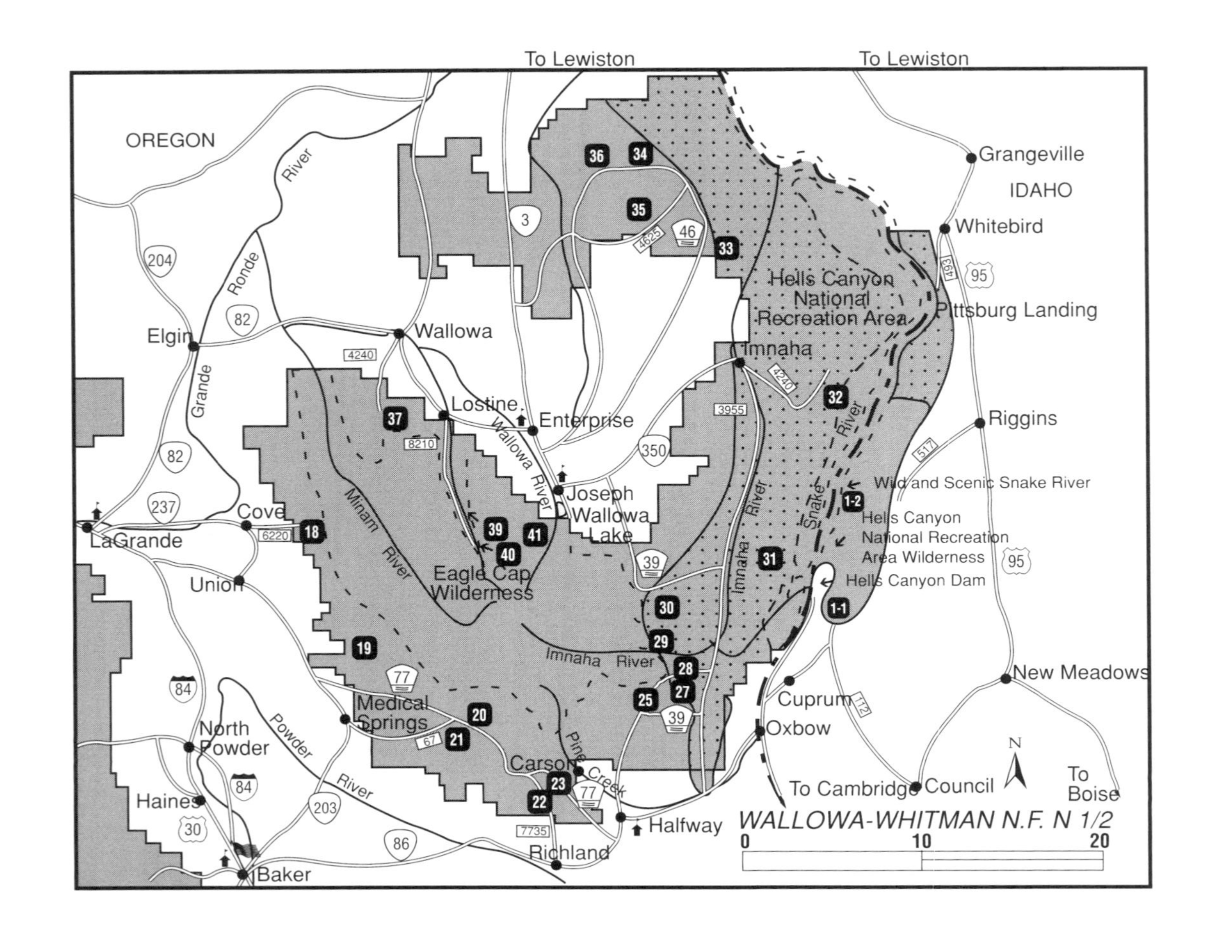
To Lewiston
To Lewiston
OREGON
Grangeville
IDAHO
Whitebird
Pittsburg Landing
Hells Canyon National Recreation Area
Imnaha
Riggins
Wild and Scenic Snake River
Hells Canyon National Recreation Area Wilderness
Hells Canyon Dam
New Meadows
Cuprum
Oxbow
To Cambridge
Council
To Boise
WALLOWA-WHITMAN N.F. N 1/2
N
0
10
20
Elgin
Wallowa
Lostine
Enterprise
Wallowa River
Joseph
Wallowa Lake
Cove
LaGrande
Union
Minam River
Eagle Cap Wilderness
Imnaha River
Snake River
Grande Ronde River
Medical Springs
Pine Creek
Carson
Halfway
Richland
North Powder
Powder River
Haines
Baker
204
82
82
237
4240
4240
3955
350
3
46
4625
8210
6220
39
39
77
77
67
7735
84
84
30
203
86
493
95
95
517
112
36
34
35
33
32
37
18
39
40
41
1-2
31
1-1
30
29
28
27
25
19
20
21
23
22

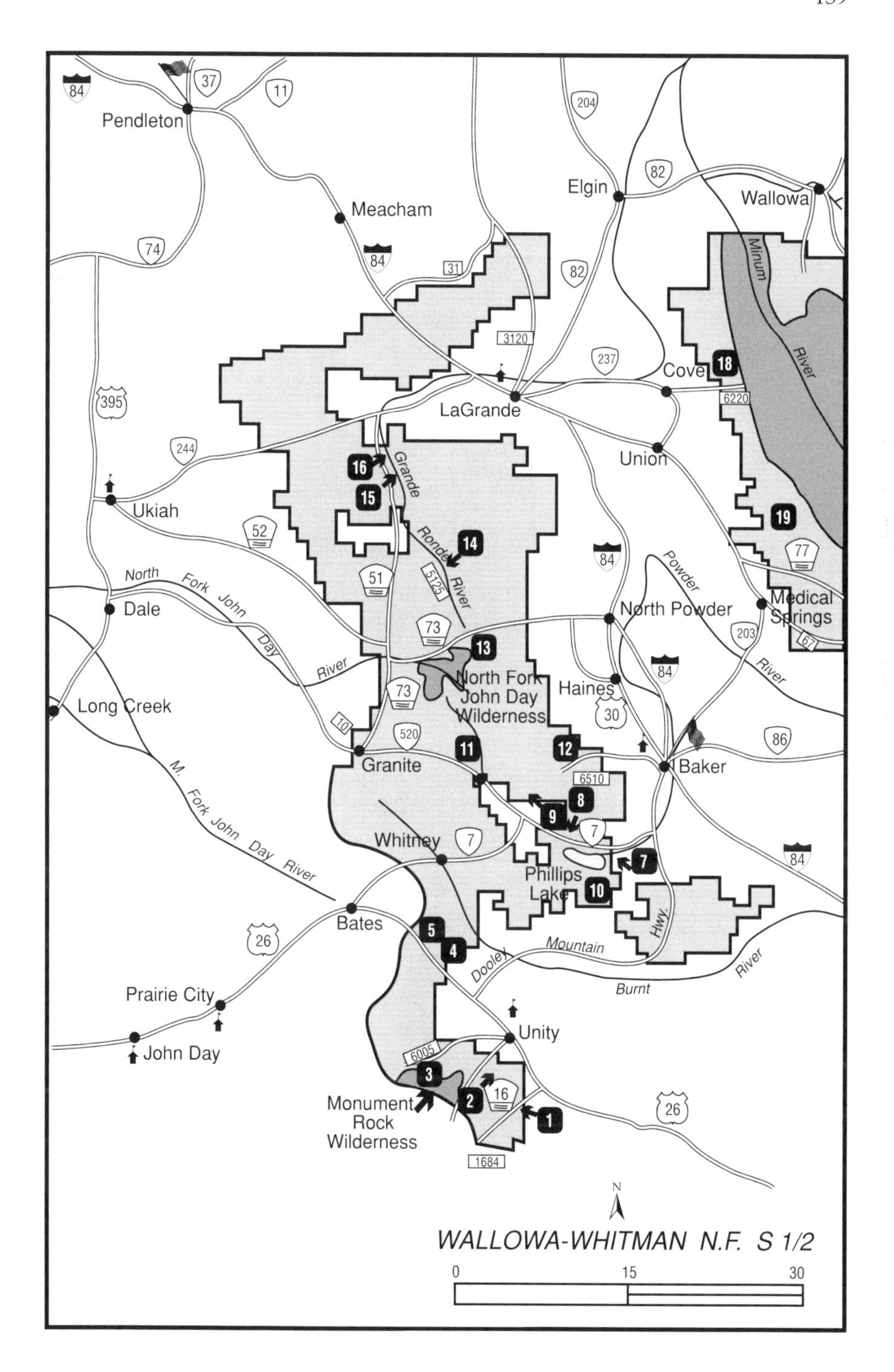
Pendleton
Meacham
Elgin
Wallowa
LaGrande
Cove
Union
Ukiah
Dale
North Powder
Medical Springs
Long Creek
Haines
Baker
Granite
Whitney
Phillips Lake
Bates
Prairie City
John Day
Unity
North Fork John Day Wilderness
Monument Rock Wilderness
North Fork John Day River
M. Fork John Day River
Grande Ronde River
Minum River
Powder River
Burnt River
Dooley Mountain Hwy.
WALLOWA-WHITMAN N.F. S 1/2
0
15
30
N

Map Location	Elevation	Picnic Units	Tent Units	Tent-Trailer Units	Fee	Drinking Water

Baker Ranger District

Anthony Lakes

Access: 21 miles W of Haines via St. Hwy. 411, FR 73.
Special Activities & Facilities: Fishing, hiking, boating, mountain climbing, winter sports, trailhead.

Map Location	Elevation	Picnic Units	Tent Units	Tent-Trailer Units	Fee	Drinking Water
13	7100	13 ❸	21❶	26❶	x	x

Deer Creek

Access: 6 miles E of Sumpter via FR 6550.
Special Activities & Facilities: Fishing, hiking, RVs to 16'.

Map Location	Elevation	Picnic Units	Tent Units	Tent-Trailer Units	Fee	Drinking Water
9	4600	2	8			

Grande Ronde Lake

Access: 21 miles W of Haines via St. Hwy. 411, FRs 73 & 43.
Special Activities & Facilities: Fishing, hiking, swimming, winter sports.

Map Location	Elevation	Picnic Units	Tent Units	Tent-Trailer Units	Fee	Drinking Water
13	6800	4	4	6	x	x

Marble Creek Picnic Site

Access: 11.5 miles W of Baker via US 30, Cty. Rd. 808, FR 6510.
Special Activities & Facilities: Hiking.

Map Location	Elevation	Picnic Units	Tent Units	Tent-Trailer Units	Fee	Drinking Water
12	4600	9				

Mason Dam Picnic Site

Access: 16 miles SW of Baker via St. Hwy. 7.
Special Activities & Facilities: Fishing.

Map Location	Elevation	Picnic Units	Tent Units	Tent-Trailer Units	Fee	Drinking Water
7	4000	16				

McCully Forks

Access: 3 miles W of Sumpter on Cty. Rd. 520.
Special Activities & Facilities: Fishing, hiking.

Map Location	Elevation	Picnic Units	Tent Units	Tent-Trailer Units	Fee	Drinking Water
11	4600		3	4		

Millers Lane

Access: 27 miles SW of Baker via St. Hwy. 7, FR 2226.
Special Activities & Facilities: Boating, fishing, hiking, swimming, RVs to 16', lightly improved.

Map Location	Elevation	Picnic Units	Tent Units	Tent-Trailer Units	Fee	Drinking Water
10	4120		3	4		

Mowich Loop Picnic Site

Access: 23 miles SW of Baker via St. Hwy. 7.
Special Activities & Facilities: Fishing.

Map Location	Elevation	Picnic Units	Tent Units	Tent-Trailer Units	Fee	Drinking Water
8	4100	5				

Mud Lake

Access: 21 miles W of Haines via St. Hwy. 411, FR 73.
Special Activities & Facilities: Fishing, hiking, winter sports.

Map Location	Elevation	Picnic Units	Tent Units	Tent-Trailer Units	Fee	Drinking Water
13	7100		3	5	x	x

Southwest Shore

Access: 26 miles SW of Baker via St. Hwy. 7, FR 2226.
Special Activities & Facilities: Boating, fishing, hiking, swimming, lightly improved.

Map Location	Elevation	Picnic Units	Tent Units	Tent-Trailer Units	Fee	Drinking Water
10	4120			18		

Union Creek

Access: 20 miles SW of Baker via St. Hwy. 7.
Special Activities & Facilities: Boating, fishing, hiking, swimming, winter sports, group picnic, operated by concessionaire.

Map Location	Elevation	Picnic Units	Tent Units	Tent-Trailer Units	Fee	Drinking Water
7	4120	80 ❶		58 ❶	x	x

La Grande Ranger District

Spool Cart

Access: 27 miles SW of La Grande via I-84, St. Hwy. 244, FR 51.
Special Activities & Facilities: Fishing, hiking.

Map Location	Elevation	Picnic Units	Tent Units	Tent-Trailer Units	Fee	Drinking Water
16	3500			5		

River

Access: 32 miles SW of La Grande via I-84, St. Hwy. 244, FR 51.
Special Activities & Facilities: Fishing, hiking.

Map Location	Elevation	Picnic Units	Tent Units	Tent-Trailer Units	Fee	Drinking Water
15	3800	10		6		x

Map Location	Elevation	Picnic Units	Tent Units	Tent-Trailer Units	Fee	Drinking Water

Time and a Half

Access: 29 miles SW of La Grande via I-84, St. Hwy. 244, FR 51.
Special Activities & Facilities: Fishing, hiking.

Map Location	Elevation	Picnic Units	Tent Units	Tent-Trailer Units	Fee	Drinking Water
15	*3700*			*5*		

Woodley

Access: 39 miles SW of La Grande via I-84, St. Hwy. 244, FRs 51, 5125.
Special Activities & Facilities: Fishing, hiking.

Map Location	Elevation	Picnic Units	Tent Units	Tent-Trailer Units	Fee	Drinking Water
14	*4500*	*4*		*7*		*x*

Moss Springs

Access: 8 miles E of Cove via Cty. Rd. 602, FR 6220 (Cove is E of La Grande on St. Hwy. 237).
Special Activities & Facilities: Hiking, trailhead, horse facilities.

Map Location	Elevation	Picnic Units	Tent Units	Tent-Trailer Units	Fee	Drinking Water
18	*5400*			*7*		

North Fork Catherine

Access: 17 miles SE of Union via St. Hwy. 203, FR 7785.
Special Activities & Facilities: Fishing, hiking, trailhead.

Map Location	Elevation	Picnic Units	Tent Units	Tent-Trailer Units	Fee	Drinking Water
19	*4400*			*6*		

Two Color

Access: 14 miles E of Medical Springs via FRs 67, 7755.
Special Activities & Facilities: Fishing, hiking.

Map Location	Elevation	Picnic Units	Tent Units	Tent-Trailer Units	Fee	Drinking Water
20	*4800*		*14*			*x*

Unity Ranger District

Eldorado

Access: 12 miles S of Unity via US 26, FR 1684.
Special Activities & Facilities: Hiking.

Map Location	Elevation	Picnic Units	Tent Units	Tent-Trailer Units	Fee	Drinking Water
1	*4600*	*Group area, no units designated*				

Elk Creek

Access: 8 miles W of Unity via Cty. Rd. 1300, FR 6005.
Special Activities & Facilities: Fishing.

Map Location	Elevation	Picnic Units	Tent Units	Tent-Trailer Units	Fee	Drinking Water
3	*4520*	*Group area, no sites designated*				

	Map Location	Elevation	Picnic Units	Tent Units	Tent-Trailer Units	Fee	Drinking Water

Long Creek

Access: 10 miles S of Unity via US 26, FR 16.
Special Activities & Facilities: Fishing.

	Map Location	Elevation	Picnic Units	Tent Units	Tent-Trailer Units	Fee	Drinking Water
	2	*4430*	*Group area, no units designated*				

Mammoth Springs

Access: 9 miles W of Unity via Cty. Rd. 1300, FRs 6005 & 2640.
Special Activities & Facilities: Fishing, hiking.

	Map Location	Elevation	Picnic Units	Tent Units	Tent-Trailer Units	Fee	Drinking Water
	3	*4550*	*group area, no units designated*				

Oregon

Access: 12 miles NW of Unity on US 26.
Special Activities & Facilities: Hiking, RVs to 16'.

	Map Location	Elevation	Picnic Units	Tent Units	Tent-Trailer Units	Fee	Drinking Water
	5	*4880*	*3*		*8*		*x*

South Fork

Access: 6 miles W of Unity via Cty. Rd. 1300, FR 6005.
Special Activities & Facilities: Fishing, hiking, RVs to 16'.

	Map Location	Elevation	Picnic Units	Tent Units	Tent-Trailer Units	Fee	Drinking Water
	3	*4400*	*7*	*7*	*12*		*x*

Stevens Creek

Access: 7 miles W of Unity Via Cty. Rd. 1300, FR 6005.
Special Activities & Facilities: Fishing, hiking.

	Map Location	Elevation	Picnic Units	Tent Units	Tent-Trailer Units	Fee	Drinking Water
	3	*4480*	*Group area, no units designated*				

Wetmore

Access: 10 miles NW of Unity via US 26.
Special Activities & Facilities: Hiking, trail to Yellow Pine, RVs to 16'.

	Map Location	Elevation	Picnic Units	Tent Units	Tent-Trailer Units	Fee	Drinking Water
♿	*4*	*4320*	*9*		*10* ❷		*x*

Yellow Pine

Access: 9 miles NW of Unity via US 26.
Special Activities & Facilities: Hiking, trail to Wetmore, dump station.

	Map Location	Elevation	Picnic Units	Tent Units	Tent-Trailer Units	Fee	Drinking Water
♿	*4*	*4450*	*23*		*21* ❷		*x*

Map Location	Elevation	Picnic Units	Tent Units	Tent-Trailer Units	Fee	Drinking Water

Eagle Cap Ranger District

Boundary

Access: 9 miles S of Wallowa via FRs 8250, 040.
Special Activities & Facilities: Fishing, hiking, trailhead.

37	*3600*		*8*			

Hurricane Creek

Access: 4 miles SW of Joseph on FR 8205.
Special Activities & Facilities: Fishing, hiking, riding, trailhead.

41	*5000*	*2*	*8*			

Shady

Access: 17 miles S of Lostine on FR 8210.
Special Activities & Facilities: Fishing, hiking, riding, trailhead.

40	*5400*			*16*		

Two Pan

Access: 17 miles S of Lostine on FR 8210.
Special Activities & Facilities: Fishing, hiking, trailhead.

40	*5600*		*6*			

Williamson

Access: 11 miles S of Lostine on FR 8210.
Special Activities & Facilities: Fishing, hiking.

39	*4900*		*10*			

Hells Canyon National Recreation Area

Blackhorse

Access: 36 miles SE of Joseph via St. Hwy. 350, FR 39.
Special Activities & Facilities: Fishing, hiking.

31	*4000*			*16*	*x*	*x*

Buckhorn

Access: 43 miles NE of Enterprise on Zumwalt Rd. & FRs 46, 780.
Special Activities & Facilities: Berry picking, view, mushroom picking.

33	*5200*		*6*			

Coverdale

Access: 41 miles SE of Joseph via St. Hwy. 350, FRs 39, 3960.
Special Activities & Facilities: Fishing, hiking.

Map Location	Elevation	Picnic Units	Tent Units	Tent-Trailer Units	Fee	Drinking Water
28	4300		9	1		x

Dougherty Springs

Access: 45 miles NE of Enterprise via St. Hwy. 3, FR 46.
Special Activities & Facilities: Fishing, hiking, hunting.

Map Location	Elevation	Picnic Units	Tent Units	Tent-Trailer Units	Fee	Drinking Water
34	4900		6	4		

Duck Lake

Access: 30 miles N of Halfway via St. Hwy. 86, FRs 39, 66.
Special Activities & Facilities: Fishing, hiking.

Map Location	Elevation	Picnic Units	Tent Units	Tent-Trailer Units	Fee	Drinking Water
27	5200		2			

Evergreen

Access: 44 miles SE of Joseph via St. Hwy. 350, FRs 39, 3960.
Special Activities & Facilities: Fishing, hiking.

Map Location	Elevation	Picnic Units	Tent Units	Tent-Trailer Units	Fee	Drinking Water
29	4500	*Group area, no units designated*				

Hat Point

Access: 56 miles NE of Joseph via St. Hwy. 350, FRs 4240 & 315.
Special Activities & Facilities: Hiking, view, horse ramps, trailhead. Long, steep access road.

Map Location	Elevation	Picnic Units	Tent Units	Tent-Trailer Units	Fee	Drinking Water
32	6982		6			

Hidden

Access: 43 miles SE Joseph via St. Hwy. 350, FRs 39, 3960.
Special Activities & Facilities: Fishing, hiking.

Map Location	Elevation	Picnic Units	Tent Units	Tent-Trailer Units	Fee	Drinking Water
29	4400			10	x	x

Indian Crossing

Access: 45 miles SE of Joseph via St. Hwy. 350, FRs 39, 3960.
Special Activities & Facilities: Fishing, hiking, horse ramp, riding, trailhead.

Map Location	Elevation	Picnic Units	Tent Units	Tent-Trailer Units	Fee	Drinking Water
29	4500			15	x	x

Lake Fork

Access: 18 miles NE of Halfway via St. Hwy. 86, FR 39.
Special Activities & Facilities: Fishing, hiking.

Map Location	Elevation	Picnic Units	Tent Units	Tent-Trailer Units	Fee	Drinking Water
27	3200			10	x	x

Map Location	Elevation	Picnic Units	Tent Units	Tent-Trailer Units	Fee	Drinking Water

Lick Creek

Access: 23 miles SE of Joseph via St. Hwy. 350, FR 39.
Special Activities & Facilities: Fishing, hiking.

Map Location	Elevation	Picnic Units	Tent Units	Tent-Trailer Units	Fee	Drinking Water
30	5400			12	x	x

Ollokot

Access: 37 miles SE of Joseph via St. Hwy. 350, FR 39.
Special Activities & Facilities: Fishing, berry picking.

Map Location	Elevation	Picnic Units	Tent Units	Tent-Trailer Units	Fee	Drinking Water
31	4000			12	x	x

Saddle Creek

Access: 50 miles NE of Joseph via St. Hwy. 350, FR 4240.
Special Activities & Facilities: Hiking, viewing, RVs to 16'. Long steep access road.

Map Location	Elevation	Picnic Units	Tent Units	Tent-Trailer Units	Fee	Drinking Water
32	6800		6			

Twin Lakes

Access: 35 miles N of Halfway on FR 66.
Special Activities & Facilities: Fishing, hiking.

Map Location	Elevation	Picnic Units	Tent Units	Tent-Trailer Units	Fee	Drinking Water
25	6500		9			

Black Lake

Access: 40 miles N of Council, Idaho, via St. Hwy. 71, FRs 002, 105, 112.
Special Activities & Facilities: Fishing, hiking, trailhead.

Map Location	Elevation	Picnic Units	Tent Units	Tent-Trailer Units	Fee	Drinking Water
1-1	7200			4		

Seven Devils

Access: 17 miles SW of Riggins, Idaho, via US 95, FR 517.
Special Activities & Facilities: Fishing, hiking, trailhead, RVs to 16'. Long steep access road.

Map Location	Elevation	Picnic Units	Tent Units	Tent-Trailer Units	Fee	Drinking Water
1-2	7400			8❸		

Windy Saddle

Access: 17 miles SW of Riggins, Idaho, via US 95, FR 517
Special Activities & Facilities: Fishing, hiking, horse ramp, trailhead. Long steep access road.

Map Location	Elevation	Picnic Units	Tent Units	Tent-Trailer Units	Fee	Drinking Water
1-2	7500		6❸			

Pine Ranger District

Eagle Forks

Access: 10 miles N of Richland on FR 7735.
Special Activities & Facilities: Fishing, hiking, trailhead.

Map Location	Elevation	Picnic Units	Tent Units	Tent-Trailer Units	Fee	Drinking Water
22	3000	3	7			

Fish Lake

Access: 29 miles N of Halfway on FR 66.
Special Activities & Facilities: Fishing, hiking, swimming, boating.

Map Location	Elevation	Picnic Units	Tent Units	Tent-Trailer Units	Fee	Drinking Water
25	6600		9	6		

McBride

Access: 11 miles W of Halfway via St. Hwy. 413, Cty. Rd. 983, FRs 7710, 77.
Special Activities & Facilities: Fishing, hiking, barrier-free toilet.

Map Location	Elevation	Picnic Units	Tent Units	Tent-Trailer Units	Fee	Drinking Water
♿ 23	4800			5		

Tamarack

Access: 12 miles E of Medical Springs on FR 67.
Special Activities & Facilities: Fishing, hiking.

Map Location	Elevation	Picnic Units	Tent Units	Tent-Trailer Units	Fee	Drinking Water
♿ 21	4600			10 ❶		x

Wallowa Valley Ranger District

Coyote

Access: 45 miles N of Enterprise via St. Hwy. 3, FR 46.
Special Activities & Facilities: Fishing, hiking, hunting, horseback riding.

Map Location	Elevation	Picnic Units	Tent Units	Tent-Trailer Units	Fee	Drinking Water
36	4800			21		

Vigne

Access: 42 miles NE of Enterprise via St. Hwy. 3, FRs 46, 4625.
Special Activities & Facilities: Fishing, hiking, horseback riding, hunting.

Map Location	Elevation	Picnic Units	Tent Units	Tent-Trailer Units	Fee	Drinking Water
35	3500			12		x

Handicapped Accessibility Codes
❶ Fully Accessible
❷ Usable
❸ Difficult
See page 7 for full description.

Wenatchee National Forest

Glacier Peak, Wenatchee National Forest. Photo by Jim Hughes.

"Something for everyone" probably best describes this forest. A wide range of recreation activities are available with over 2,500 miles of recreation trails and 4,700 miles of forest roads. Visitors can enjoy the pristine beauty of alpine meadows, sparkling mountain lakes, and jagged peaks that touch the sky. The shores of narrow 1,500-feet-deep Lake Chelan offer boat-in camping. In addition to Lake Chelan and 7-mile-long Lake Wenatchee, five major reservoirs offer an abundance of fishing and other recreation opportunities. Exceptional beauty is found in all of the seven wildernesses: Alpine Lakes, Glacier Peak, Henry M. Jackson, Goat Rocks, William O. Douglas, Norse Peak, and Lake Chelan-Sawtooth.

Special places of interest include Lake Chelan boat tour of its 55-mile length; White River auto tour from Lake Wenatchee; White River Falls; the scenery of Bumping River Road; Blewett mining area; Red Top agate beds for rockhounding; Liberty National Historic District; Naches Trail wagon road; Ravens Roost viewpoint; 400-foot Boulder Cave; Miners Ridge viewpoint; Wildcat Post Piles geologic formations; Blue Slide, a huge prehistoric slide; Holden mine and tailings; Entiat Falls; Silver Falls; White River viewpoint; and Tumwater Canyon on the Wenatchee River.

Further information about recreation opportunities, campground locations and facilities, as well as current maps of the area, are available at the following offices:

Wenatchee National Forest
Supervisor's Office
301 Yakima Street
P.O. Box 811 (98807)
Wenatchee, WA 98801
(509) 662-4335

Chelan Ranger District
428 Woodin Ave.
P.O. Box 189
Chelan, WA 98816
(509) 682-2576

Cle Elum Ranger District
803 W. 2nd Street
Cle Elum, WA 98922
(509) 674-4411

Lake Wenatchee Ranger District
22976 Highway 207
Leavenworth, WA 98826
(509) 763-3103

Leavenworth Ranger District
600 Sherbourne Street
Leavenworth, WA 98826
(509) 782-1413

Naches Ranger District
10061 Highway 12
Naches, WA 98937
(509) 653-2205

Entiat Ranger District
2108 Entiat Way
P.O. Box 476
Entiat, WA 98822
(509) 784-1511

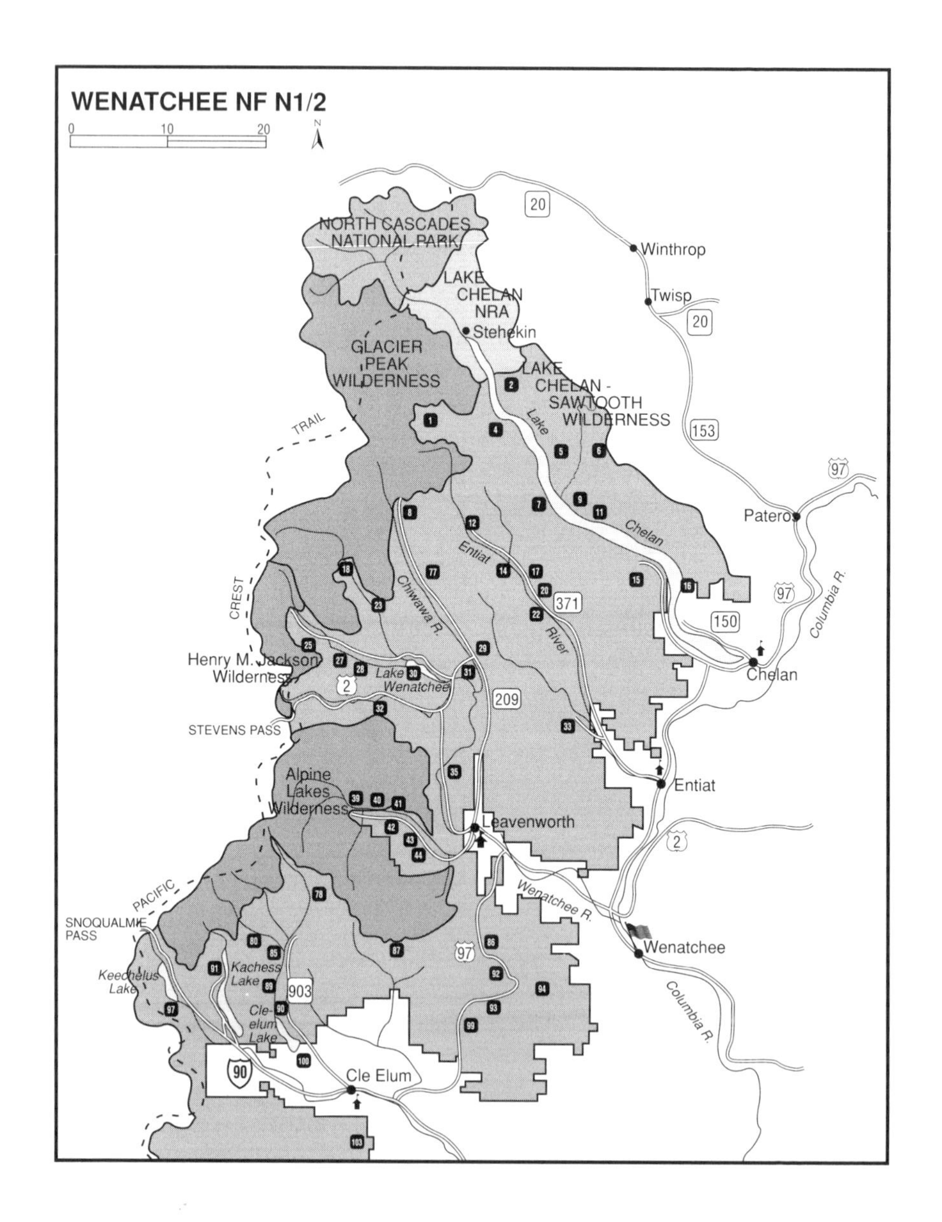
WENATCHEE NF N1/2
0
10
20
N
NORTH CASCADES
NATIONAL PARK
LAKE
CHELAN
NRA
Stehekin
GLACIER
PEAK
WILDERNESS
LAKE
CHELAN -
SAWTOOTH
WILDERNESS
Winthrop
Twisp
Pateros
Chelan
Entiat
Leavenworth
Wenatchee
Cle Elum
Henry M. Jackson
Wilderness
Alpine
Lakes
Wilderness
STEVENS PASS
SNOQUALMIE
PASS
PACIFIC
CREST
TRAIL
Lake
Chelan
Entiat
River
Chiwawa R.
Lake
Wenatchee
Wenatchee R.
Columbia R.
Kachess
Lake
Keechelus
Lake
Cle-
elum
Lake
20
153
97
371
150
2
209
903
90

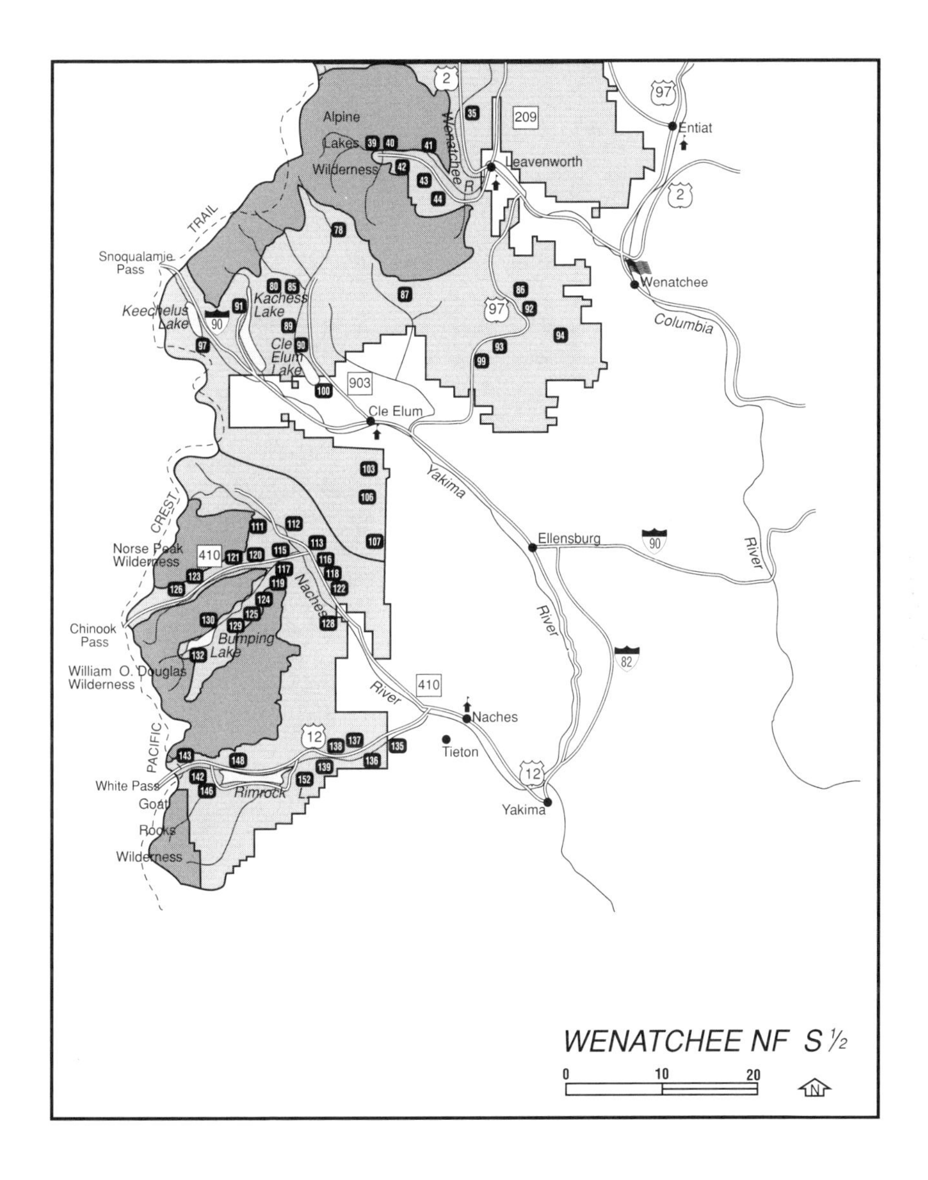
Alpine
Lakes
Wilderness
Wenatchee R
Leavenworth
Entiat
Snoqualamie Pass
TRAIL
Keechelus Lake
Kachess Lake
Cle Elum Lake
Wenatchee
Columbia
Cle Elum
Yakima
Ellensburg
River
CREST
Norse Peak Wilderness
Naches
Chinook Pass
Bumping Lake
William O. Douglas Wilderness
River
Naches
Tieton
PACIFIC
White Pass
Goat Rocks Wilderness
Rimrock L.
Yakima
WENATCHEE NF S 1/2
0
10
20
N

Map Location	Elevation	Picnic Units	Tent Units	Tent-Trailer Units	Fee	Drinking Water

Chelan Ranger District

Ramona Park

Access: 26 miles NW of Chelan via US 97, Cty. Rd. 23, FRs 5900, 8410.
Special Activities & Facilities: Hiking, motorbiking.

Map Location	Elevation	Picnic Units	Tent Units	Tent-Trailer Units	Fee	Drinking Water
15	1900		5			

South Navarre

Access: 33 miles NW of Chelan via St. Hwy. 150, FR 8200.
Special Activities & Facilities: Horse facilities, hiking, scenic.

Map Location	Elevation	Picnic Units	Tent Units	Tent-Trailer Units	Fee	Drinking Water
6	6000		4			

Lucerne

Access: 36.5 miles NW of Chelan via Lake Chelan.
Special Activities & Facilities: Boating, swimming, fishing, water skiing, hiking.

Map Location	Elevation	Picnic Units	Tent Units	Tent-Trailer Units	Fee	Drinking Water
4*	1100		2			

Prince Creek

Access: 30.8 miles NW of Chelan via Lake Chelan.
Special Activities & Facilities: Boating, swimming, fishing, waterskiing, hiking.

Map Location	Elevation	Picnic Units	Tent Units	Tent-Trailer Units	Fee	Drinking Water
5	1100		5			

Safety Harbor

Access: 22.1 mile NW of Chelan via Lake Chelan.
Special Activities & Facilities: Boating, swimming, fishing, waterskiing.

Map Location	Elevation	Picnic Units	Tent Units	Tent-Trailer Units	Fee	Drinking Water
9	1100		3			

Moore Point

Access: 6 miles S of Stehekin via Lake Chelan.
Special Activities & Facilities: Boating, swimming, fishing, waterskiing, trails, shelter.

Map Location	Elevation	Picnic Units	Tent Units	Tent-Trailer Units	Fee	Drinking Water
2	1100	1	4			

Big Creek

Access: 24 miles NW Chelan via Lake Chelan.
Special Activities & Facilities: Boating, swimming, shelter.

Map Location	Elevation	Picnic Units	Tent Units	Tent-Trailer Units	Fee	Drinking Water
7*	1100		4			

Map Location	Elevation	Picnic Units	Tent Units	Tent-Trailer Units	Fee	Drinking Water

Deer Point

Access: 18.9 miles NW of Chelan via Lake Chelan.
Special Activities & Facilities: Boating, swimming, fishing, waterskiing.

Map Location	Elevation	Picnic Units	Tent Units	Tent-Trailer Units	Fee	Drinking Water
11	*1100*		*4*			

Mitchell Creek

Access: 12.2 miles NW of Chelan via Lake Chelan.
Special Activities & Facilities: Boating, swimming, fishing, waterskiing.

Map Location	Elevation	Picnic Units	Tent Units	Tent-Trailer Units	Fee	Drinking Water
16	*1100*	*1*	*10*			

Refrigerator Harbor

Access: 36.3 miles NW of Chelan via Lake Chelan.
Special Activities & Facilities: Boating, hiking, fishing, waterskiing, swimming.

Map Location	Elevation	Picnic Units	Tent Units	Tent-Trailer Units	Fee	Drinking Water
*4**	*1100*		*4*			

Domke Lake

Access: 35.7 miles NW of Chelan via Lake Chelan and trail.
Special Activities &Facilities: Boat rental, hiking, fishing.

Map Location	Elevation	Picnic Units	Tent Units	Tent-Trailer Units	Fee	Drinking Water
*4**	*2200*		*6*			

Domke Falls

Access: 37.5 miles NW of Chelan via Lake Chelan.
Special Activities & Facilities: Boating, swimming, fishing, waterskiing.

Map Location	Elevation	Picnic Units	Tent Units	Tent-Trailer Units	Fee	Drinking Water
*4**	*1100*		*3*			

Holden

Access: 44.2 miles NW of Chelan via Lake Chelan, FR 8301.
Special Activities & Facilities: Scenic, hiking, entry to Glacier Peak Wilderness.

Map Location	Elevation	Picnic Units	Tent Units	Tent-Trailer Units	Fee	Drinking Water
1	*3200*		*2*			

Graham Harbor

Access: 28 miles NW of Chelan via Lake Chelan.
Special Activities & Facilities: Boating, swimming, shelter.

Map Location	Elevation	Picnic Units	Tent Units	Tent-Trailer Units	Fee	Drinking Water
*7**	*1100*		*5*			

Map Location	Elevation	Picnic Units	Tent Units	Tent-Trailer Units	Fee	Drinking Water

Entiat Ranger District

Pine Flat

Access: 15 miles NW of Entiat via Cty. Rd. 371, FR 5700.
Special Activities & Facilities: Fishing, riding, motorcycle trails, horses.

Map Location	Elevation	Picnic Units	Tent Units	Tent-Trailer Units	Fee	Drinking Water
33	1900	1	6	1	x	x

Fox Creek

Access: 28 miles NW of Entiat via Cty. Rd. 371, FR 51.
Special Activities & Facilities: Fishing.

Map Location	Elevation	Picnic Units	Tent Units	Tent-Trailer Units	Fee	Drinking Water
22	2300	1	15		x	x

Lake Creek

Access: 29 miles NW of Entiat via Cty. Rd. 371, FR 51.
Special Activities & Facilities: Fishing, trails.

Map Location	Elevation	Picnic Units	Tent Units	Tent-Trailer Units	Fee	Drinking Water
20	2400	1	15	2	x	x

Silver Falls

Access: 32 miles NW of Entiat via Cty. Rd. 371, FR 51.
Special Activities & Facilities: Fishing, trails.

Map Location	Elevation	Picnic Units	Tent Units	Tent-Trailer Units	Fee	Drinking Water
17	2400	7		31	x	x

North Fork

Access: 35 miles NW of Entiat via Cty. Rd. 371, FR 51.
Special Activities & Facilities: Fishing.

Map Location	Elevation	Picnic Units	Tent Units	Tent-Trailer Units	Fee	Drinking Water
14	2600		7	1	x	x

Cottonwood

Access: 39 miles NW of Entiat via Cty. Rd. 371, FR 51.
Special Activities & Facilities: Trails and berry picking.

Map Location	Elevation	Picnic Units	Tent Units	Tent-Trailer Units	Fee	Drinking Water
12	3000		23	2	x	x

Lake Wenatchee Ranger District

Nason Creek

Access: 19 miles NW of Leavenworth via US 2, St. Hwy. 207.
Special Activities & Facilities: Within 1 mile–riding horses, boating, swimming, waterskiing.

Map Location	Elevation	Picnic Units	Tent Units	Tent-Trailer Units	Fee	Drinking Water
31	1800		27[2]	45[2]	x	x

Map Location	Elevation	Picnic Units	Tent Units	Tent-Trailer Units	Fee	Drinking Water

Riverside

Access: 31 miles NW of Leavenworth via US 2, St. Hwy. 207, FR 6500.

Special Activities & Facilities: Fishing.

Map Location	Elevation	Picnic Units	Tent Units	Tent-Trailer Units	Fee	Drinking Water
28	2000		3	3		

Glacier View

Access: 25 miles NW of Leavenworth via US 2, St. Hwy. 207, FR 6607.

Special Activities & Facilities: Boating, swimming, fishing, waterskiing.

Map Location	Elevation	Picnic Units	Tent Units	Tent-Trailer Units	Fee	Drinking Water
30	1900		23		x	x

Soda Springs

Access: 33 miles NW of Leavenworth via US 2, St. Hwy. 207, FR 6500.

Special Activities & Facilities: Berry picking, fishing, nature trails, no trailers.

Map Location	Elevation	Picnic Units	Tent Units	Tent-Trailer Units	Fee	Drinking Water
27	2000		5			

Lake Creek

Access: 36 miles NW of Leavenworth via US 2, St. Hwy. 207, FR 6500.

Special Activities & Facilities: Fishing, berry picking.

Map Location	Elevation	Picnic Units	Tent Units	Tent-Trailer Units	Fee	Drinking Water
25	2300			8		

White River Falls

Access: 34 miles NW of Leavenworth via US 2, St. Hwy. 207, FR 6400.

Special Activities & Facilities: Fishing, entry to Glacier Peak Wilderness, no trailers.

Map Location	Elevation	Picnic Units	Tent Units	Tent-Trailer Units	Fee	Drinking Water
18	2100		5			

Whitepine

Access: 25 miles NW of Leavenworth via US 2.

Special Activities & Facilities: Fishing, berry picking.

Map Location	Elevation	Picnic Units	Tent Units	Tent-Trailer Units	Fee	Drinking Water
32	1900			5		

Map Location	*Elevation*	*Picnic Units*	*Tent Units*	*Tent-Trailer Units*	*Fee*	*Drinking Water*

Napeequa

Access: 31 miles NW of Leavenworth via US 2, St. Hwy. 207, FR 6400.
Special Activities & Facilities: Entrance to Glacier Peak Wilderness.

23	*2000*		*4*	2		

Goose Creek (Chiwawa River Drainage)

Access: 21 miles N of Leavenworth via St. Hwy. 209, Cty. Rd. 22, FR 6100.
Special Activities & Facilities: Fishing, motorcycle trails.

29	*2200*		*10*	*20*	*x*	*x*

Phelps Creek (Chiwawa River Drainage)

Access: 42 miles NW of Leavenworth via US 2, St. Hwy. 207, Cty. Rd. 22, FRs 62, 6200.
Special Activities & Facilities: Entrance to Glacier Peak Wilderness.

8	*2800*		*7*			

Chiwawa River Campgrounds

Access: Between 20-40 miles NW of Leavenworth via US 2, St. Hwy. 207, Cty. Rd. 22, FRs 62, 6200.
Note: The following additional sites are located within the Chiwawa River Drainage. They are generally lightly improved.

Alder Creek Horse Camp

*77**	*2400*			*6*		

Grouse Creek

*77**	*2400*	*(Group site for 50 people maximum, reservations.)*				

Finner Creek

*77**	*2500*			*3*		*x*

River Bend

*77**	*2500*			*5*		

Rock Creek

*77**	*2500*			*4*		

	Map Location	Elevation	Picnic Units	Tent Units	Tent-Trailer Units	Fee	Drinking Water
Schaeffer Creek							
	77*	2500			6		
Alkinson Flat							
	77*	2550			7		
Nineteen Mile							
	77*	2600			4		
Alpine Meadow							
	8*	2700			4		
Meadow Creek (Chiwawa River Drainage) Access: NW of Leavenworth via US 2, St. Hwy. 207, Cty. Rd. 22, FRs 62, 6300.							
	29*	2400			4		

Glacier Peak Wilderness, Wenatchee National Forest

Leavenworth Ranger District

Bridge Creek

Access: 9 miles SW of Leavenworth on FR 7600.
Special Activities & Facilities: Fishing, hiking, trailers to 19'.

	Map Location	Elevation	Picnic Units	Tent Units	Tent-Trailer Units	Fee	Drinking Water
	43	1900		6		x	x

Johnny Creek

Access: 12 miles W of Leavenworth on FR 7600.
Special Activities & Facilities: Fishing, trails.

	Map Location	Elevation	Picnic Units	Tent Units	Tent-Trailer Units	Fee	Drinking Water
♿	42	2300		8	58❷	x	x

Chatter Creek

Access: 16 miles W of Leavenworth on FR 7600.
Special Activities & Facilities: Fishing.

	Map Location	Elevation	Picnic Units	Tent Units	Tent-Trailer Units	Fee	Drinking Water
	40	2800	1	9	3	x	x

Tumwater

Access: 10 miles NW of Leavenworth via US 2.
Special Activities & Facilities: Fishing, trails.

	Map Location	Elevation	Picnic Units	Tent Units	Tent-Trailer Units	Fee	Drinking Water
♿	35	2000	5❸	27	53❷	x	x

Eightmile

Access: 8 miles SW of Leavenworth on FR 7600.
Special Activities & Facilities: Fishing, trails.

	Map Location	Elevation	Picnic Units	Tent Units	Tent-Trailer Units	Fee	Drinking Water
♿	44	1800		12	32❷	x	x

Ida Creek

Access: 14 miles W of Leavenworth on FR 7600.
Special Activities & Facilities: Fishing, trails.

	Map Location	Elevation	Picnic Units	Tent Units	Tent-Trailer Units	Fee	Drinking Water
♿	41	1900		5	5❸	x	x

Rock Island

Access: 17 miles W of Leavenworth on FR 7600.
Special Activities & Facilities: Fishing, trails.

	Map Location	Elevation	Picnic Units	Tent Units	Tent-Trailer Units	Fee	Drinking Water
♿	39	2900		12	10❸	x	x

Tronsen

Access: 23 miles S of Leavenworth via US 2, US 97.
Special Activities & Facilities: Trails, picnicking.

	Map Location	Elevation	Picnic Units	Tent Units	Tent-Trailer Units	Fee	Drinking Water
	92	3900	2	13	12	x	x

	Map Location	Elevation	Picnic Units	Tent Units	Tent-Trailer Units	Fee	Drinking Water

Bonanza

Access: 18 miles S of Leavenworth via US 2, US 97.
Special Activities & Facilities: Picnicking, trails.

	86	3000		4	1	x	x

Blackpine Creek Horse Camp

Access: 18 miles W of Leavenworth on FR 7600.
Special Activities & Facilities: Fishing, trails.

♿	39	3000		6[3]	2[3]	x	x

Cle Elum Ranger District

Crystal Springs

Access: 21 miles NW of Cle Elum via I-90, FR 54.
Special Activities & Facilities: Berries, mushrooms, fishing, community kitchen.

	97	2400	5	20	10	x	x

Kachess

Access: 26 miles NW of Cle Elum via I-90, FR 49.
Special Activities & Facilities: Group site available. Water sports, hiking.

	91	2300	34	91	91	x	x

Cle Elum River

Access: 18 miles NW of Cle Elum on Cty. Rd. 903.
Special Activities & Facilities: Fishing, small group sites.

	90	2200		2	33	x	x

Red Mountain

Access: 20 miles NW of Cle Elum on Cty. Rd. 903.
Special Activities & Facilities: Fishing, small group sites.

	89	2300		2	13		

Salmon La Sac

Access: 22 miles NW of Cle Elum on Cty. Rd. 903.
Special Activities & Facilities: 15-unit horse use camp, fishing, trailhead, community kitchen, 100 person group reservation site.

♿	85	2400	11[2]	30	80[2]	x	x

Fish Lake

Access: 33 miles NW of Cle Elum via Cty. Rd. 903, FR 4330.
Special Activities & Facilities: Hunting, trailhead, group camping, rough access road–no trailers.

Map Location	Elevation	Picnic Units	Tent Units	Tent-Trailer Units	Fee	Drinking Water
78	3400		10			

Wishpoosh

Access: 10 miles NW of Cle Elum on Cty. Rd. 903.
Special Activities & Facilities: Water recreation, fishing.

Map Location	Elevation	Picnic Units	Tent Units	Tent-Trailer Units	Fee	Drinking Water
100	2400	16	17	22	x	x

Owhi

Access: 26 miles NW of Cle Elum via Cty. Rd. 903, FR 46.
Special Activities & Facilities: Fishing, swimming, boating, trails, walk-in sites only.

Map Location	Elevation	Picnic Units	Tent Units	Tent-Trailer Units	Fee	Drinking Water
80	2800	6	22			

Tamarack Spring

Access: 26 miles S of Cle Elum via I-90, FRs 33, 3330, 3120.
Special Activities & Facilities: Horse riding, hunting.

Map Location	Elevation	Picnic Units	Tent Units	Tent-Trailer Units	Fee	Drinking Water
106	4700			3		x

Taneum

Access: 21 miles SE of Cle Elum via I-90, FR 33.
Special Activities & Facilities: Fishing, camping.

Map Location	Elevation	Picnic Units	Tent Units	Tent-Trailer Units	Fee	Drinking Water
103*	2400	16	2	13	x	x

Beverly

Access: 25 miles N of Cle Elum via Cty. Rd. 970, FR 9737.
Special Activities & Facilities: Mountain climbing, trails, horse trails.

Map Location	Elevation	Picnic Units	Tent Units	Tent-Trailer Units	Fee	Drinking Water
87	3200		13	3		

Mineral Springs

Access: 18 miles NE of Cle Elum via US 97.
Special Activities & Facilities: Fishing, hunting, berries, mushrooms, picnicking, winter recreation.

Map Location	Elevation	Picnic Units	Tent Units	Tent-Trailer Units	Fee	Drinking Water
99	2700		5	7	x	x

Map Location	Elevation	Picnic Units	Tent Units	Tent-Trailer Units	Fee	Drinking Water

Buck Meadows

Access: 36 miles S of Cle Elum on FR 31.

Special Activities & Facilities: Riding horses, lightly improved.

Map Location	Elevation	Picnic Units	Tent Units	Tent-Trailer Units	Fee	Drinking Water
107	4200			5		

Swauk

Access: 22 miles NE of Cle Elum via US 97.

Special Activities & Facilities: Fishing, mushrooms, hunting, group picnics, cross-country skiing.

Map Location	Elevation	Picnic Units	Tent Units	Tent-Trailer Units	Fee	Drinking Water
93	3200	34		23	x	x

Haney Meadows

Access: 26 miles NE of Cle Elum via US 97, FR 9712.

Special Activities & Facilities: Horse trails, hunting, mountain biking.

Map Location	Elevation	Picnic Units	Tent Units	Tent-Trailer Units	Fee	Drinking Water
94	5100			16		

Ice Water

Access: 20 miles S of Cle Elum via FR 33.

Special Activities & Facilities: Motorcycle trails, fishing, hunting.

Map Location	Elevation	Picnic Units	Tent Units	Tent-Trailer Units	Fee	Drinking Water
103*	2400			17		

Naches Ranger District

Windy Point

Access: 13 miles W of Naches via US 12.

Special Activities & Facilities: Fishing.

Map Location	Elevation	Picnic Units	Tent Units	Tent-Trailer Units	Fee	Drinking Water
135	2000			15	x	x

Willows

Access: 19 miles W of Naches via US 12.

Special Activities & Facilities: Fishing.

Map Location	Elevation	Picnic Units	Tent Units	Tent-Trailer Units	Fee	Drinking Water
136	2400			16	x	x

Wild Rose

Access: 20 miles SW of Naches via US 12.

Special Activities & Facilities: Fishing, picnicking.

Map Location	Elevation	Picnic Units	Tent Units	Tent-Trailer Units	Fee	Drinking Water
137	2400			8		

River Bend

Access: 21 miles SW of Naches via US 12.
Special Activities & Facilities: Fishing.

Map Location	Elevation	Picnic Units	Tent Units	Tent-Trailer Units	Fee	Drinking Water
138	2500		6		x	x

Hause Creek

Access: 22 miles SW of Naches via US 12.
Special Activities & Facilities: Fishing, barrier free.

	Map Location	Elevation	Picnic Units	Tent Units	Tent-Trailer Units	Fee	Drinking Water
♿	139	2500			42❷	x	x

South Fork Tieton

Access: 27 miles SW of Naches via US 12, Cty. Rd. 1200, FR 1203.
Special Activities & Facilities: Fishing, hiking.

Map Location	Elevation	Picnic Units	Tent Units	Tent-Trailer Units	Fee	Drinking Water
152	3000			15		

Indian Creek

Access: 32 miles SW of Naches via US 12.
Special Activities & Facilities: Near Rim Rock Lake, hiking, boating, fishing.

Map Location	Elevation	Picnic Units	Tent Units	Tent-Trailer Units	Fee	Drinking Water
148	3000			39	x	x

Dog Lake

Access: 22 miles NE of Packwood via US 12.
Special Activities & Facilities: Fishing, boating, hiking, RVs to 16'.

Map Location	Elevation	Picnic Units	Tent Units	Tent-Trailer Units	Fee	Drinking Water
142	4300			8		

White Pass Lake

Access: 19 miles NE of Packwood via US 12.
Special Activities & Facilities: Trailhead to PCT, boating, fly-fishing only, hiking.

Map Location	Elevation	Picnic Units	Tent Units	Tent-Trailer Units	Fee	Drinking Water
143	4500			16		

White Pass Lake Horse Camp

Access: 19 miles NE of Packwood via US 12.
Special Activities & Facilities: Hunting, trails.

Map Location	Elevation	Picnic Units	Tent Units	Tent-Trailer Units	Fee	Drinking Water
143	4500			18		

	Map Location	Elevation	Picnic Units	Tent Units	Tent-Trailer Units	Fee	Drinking Water

Clear Lake

Access: 37 miles SW of Naches via US 12, Cty. Rd. 1200, FR 1200-840.
Special Activities & Facilities: Fishing, boating, includes group reservation area, barrier-free toilet.

♿	*146*	*3100*	*4*		*63* ❸	*x*	*x*

Peninsula

Access: 26 miles SW of Naches via US 12, off Cty. Rd. 1200.
Special Activities & Facilities: Boating, fishing, waterskiing, on Rim Rock Lake.

	152	*3000*			*19*		

Cottonwood

Access: 22 miles NW of Naches on St. Hwy. 410.
Special Activities & Facilities: Fishing.

	128	*2300*			*16*		

Sawmill Flat

Access: 25 miles NW of Naches on St. Hwy. 410.
Special Activities & Facilities: Fishing, shelter.

♿	*118*	*2500*	*10* ❶		*25* ❷	*x*	*x*

Little Naches

Access: 26 miles NW of Naches on St. Hwy. 410.
Special Activities & Facilities: Fishing

	113	*2500*			*23*	*x*	*x*

Kaner Flat

Access: 32 miles NW of Naches via St. Hwy. 410, FR 1900.
Special Activities & Facilities: Motorcycle trails, group reservations, hiking, near fish ladder.

	112	*2600*	*27*		*41*	*x*	*x*

Soda Springs

Access: 38 miles NW of Naches via St. Hwy. 410, Cty. Rd. 1800.
Special Activities & Facilities: Fishing, geological, shelter, hiking.

	124	*3100*	*6*		*26*	*x*	*x*

<table>
<tr><th>Map Location</th><th>Elevation</th><th>Picnic Units</th><th>Tent Units</th><th>Tent-Trailer Units</th><th>Fee</th><th>Drinking Water</th></tr>
<tr><td colspan="7">Cougar Flat
Access: 39 miles NW of Naches via St. Hwy. 410, Cty. Rd. 1800.
Special Activities & Facilities: Fishing, hiking.</td></tr>
<tr><td>125</td><td>3100</td><td></td><td></td><td>12</td><td>x</td><td>x</td></tr>
<tr><td colspan="7">Bumping Crossing
Access: 44 miles NW of Naches via St. Hwy. 410, Cty. Rd. 1800.
Special Activities & Facilities: Fishing, hiking.</td></tr>
<tr><td>129</td><td>3200</td><td></td><td></td><td>12</td><td></td><td></td></tr>
<tr><td colspan="7">Bumping Lake
Access: 44 miles NW of Naches via St. Hwy. 410, Cty. Rd. 1800.
Special Activities & Facilities: Sailing, boating, fishing.</td></tr>
<tr><td>132</td><td>3400</td><td></td><td></td><td>45</td><td>x</td><td>x</td></tr>
<tr><td colspan="7">Bumping Dam
Access: 43 miles NW of Naches via St. Hwy. 410, Cty. Rd. 1800.
Special Activities & Facilities: Fishing, boating, sailing.</td></tr>
<tr><td>130</td><td>3400</td><td></td><td></td><td>23</td><td>x</td><td></td></tr>
<tr><td colspan="7">Halfway Flat
Access: 28 miles NW of Naches via St. Hwy. 410, FR 1704.
Special Activities & Facilities: Fishing.</td></tr>
<tr><td>116</td><td>2500</td><td></td><td></td><td>12</td><td></td><td></td></tr>
<tr><td colspan="7">Boulder Cave
Access: 26 miles NW of Naches via St. Hwy. 410, FR 1704.
Special Activities & Facilities: Fishing, hiking, cave exploring, shelter, barrier-free trail and facilities, interpretive program.</td></tr>
<tr><td>122</td><td>2500</td><td>8</td><td></td><td></td><td></td><td></td></tr>
<tr><td colspan="7">Indian Flat
Access: 31 miles NW of Naches via St. Hwy. 410.
Special Activities & Facilities: Fishing, hiking.</td></tr>
<tr><td>115</td><td>2600</td><td></td><td></td><td>11</td><td>x</td><td>x</td></tr>
<tr><td colspan="7">Cedar Springs
Access: 33 miles NW of Naches via St. Hwy. 410, Cty. Rd. 1800.
Special Activities & Facilities: Fishing, hiking.</td></tr>
<tr><td>119</td><td>2800</td><td></td><td></td><td>15</td><td></td><td></td></tr>
</table>

Map Location	Elevation	Picnic Units	Tent Units	Tent-Trailer Units	Fee	Drinking Water

American Forks

Access: 32 miles NW of Naches via St. Hwy. 410.
Special Activities & Facilities: Fishing, hiking, shelter.

Map Location	Elevation	Picnic Units	Tent Units	Tent-Trailer Units	Fee	Drinking Water
117	*2800*	*12*		*16*	*x*	*x*

Lodge Pole

Access: 45 miles NW of Naches via St. Hwy. 410.
Special Activities & Facilities: Fishing, berry picking.

Map Location	Elevation	Picnic Units	Tent Units	Tent-Trailer Units	Fee	Drinking Water
126	*3500*			*34*	*x*	*x*

Pleasant Valley

Access: 41 miles NW of Naches via St. Hwy. 410.
Special Activities & Facilities: Fishing, hiking, shelter.

Map Location	Elevation	Picnic Units	Tent Units	Tent-Trailer Units	Fee	Drinking Water
123	*3300*	*5*		*19*	*x*	*x*

Hellscrossing

Access: 38 miles NW of Naches via St. Hwy. 410.
Special Activities & Facilities: Fishing, hiking.

Map Location	Elevation	Picnic Units	Tent Units	Tent-Trailer Units	Fee	Drinking Water
121	*3200*			*18*	*x*	*x*

Pine Needle

Access: 31 miles NW of Naches via St. Hwy. 410.
Special Activities & Facilities: Fishing, reservations and fee required for groups.

Map Location	Elevation	Picnic Units	Tent Units	Tent-Trailer Units	Fee	Drinking Water
120	*3000*			*8*	*x*	

Crow Creek

Access: 32 miles NW of Naches via St. Hwy. 410, FRs 1900, 1904.
Special Activities & Facilities: Hunting, fishing, ORV trails.

Map Location	Elevation	Picnic Units	Tent Units	Tent-Trailer Units	Fee	Drinking Water
111	*2900*			*15*		

*Sites in close proximity to others

Handicapped Accessibility Codes
- ❶ Fully Accessible
- ❷ Usable
- ❸ Difficult

See page 7 for full description.

Willamette National Forest

Mt. Washington, Willamette National Forest. Photo by Gerald W. Gause.

Recreational opportunities abound on the forest. There are 1300 miles of trail, 1200 camp sites, and 380,000 acres of wilderness in eight Wilderness Areas. Mt. Jefferson, among the most beautiful mountains in the world, looks down upon deep blue lakes, while vast plains of lava in the Mt. Washington Wilderness create a different, desolate landscape. Active glaciers lie on the upper slopes of each of the imposing Three Sisters Mountains. The Pacific Crest National Scenic Trail follows the crest of the Cascades through the wildernesses. Six major reservoirs provide hydroelectric power and flood control, as well as recreation activities.

Special places of interest include breathtaking views from the McKenzie Pass Scenic Highway and Scott Lake; Proxy Falls; Clear Lake with its submerged forest; the plunges of the McKenzie River over Sahalie and Koosah falls; McKenzie River trail; McKenzie River Canyon; the appearing and disappearing Fish Lake; Mt. Washington, framed in Big Lake; 286-foot Salt Creek Falls; Sawyers Lava Caves; crystal clear Waldo Lake, one of the purest in the world; Detroit Dam and reservoir; winter sports areas at Willamette Pass and Hoodoo.

Further information about recreation opportunities, campground location and facilities, as well as current maps of the area, are available at the following offices:

Willamette National Forest
Supervisor's Office
211 E. 7th Ave.
P.O. Box 10607
Eugene, OR 97440
(503) 465-6521
recording 465-6561

Blue River Ranger District
Blue River, OR 97413
(503) 822-3317

Detroit Ranger District
HC-73, Box 320
Mill City, OR 97360
(503) 854-3366

Lowell Ranger District
Lowell, OR 97452
(503) 937-2129

McKenzie Ranger District
McKenzie Bridge, OR 97413
(503) 822-3381

Oakridge Ranger District
46375 Highway 58
Westfir, OR 97492
(503) 782-2291

Rigdon Ranger District
49098 Salmon Creek Road
Oakridge, OR 97463
(503) 782-2283

Sweet Home Ranger District
3225 Highway 20
Sweet Home, OR 97386
(503) 367-5168

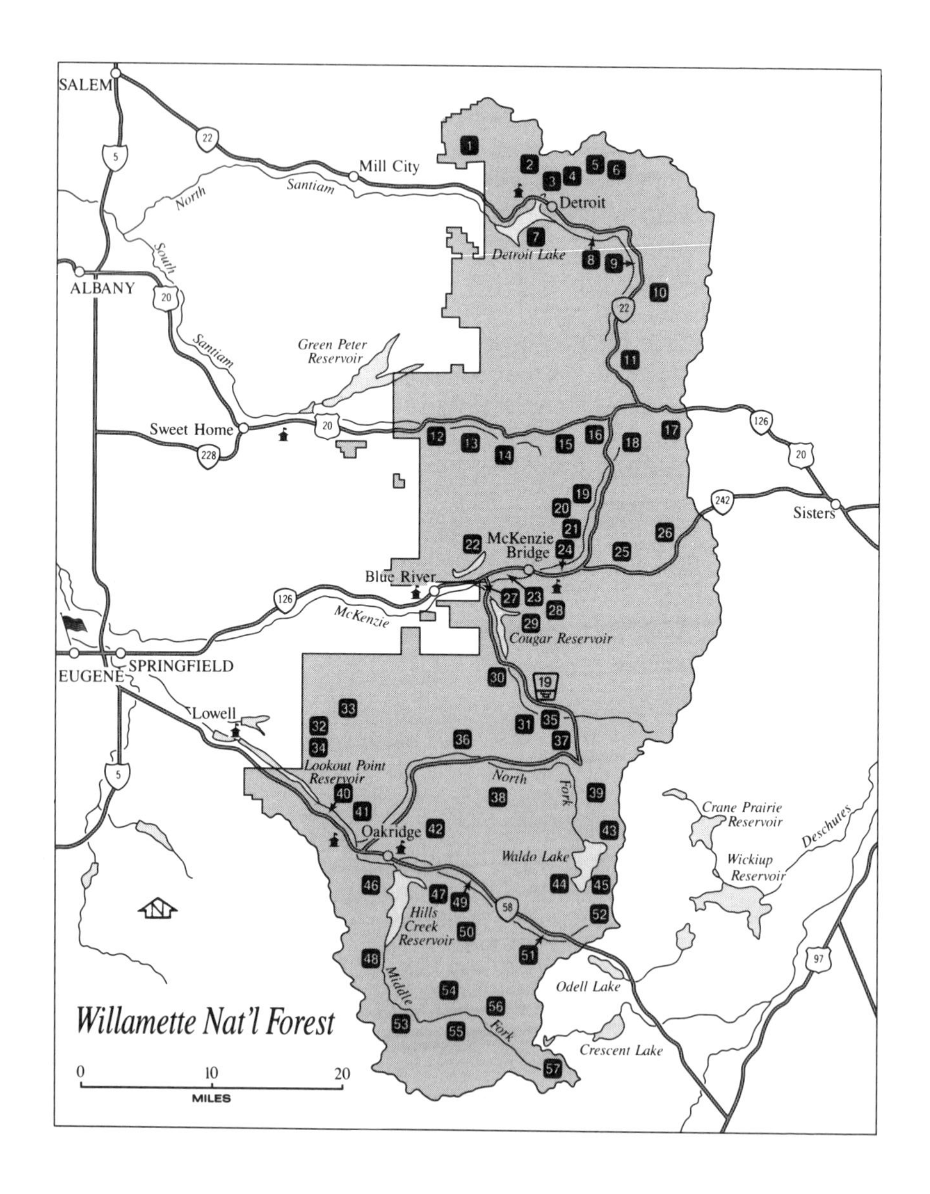
SALEM
Mill City
North
Santiam
Detroit
Detroit Lake
South
ALBANY
Santiam
Green Peter
Reservoir
Sweet Home
McKenzie
Bridge
Blue River
Sisters
McKenzie
Cougar Reservoir
EUGENE
SPRINGFIELD
Lowell
Lookout Point
Reservoir
North
Fork
Oakridge
Waldo Lake
Hills
Creek
Reservoir
Crane Prairie
Reservoir
Wickiup
Reservoir
Deschutes
Middle
Fork
Odell Lake
Crescent Lake
Willamette Nat'l Forest
0
10
20
MILES

WILLAMETTE NATIONAL FOREST

Alder Springs
Access: 12 miles E of McKenzie Bridge via St. Hwys. 126, 242.
Special Activities & Facilities: Fishing, hiking.

Map Location	Elevation	Picnic Units	Tent Units	Tent-Trailer Units	Fee	Drinking Water
26	3600		6			

Bedrock
Access: 16 miles NE of Lowell via Cty. Rds. 6220, 6204, FR 18.
Special Activities & Facilities: Swimming, fishing,hiking.

Map Location	Elevation	Picnic Units	Tent Units	Tent-Trailer Units	Fee	Drinking Water
33	1100		6	13[3]	x	x

Big Lake
Access: 4 miles S of Santiam Pass via US 20, FR 2690.
Special Activities & Facilities: Fishing, swimming, waterskiing, boating.

Map Location	Elevation	Picnic Units	Tent Units	Tent-Trailer Units	Fee	Drinking Water
17	4650	5		21	x	x

Big Lake West
Access: 4 miles S of Santiam Pass via US 20, FR 2690.
Special Activities & Facilities: Boating, waterskiing, hiking.

Map Location	Elevation	Picnic Units	Tent Units	Tent-Trailer Units	Fee	Drinking Water
17	4650		13			

Big Meadows Horsecamp
Access: 27 miles SE of Detroit via Hwy. 22, FRs 2267, 2257.
Special Activities & Facilities: Hiking, fishing, horse use.

Map Location	Elevation	Picnic Units	Tent Units	Tent-Trailer Units	Fee	Drinking Water
11	3600			9	x	x

Big Pool
Access: 14 miles E of Lowell via Cty. Rds. 6220, 6204, FR 18.
Special Activities & Facilities: Swimming, fishing, hiking.

Map Location	Elevation	Picnic Units	Tent Units	Tent-Trailer Units	Fee	Drinking Water
32	1000		3	2	x	x

Black Canyon
Access: 8 miles W of Oakridge via St. Hwy. 58.
Special Activities & Facilities: Boating, fishing, hiking, waterskiing, swimming, Lookout Point Reservoir.

Map Location	Elevation	Picnic Units	Tent Units	Tent-Trailer Units	Fee	Drinking Water
40	1000	3[1]	13	59[1]	x	x

Blue Pool
Access: 9 miles E of Oakridge via St. Hwy. 58.
Special Activities & Facilities: Swimming, fishing, barrier-free toilet.

Map Location	Elevation	Picnic Units	Tent Units	Tent-Trailer Units	Fee	Drinking Water
49	1900	5		24	x	x

	Map Location	Elevation	Picnic Units	Tent Units	Tent-Trailer Units	Fee	Drinking Water

Box Canyon Horsecamp

Access: 30.5 miles SE of Blue River via St. Hwy. 126, FR 19.
Special Activities & Facilities: Hiking, corrals.

	Map Location	Elevation	Picnic Units	Tent Units	Tent-Trailer Units	Fee	Drinking Water
	37	*3600*			*14*		

Breitenbush

Access: 10 miles NE of Detroit via FR 46.
Special Activities & Facilities: Swimming, fishing, hiking.

	Map Location	Elevation	Picnic Units	Tent Units	Tent-Trailer Units	Fee	Drinking Water
	6	*2200*			*30*	*x*	*x*

Broken Bowl

Access: 12 miles NE of Lowell via Cty. Rds. 6220, 6204, FR 18.
Special Activities & Facilities: Picnicking, fishing, swimming, group sites.

	Map Location	Elevation	Picnic Units	Tent Units	Tent-Trailer Units	Fee	Drinking Water
♿	*32*	*1000*	*7*	*3*	*6*❸	*x*	*x*

Campers Flat

Access: 23 miles S of Oakridge via FR 21.
Special Activities & Facilities: Camping, fishing, picnicking.

	Map Location	Elevation	Picnic Units	Tent Units	Tent-Trailer Units	Fee	Drinking Water
	53	*2000*		*5*		*x*	*x*

Clear Lake Picnic Area

Access: 3 miles S of Hwys. 20/126 junction via Hwy. 126.
Special Activities & Facilities: Nonmotorized boating, fishing.

	Map Location	Elevation	Picnic Units	Tent Units	Tent-Trailer Units	Fee	Drinking Water
	18	*3100*	*17*				

Cleator Bend

Access: 9 miles NE of Detroit on FR 46.
Special Activities & Facilities: Fishing, hiking.

	Map Location	Elevation	Picnic Units	Tent Units	Tent-Trailer Units	Fee	Drinking Water
	5	*2200*			*9*	*x*	*x*

Coldwater Cove

Access: 18 miles NE of McKenzie Bridge via St. Hwy. 126.
Special Activities & Facilities: Hiking, nonmotorized boating, fishing on Clear Lake.

	Map Location	Elevation	Picnic Units	Tent Units	Tent-Trailer Units	Fee	Drinking Water
♿	*18*	*3100*			*35*❷	*x*	*x*

C.T. Beach Picnic Area/Boat Launch

Access: 5 miles SE of Oakridge on FR 23.
Special Activities & Facilities: Picnicking, boating, fishing on Hills Cr Reservoir.

	Map Location	Elevation	Picnic Units	Tent Units	Tent-Trailer Units	Fee	Drinking Water
	47	*1600*	*8*				

<table>
<tr><th></th><th>Map Location</th><th>Elevation</th><th>Picnic Units</th><th>Tent Units</th><th>Tent-Trailer Units</th><th>Fee</th><th>Drinking Water</th></tr>
<tr><td colspan="8">Delta
Access: 6 miles E of Blue River via St. Hwy. 126, FRs 19, 19400.
Special Activities & Facilities: Fishing, nature trail.</td></tr>
<tr><td>♿</td><td>27</td><td>1200</td><td>3</td><td></td><td>39❷</td><td>x</td><td>x</td></tr>
<tr><td colspan="8">Dolly Varden
Access: 12 miles NE of Lowell via Cty. Rds. 6220, 6204, FR 18.
Special Activities & Facilities: Picnicking, hiking, swimming, fishing, camping.</td></tr>
<tr><td></td><td>32</td><td>1000</td><td></td><td>2</td><td>4</td><td></td><td></td></tr>
<tr><td colspan="8">Echo Picnic Area/Boat Launch
Access: 9 miles SE of Blue River via St. Hwy. 126, FRs 19, 1993.
Special Activities & Facilities: Boating, swimming, fishing, waterskiing, hiking.</td></tr>
<tr><td></td><td>29</td><td>1700</td><td>7</td><td></td><td></td><td></td><td></td></tr>
<tr><td colspan="8">Fernview
Access: 23 miles E of Sweet Home via US 20.
Special Activities & Facilities: Fishing, swimming, hiking.</td></tr>
<tr><td></td><td>13</td><td>1400</td><td></td><td>2</td><td>9</td><td>x</td><td>x</td></tr>
<tr><td colspan="8">Ferrin
Access: 2 miles W of Oakridge via St. Hwy. 58.
Special Activities & Facilities: Fishing, hiking, boating</td></tr>
<tr><td></td><td>41</td><td>1200</td><td>7</td><td></td><td></td><td></td><td></td></tr>
<tr><td colspan="8">Fish Lake
Access: 22 miles NE of McKenzie Bridge via St. Hwy. 126.
Special Activities & Facilities: Camping, picnicking, low water in summer.</td></tr>
<tr><td></td><td>16</td><td>3200</td><td></td><td></td><td>8</td><td></td><td>x</td></tr>
<tr><td colspan="8">French Pete
Access: 20 miles SE of Blue River via St. Hwy. 126, FR 19.
Special Activities & Facilities: Camping, picnicking, fishing, hiking.</td></tr>
<tr><td></td><td>30</td><td>1800</td><td></td><td></td><td>17</td><td>x</td><td>x</td></tr>
</table>

Scott Lake, Willamette National Forest

Frissell Crossing

Access: 31 miles SE of Blue River via St. Hwy. 126, FR 19.
Special Activities & Facilities: Camping, picnicking, fishing, hiking.

Map Location	Elevation	Picnic Units	Tent Units	Tent-Trailer Units	Fee	Drinking Water
35	2600			12	x	x

Gold Lake

Access: 28 miles E of Oakridge via St. Hwy. 58, FRs 58, 500.
Special Activities & Facilities: Nonmotorized boating, fly fishing, barrier-free toilet.

♿

Map Location	Elevation	Picnic Units	Tent Units	Tent-Trailer Units	Fee	Drinking Water
52	4800	5		20	x	x

Hampton

Access: 10 miles W of Oakridge via St. Hwy. 58.
Special Activities & Facilities: Boating, swimming, fishing, water skiing, Lookout Point Reservoir.

Map Location	Elevation	Picnic Units	Tent Units	Tent-Trailer Units	Fee	Drinking Water
40	1100			5	x	x

Harralson Horse Camp

Access: 35 miles NE of Oakridge via St. Hwy. 58, FRs 5897, 5898.
Special Activities & Facilities: Trail access to Waldo Lake area.

Map Location	Elevation	Picnic Units	Tent Units	Tent-Trailer Units	Fee	Drinking Water
43	5500			6		

Homestead

Access: 27 miles SE of Blue River via St. Hwy. 126, FR 19.
Special Activities & Facilities: Fishing.

Map Location	Elevation	Picnic Units	Tent Units	Tent-Trailer Units	Fee	Drinking Water
31	2200		7			

Hoover

Access: 5.5 miles SE of Detroit via FR 10.
Special Activities & Facilities: Boat ramp, boating, waterskiing, fishing, adjacent group area S side of Detroit Reservoir, hiking.

♿

Map Location	Elevation	Picnic Units	Tent Units	Tent-Trailer Units	Fee	Drinking Water
7	1600		2	35[3]	x	x

House Rock

Access: 26 miles E of Sweet Home via US 20.
Special Activities & Facilities: Swimming, fishing, hiking.

Map Location	Elevation	Picnic Units	Tent Units	Tent-Trailer Units	Fee	Drinking Water
14	1800	6	11	4	x	x

Map Location	Elevation	Picnic Units	Tent Units	Tent-Trailer Units	Fee	Drinking Water

Horse Creek

Access: 1 mile SE Of McKenzie Bridge via Horse Creek Rd.
Special Activities and Facilities: Group Camping.

	1200			21	x	x

Humbug

Access: 5 miles NE of Detroit on FR 46.
Special Activities & Facilities: Fishing, hiking.

4	1800			21	x	x

Ice Cap Creek

Access: 19 miles NE of McKenzie Bridge via St. Hwy. 126.
Special Activities & Facilities: Fishing, hiking.

19	3000	2	8	14	x	x

Indigo Springs

Access: 31 miles SE of Oakridge on FR 21.
Special Activities & Facilities: Fishing, hiking.

56	2800		2	1		

Islet

Access: 37 miles E of Oakridge via St. Hwy. 58, FRs 5897 & 5898.
Special Activities & Facilities: Fishing, boating, hiking, swimming.

43	5400			55	x	x

Kiahanie

Access: 18 miles NE of Westfir on FR 19.
Special Activities & Facilities: Camping, picnicking, fishing, RVs to 16'.

36	2200			21	x	x

Lake's End (Boat-in access)

Access: 13 miles NE of McKenzie Bridge via Hwy. 126, FR 730.
Special Activities & Facilities: Boating, swimming, fishing, Smith Reservoir.

20	3000		17			

Map Location	Elevation	Picnic Units	Tent Units	Tent-Trailer Units	Fee	Drinking Water

Limberlost

Access: 5 miles E of McKenzie Bridge via St. Hwys. 126, 242.
Special Activities & Facilities: Fishing.

Map Location	Elevation	Picnic Units	Tent Units	Tent-Trailer Units	Fee	Drinking Water
25	1800		12			

Lost Prairie

Access: 37 miles E of Sweet Home via US 20.
Special Activities & Facilities: Camping, picnicking, hiking.

Map Location	Elevation	Picnic Units	Tent Units	Tent-Trailer Units	Fee	Drinking Water
15	3300	6	2	2	x	x

McKenzie Bridge

Access: 1 mile W of McKenzie Bridge via St. Hwy. 126.
Special Activities & Facilities: Fishing on McKenzie River.

Map Location	Elevation	Picnic Units	Tent Units	Tent-Trailer Units	Fee	Drinking Water
23	1400	5		20	x	x

Marion Forks

Access: 16 miles SE of Detroit via St. Hwy. 22.
Special Activities & Facilities: Fishing, hiking.

Map Location	Elevation	Picnic Units	Tent Units	Tent-Trailer Units	Fee	Drinking Water
10	2500			15	x	x

Mona

Access: 7 miles NE of Blue River via St. Hwy. 126, FRs 15, 120.
Special Activities & Facilities: Boating, swimming, fishing, waterskiing, on Blue River Lake.

Map Location	Elevation	Picnic Units	Tent Units	Tent-Trailer Units	Fee	Drinking Water
♿ 22	1360			23 ❸	x	x

North Waldo

Access: 36 miles E of Oakridge, via St. Hwy. 58, FRs 5897, 5898.
Special Activities & Facilities: Boating, swimming, fishing, hiking.

Map Location	Elevation	Picnic Units	Tent Units	Tent-Trailer Units	Fee	Drinking Water
43	5400	6		58	x	x

Olallie

Access: 11 miles NE of McKenzie Bridge via St. Hwy. 126.
Special Activities & Facilities: Fishing.

Map Location	Elevation	Picnic Units	Tent Units	Tent-Trailer Units	Fee	Drinking Water
21	2000			17	x	x

Packard Creek

Access: 7 miles S of Oakridge on FR 21.
Special Activities & Facilities: Boating, swimming, fishing, waterskiing, Hills Cr Reservoir, hiking.

Map Location	*Elevation*	*Picnic Units*	*Tent Units*	*Tent-Trailer Units*	*Fee*	*Drinking Water*
46	1600	7		33	x	x

Paradise

Access: 4 miles E of McKenzie Bridge via St. Hwy. 126.
Special Activities & Facilities: Fishing, boating, hiking, McKenzie River.

Map Location	*Elevation*	*Picnic Units*	*Tent Units*	*Tent-Trailer Units*	*Fee*	*Drinking Water*
24	1600	5		64	x	x

Piety Island

Access: By boat.
Special Activities & Facilities: Boating, swimming, fishing, waterskiing, on Detroit Reservoir.

Map Location	*Elevation*	*Picnic Units*	*Tent Units*	*Tent-Trailer Units*	*Fee*	*Drinking Water*
7	1600		11			

Puma

Access: 18 miles NE of Lowell via Cty. Rds. 6220, 6204, FR 18.
Special Activities & Facilities: Swimming, fishing, hiking.

Map Location	*Elevation*	*Picnic Units*	*Tent Units*	*Tent-Trailer Units*	*Fee*	*Drinking Water*
♿ 33	1100		1	10❸	x	x

Riverside

Access: 17 miles SE of Detroit via St. Hwy. 22.
Special Activities & Facilities: Fishing, hiking.

Map Location	*Elevation*	*Picnic Units*	*Tent Units*	*Tent-Trailer Units*	*Fee*	*Drinking Water*
9	2400			37	x	x

Roaring River

Access: 32 miles SE of Blue River via St. Hwy. 126, FR 19.
Special Activities & Facilities: Camping, fishing, group site-reservations required. Maximum group size is 50.

Map Location	*Elevation*	*Picnic Units*	*Tent Units*	*Tent-Trailer Units*	*Fee*	*Drinking Water*
35	2600		5			

Sacandaga

Access: 26 miles SE of Oakridge on FR 21.
Special Activities & Facilities: Fishing.

Map Location	*Elevation*	*Picnic Units*	*Tent Units*	*Tent-Trailer Units*	*Fee*	*Drinking Water*
55	2400			17		

Salmon Creek Falls

Access: 4 miles E of Oakridge on FR 24.
Special Activities & Facilities: Fishing, barrier-free toilet.

	Map Location	Elevation	Picnic Units	Tent Units	Tent-Trailer Units	Fee	Drinking Water
♿	42	1520	3		14	x	x

Salt Creek Falls

Access: 23 miles SE of Oakridge via St. Hwy. 58.
Special Activities & Facilities: Fishing, 2nd highest waterfall in Oregon.

	Map Location	Elevation	Picnic Units	Tent Units	Tent-Trailer Units	Fee	Drinking Water
	51	4000	15				

Sand Prairie

Access: 14 miles S of Oakridge on FR 21.
Special Activities & Facilities: Boating, swimming, fishing, Hills Creek Reservoir, launching ramp.

	Map Location	Elevation	Picnic Units	Tent Units	Tent-Trailer Units	Fee	Drinking Water
	48	1600			21	x	x

Secret

Access: 21 miles S of Oakridge on FR 21.
Special Activities & Facilities: Fishing.

	Map Location	Elevation	Picnic Units	Tent Units	Tent-Trailer Units	Fee	Drinking Water
	53	2000			6		

Shadow Bay

Access: 31 miles E of Oakridge via St. Hwy. 58, FRs 5897 & 5896.
Special Activities & Facilities: Reservations for groups, swimming, fishing, hiking, boating.

	Map Location	Elevation	Picnic Units	Tent Units	Tent-Trailer Units	Fee	Drinking Water
	45	5400			92	x	x

Shady Cove

Access: 19 miles NE of Mechama on Little North Santiam Rd.
Special Activities & Facilities: Fishing, hiking.

	Map Location	Elevation	Picnic Units	Tent Units	Tent-Trailer Units	Fee	Drinking Water
	1	1500			11		

Shady Dell

Access: 5 miles W of Oakridge via St. Hwy. 58.
Special Activities & Facilities: Fishing.

	Map Location	Elevation	Picnic Units	Tent Units	Tent-Trailer Units	Fee	Drinking Water
♿	40	1000		6	32	x	x

Map Location	Elevation	Picnic Units	Tent Units	Tent-Trailer Units	Fee	Drinking Water

Skookum Creek

Access: 35 miles NE of Westfir via FRs 19, 1957.
Special Activities & Facilities: Hiking, horse facilities.

39	*4500*		*9*			*x*

Slide Creek

Access: 17 miles SE of Blue River via St. Hwy. 126, FRs 19, 1993, 1994, 500.
Special Activities & Facilities: Boating, swimming, fishing, waterskiing, Cougar Reservoir.

29	*1700*			*16*	*x*	*x*

Southshore

Access: 8 miles S of Detroit on FR 10.
Special Activities & Facilities: Boating, swimming, fishing, waterskiing, hiking, boat ramp.

♿	*7*	*1600*	*8*	*8*	*24❸*	*x*	*x*

Timpanogas Lake

Access: 43 miles SE of Oakridge via FRs 21, 2154.
Special Activities & Facilities: Nonmotorized boating, swimming, fishing, hiking.

57	*5200*			*10*		*x*

Trail Bridge

Access: 13 miles NE of McKenzie Bridge via St. Hwy. 126, FR 730.
Special Activities & Facilities: Boating, swimming, fishing, hiking, Trail Bridge Reservoir.

21	*2000*			*26*	*x*	*x*

Trout Creek

Access: 19 miles E of Sweethome via US 20.
Special Activities & Facilities: Swimming, fishing.

12	*1300*		*4*	*20*	*x*	*x*

Twin Springs

Access: 29 miles SE of Blue River via St. Hwy. 126, FR 19.
Special Activities & Facilities: Camping, picnicking, fishing.

31	*2400*		*3*	*5*		

Map Location	*Elevation*	*Picnic Units*	*Tent Units*	*Tent-Trailer Units*	*Fee*	*Drinking Water*

Upper Arm

Access: 1 mile NE of Detroit on FR 46.
Special Activities & Facilities: Boating, Detroit Reservoir, swimming, fishing, waterskiing.

3	*1600*		*2*	*3*		*x*

Whispering Falls

Access: 8 miles SE of Detroit via St. Hwy. 22.
Special Activities & Facilities: Fishing, N. Santiam, hiking.

8	*1900*			*16*	*x*	*x*

Winberry

Access: 12 miles E of Lowell, via Cty. Rds. 6220, 6245, FR 1802.
Special Activities & Facilities: Fishing, hiking.

34	*1900*		*4*	*2*	*x*	*x*

Yukwah

Access19 miles E of Sweet Home via US 20.
Special Activities & Facilities: Hiking, swimming, fishing.

12	*1300*			*20*	*x*	*x*

Handicapped Accessibility Codes
- ❶ Fully Accessible
- ❷ Usable
- ❸ Difficult

See page 7 for full description.

Winema National Forest

Winema National Forest

The Winema National Forest, the newest in Oregon, was created in 1961 from portions of the former Klamath Indian Reservation and adjacent forests. History records a visit to the area by Peter Ogden of the Hudson's Bay Company in 1826 and exploration by Lt. John Fremont in 1843. The forest is named for Wi-Ne-Ma, an interpreter and peacemaker, who was a heroine of the Modoc War of 1872.

The area is known for its sunny skies and diverse landscape of marshes, lakes, forested slopes, and wide basins, which serve as home to deer, elk and large populations of eagles, osprey, pelicans and herons. Beautiful mountain lakes are a prime feature of the forest and Mountain Lakes and Sky Lakes wildernesses are dotted with over 300 picturesque lakes. The unusual volcanic cones, Goose Egg and Goose Nest, and extensive pumice deposits testify to the fury of Mt. Mazama that created neighboring Crater Lake.

Special places and activities of interest to the visitor include the Pacific Crest National Scenic Trail; the Upper Klamath Canoe Trail where marsh, lake and forest meet; hundreds of miles of snowmobile and cross-country ski trails; Lake of the Woods, Miller Lake and Fourmile Lake; the Upper Klamath Lake Loop tour; the tortured landscapes of Devils Garden and The Badlands and the erosion-carved Sand Creek Pinnacles; Mare's Eggs Springs with its rare aquatic "eggs"; Oux Kanee Overlook; historic Lake of the Woods Visitor Center constructed by the CCC; pristine Mt. Thielsen Wilderness; and the views from the top of Pelican Butte (primitive road access) and Mt. McLoughlin and Yamsey Mtn. (trail access).

Further information about recreation opportunities, campground locations and facilities, as well as current maps of the area, are available at the following offices:

Winema National Forest
Supervisor's Office
2819 Dahlia Street
Klamath Falls, OR 97601
(503) 883-6714

Chemult Ranger District
P.O. Box 150
Chemult, OR 97731
(503) 365-2229

Chiloquin Ranger District
P.O. Box 357
Chiloquin, OR 97624
(503) 783-2221

Klamath Ranger District
1936 California Ave.
Klamath Falls, OR 97601
(503) 883-6824

Lakes of the Woods Visitor Center
Highway 140 at
Lake-of-the Woods
(503) 949-8800
Mail: Harriman Route
Box 905
Klamath Falls, OR 97601

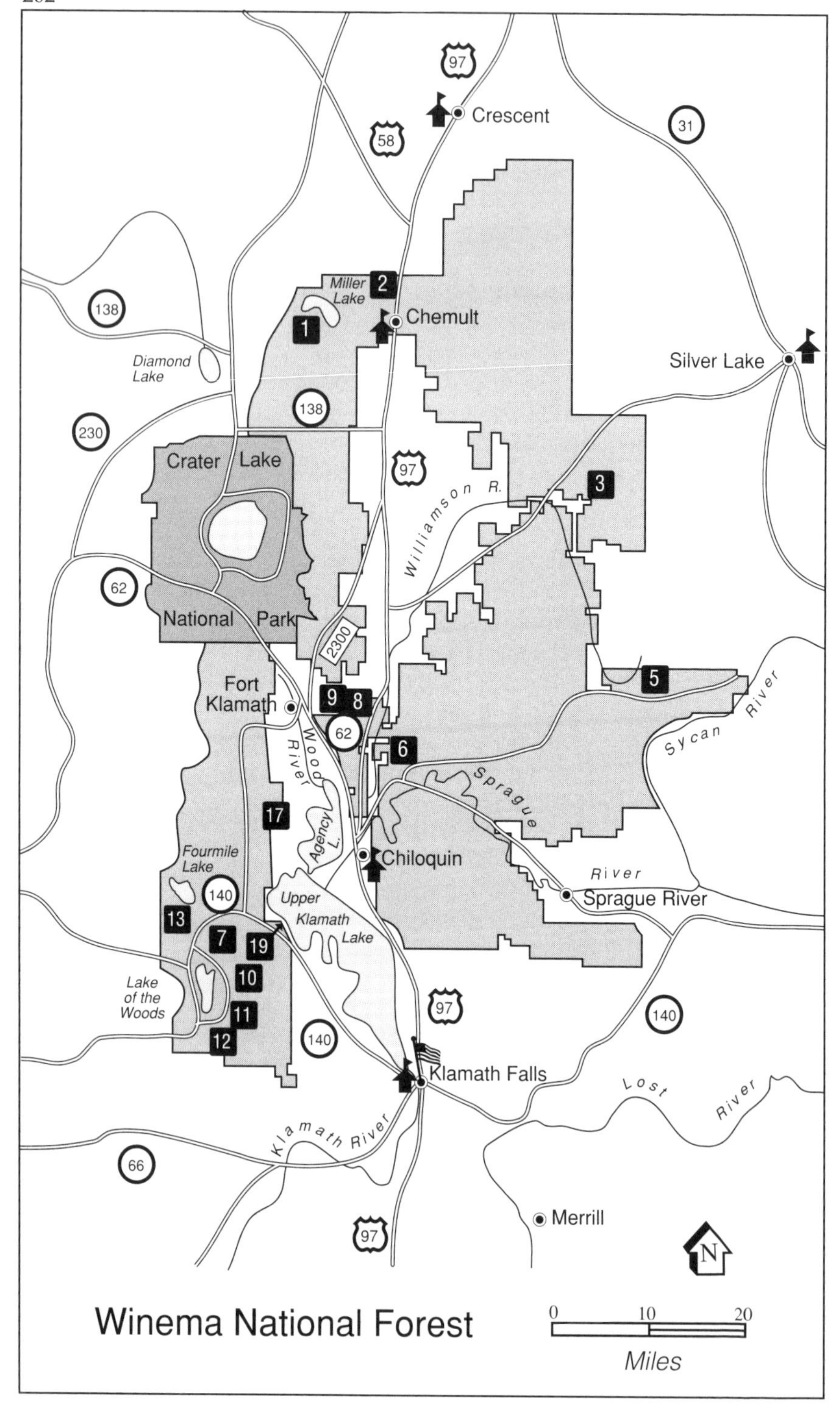

97
Crescent
31
58
Miller Lake
2
1
Chemult
138
Diamond Lake
Silver Lake
230
138
Crater Lake
97
3
Williamson R.
62
National Park
2300
5
Fort Klamath
9
8
62
Wood River
6
Sycan River
Sprague
17
Agency L.
Fourmile Lake
Chiloquin
River
140
Sprague River
13
Upper Klamath Lake
7
19
10
Lake of the Woods
11
97
140
12
140
Klamath Falls
Lost River
Klamath River
66
Merrill
97
N
Winema National Forest
0
10
20
Miles

WINEMA NATIONAL FOREST

	Map Location	*Elevation*	*Picnic Units*	*Tent Units*	*Tent-Trailer Units*	*Fee*	*Drinking Water*

Chemult Ranger District

Digit Point

Access: At Miller Lake 13 miles W of Chemult on FR 9772.
Special Activities & Facilities: Boating, swimming, fishing, hiking.

	Map Location	*Elevation*	*Picnic Units*	*Tent Units*	*Tent-Trailer Units*	*Fee*	*Drinking Water*
♿	*1*	*5600*	*11*❸		*64*❷	*x*	*x*

Corral Springs

Access: 2 miles N of Chemult via FR 9774.
Special Activities & Facilities: Hunting.

	Map Location	*Elevation*	*Picnic Units*	*Tent Units*	*Tent-Trailer Units*	*Fee*	*Drinking Water*
	2	*4900*		*7*			

Jackson Creek

Access: 27 miles E of US 97 via Silver Lake Cty. Rd., FR 49.
Special Activities & Facilities: Fishing, horse corral, hunting.

	Map Location	*Elevation*	*Picnic Units*	*Tent Units*	*Tent-Trailer Units*	*Fee*	*Drinking Water*
	3	*4600*			*12*		

Chiloquin Ranger District

Head of the River

Access: 25 miles NE of Chiloquin via Cty. Rds. 858, 600, FR 4648.
Special Activities & Facilities: Fishing.

	Map Location	*Elevation*	*Picnic Units*	*Tent Units*	*Tent-Trailer Units*	*Fee*	*Drinking Water*
♿	*5*	*4600*			*6*❸		

Williamson River

Access: 6 miles N of Chiloquin via US 97, FR 9730.
Special Activities & Facilities: Camping, fishing, rafting.

	Map Location	*Elevation*	*Picnic Units*	*Tent Units*	*Tent-Trailer Units*	*Fee*	*Drinking Water*
♿	*6*	*4200*		*3*	*7*❸	*x*	*x*

Oux Kanee

Access: 33 miles N of Klamath Falls via US 97, FR 9732.
Special Activities & Facilities: Viewpoint, picnicking, interpretive trail.

	Map Location	*Elevation*	*Picnic Units*	*Tent Units*	*Tent-Trailer Units*	*Fee*	*Drinking Water*
	8	*4600*	*6*				

Wood River

Access: .3 miles E of Fort Klamath off St. Hwy. 62.
Special Activities & Facilities: Fishing, picnicking, rafting.

	Map Location	*Elevation*	*Picnic Units*	*Tent Units*	*Tent-Trailer Units*	*Fee*	*Drinking Water*
	9	*4200*	*4*				

Map Location	Elevation	Picnic Units	Tent Units	Tent-Trailer Units	Fee	Drinking Water

Klamath Ranger District

Aspen Point

Access: 33 miles NW of Klamath Falls via St. Hwy. 140, FR 3704.
Special Activities & Facilities: Boating, swimming, fishing, waterskiing, trails, Lake of the Woods.

Map Location	Elevation	Picnic Units	Tent Units	Tent-Trailer Units	Fee	Drinking Water
10	5000	20	6	55[3]	x	x

Rainbow Bay

Access: 35 miles NW of Klamath Falls via St. Hwy. 140, FR 3704.
Special Activities & Facilities: Lake of the Woods, swimming, waterskiing, trails, picnicking, boating, group picnicking, fees for group use only.

Map Location	Elevation	Picnic Units	Tent Units	Tent-Trailer Units	Fee	Drinking Water
11	5000	67[2]			x	x

Sunset

Access: 35 miles NW of Klamath Falls via St. Hwy. 140, Cty. Rd. 533.
Special Activities & Facilities: Boating, swimming, fishing, waterskiing, barrier-free trails and toilets, Lake of the Woods.

Map Location	Elevation	Picnic Units	Tent Units	Tent-Trailer Units	Fee	Drinking Water
12	5000	5		67	x	x

Fourmile Lake

Access: 39 miles NW of Klamath Falls via St. Hwy. 140, FR 3661.
Special Activities & Facilities: Boating, hiking, swimming, fishing.

Map Location	Elevation	Picnic Units	Tent Units	Tent-Trailer Units	Fee	Drinking Water
13	5800	6		25	x	x

Crystal

Access: 33 miles NW of Klamath Falls via St. Hwy. 140, Cty. Rd. 531.
Special Activities & Facilities: Picnicking.

Map Location	Elevation	Picnic Units	Tent Units	Tent-Trailer Units	Fee	Drinking Water
17	4200	4				

Odessa

Access: 22 miles NW of Klamath Falls via St. Hwy. 140, FR 3639.
Special Activities & Facilities: Fishing, boating, picnicking.

Map Location	Elevation	Picnic Units	Tent Units	Tent-Trailer Units	Fee	Drinking Water
19	4100		5			

Lake of the Woods Visitor Center

Access: 33 miles NW of Klamath Falls on St. Hwy. 140.
Special Activities & Facilities: Information, book and map sales.

Map Location	Elevation	Picnic Units	Tent Units	Tent-Trailer Units	Fee	Drinking Water
7	5000					

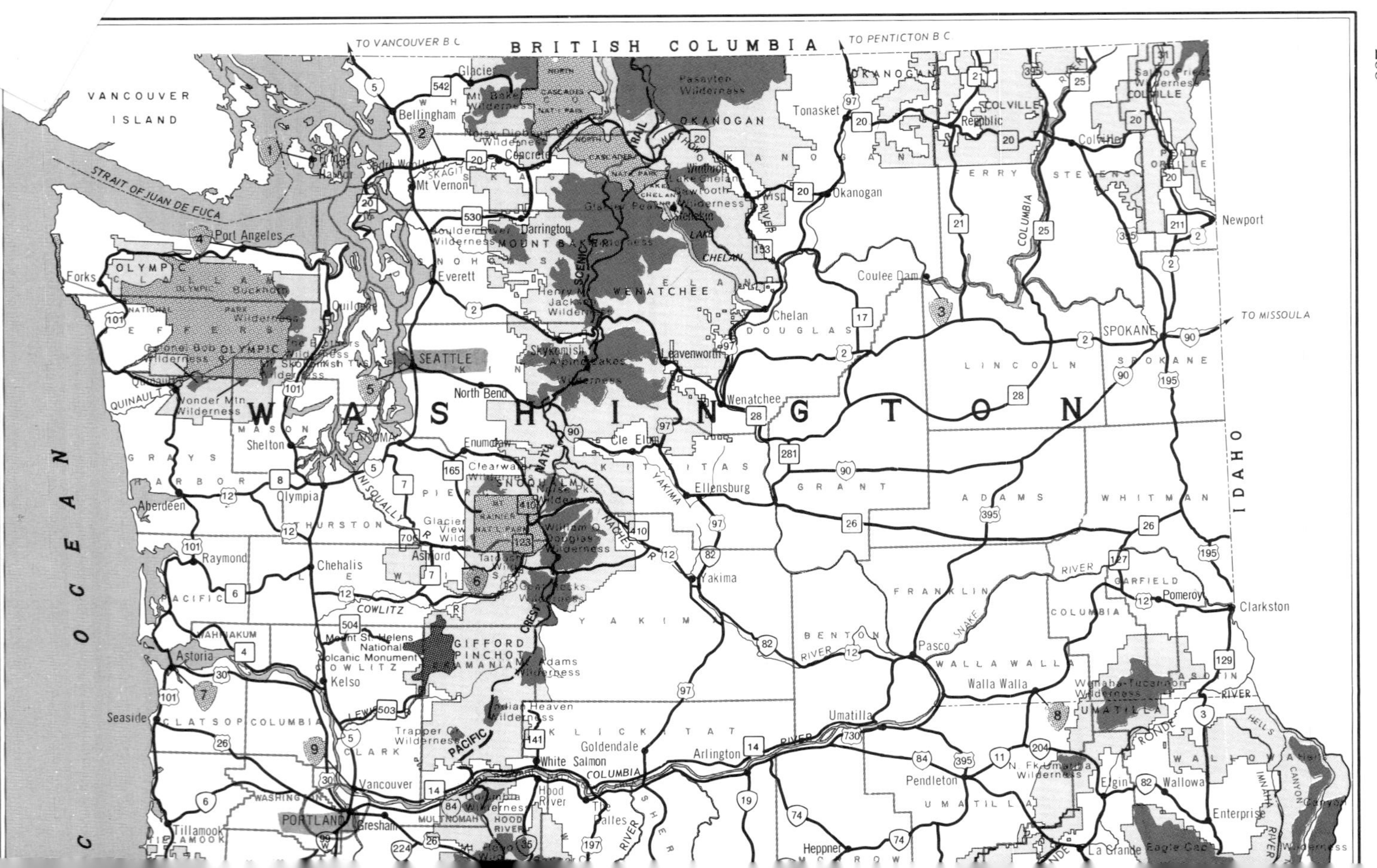
BRITISH COLUMBIA
TO VANCOUVER B C
TO PENTICTON B C
TO MISSOULA
IDAHO
VANCOUVER ISLAND
STRAIT OF JUAN DE FUCA
OCEAN
W A S H I N G T O N
SEATTLE
PORTLAND
SPOKANE
Newport
Clarkston
Pomeroy
Walla Walla
Pasco
Pendleton
Umatilla
Heppner
Arlington
Goldendale
White Salmon
Hood River
Yakima
Ellensburg
Cle Elum
Wenatchee
Leavenworth
Chelan
Coulee Dam
Okanogan
Tonasket
Republic
Colville
Bellingham
Mt Vernon
Everett
Darrington
Concrete
Skykomish
North Bend
Enumclaw
Ashford
Olympia
Shelton
Chehalis
Kelso
Vancouver
Gresham
Port Angeles
Forks
Aberdeen
Raymond
Astoria
Seaside
Tillamook
Enterprise
Wallowa
Elgin
La Grande
OKANOGAN
LINCOLN
ADAMS
WHITMAN
GARFIELD
COLUMBIA
FRANKLIN
WALLA WALLA
BENTON
GRANT
DOUGLAS
KITTITAS
KLICKITAT
SKAMANIA
CLARK
COWLITZ
THURSTON
MASON
GRAYS HARBOR
PACIFIC
WAHKIAKUM
CLATSOP
FERRY
SPOKANE
WENATCHEE
SNAKE
YAKIMA
NISQUALLY
QUINAULT
SCENIC
CHELAN
MULTNOMAH
GIFFORD PINCHOT
Pasayten Wilderness
Mount St Helens National Volcanic Monument
Trapper Creek Wilderness
Indian Heaven Wilderness
Adams Wilderness
Glacier View Wilderness
Wonder Mtn Wilderness
Henry M Jackson Wilderness
Alpine Lakes Wilderness
Wenaha-Tucannon Wilderness
N Fk Umatilla Wilderness
Columbia Wilderness
PACIFIC CREST